A Union Tested

New Perspectives on the Civil War Era

SERIES EDITORS

Judkin Browning, Appalachian State University
Susanna Lee, North Carolina State University

SERIES ADVISORY BOARD

Stephen Berry, University of Georgia
Jane Turner Censer, George Mason University
Paul Escott, Wake Forest University
Lorien Foote, Texas A&M University
Anne Marshall, Mississippi State University
Barton Myers, Washington & Lee University
Michael Thomas Smith, McNeese State University
Susannah Ural, University of Southern Mississippi
Heather Andrea Williams, University of Pennsylvania
Kidada Williams, Wayne State University

A Union Tested

The Civil War Letters of Cimbaline and Henry Fike

Edited by Jeremy Neely

The University of Georgia Press
ATHENS

Large portions of chapter 5 appeared previously in
"'The Terrors and Trials of War': The Civil War Papers
of Henry and Cimbaline Fike," *Missouri Historical
Review* 115, no. 2 (January 2021): 107–133.

© 2024 by the University of Georgia Press
Athens, Georgia 30602
www.ugapress.org
All rights reserved
Designed by Mary McKeon
Set in 10/13 ITC New Baskerville

Most University of Georgia Press titles are
available from popular e-book vendors.

Printed digitally

Library of Congress Cataloging-in-Publication Data
Names: Fike, Lucy Cimbaline, 1833–1906. | Neely,
Jeremy, 1975– editor. | Fike, Henry C., 1832–1919.
Title: A union tested : the Civil War letters of
Cimbaline and Henry Fike / Jeremy Neely.
Other titles: Civil War letters of Cimbaline and Henry Fike
Description: Athens : The University of Georgia Press,
[2025] | Series: New perspectives on the Civil War era
| Includes bibliographical references and index.
Identifiers: LCCN 2024025224 | ISBN 9780820369440
(hardback) | ISBN 9780820369457 (paperback) | ISBN
9780820369464 (epub) | ISBN 9780820369471 (pdf)
Subjects: LCSH: Fike, Lucy Cimbaline, 1833–1906—
Correspondence. | Fike, Henry, 1832–1919—Correspondence.
| United States—History—Civil War, 1861–1865—Personal
narratives. | Illinois—History—Civil War, 1861–1865—
Personal narratives. | United States. Army. Illinois Infantry
Regiment, 117th (1862–1865) | Quartermasters—Illinois—
Correspondence. | Women—Illinois—Mascoutah—
Correspondence. | Fike family. | Mascoutah (Ill.)–Biography.
Classification: LCC E505.5 117th .F55 2025
LC record available at https://lccn.loc.gov/2024025224

Contents

List of Illustrations *vii*

Acknowledgments *ix*

Introduction. The Epistolary Bridge *1*

Editorial Note *17*

Chapter 1. "Do My Duty" *19*

Chapter 2. "I Never Had Such Thinges to Attend to Before" *43*

Chapter 3. "Makes Me Feel like Fiting" *72*

Chapter 4. "A Hard Trip Indeed" *102*

Chapter 5. "The Terrors and Trials of War" *128*

Chapter 6. "What We Enlisted For" *156*

Chapter 7. "The War Is at an End" *180*

Epilogue. "Nothing New. Fine Weather" *209*

Bibliography *211*

Index *227*

Illustrations

Cimbaline Fike 2

Henry Fike 2

Camp Butler 22

Acknowledgments

SIFTING THROUGH HUNDREDS OF LETTERS that somehow survived fire, flood, and countless Civil War dangers, I am grateful for every small expression of care that aided their preservation: the friends, acquaintances, and postal carriers who delivered each piece across hundreds of miles; each recipient's diligence in keeping their mail safe from loss or destruction at the marauding hands of guerrillas or toddlers; and the family members who kept these papers in drawers, trunks, or attics before graciously donating them to repositories whose professional staff processed and made these collections available to researchers today. In particular, I thank the estate of Martha Rayhill, the granddaughter of Henry Fike's sister Charity Fike Rayhill, for bequeathing the Fikes' letters to the Spencer Research Library at the University of Kansas, and also Lyman W. Fike, a grandson of Henry Fike's brother Moses, and his son Stanley Fike, who donated Henry's diary to the State Historical Society of Missouri.

In that same spirit, it is my pleasure to acknowledge and thank the individuals and institutions whose assistance helped make this book possible. The summer research fellowship, course releases, and research funding that I received from Missouri State University have all been immensely beneficial, and I want to thank Victor Matthews, retired Dean of the College of Humanities and Public Affairs, and Kathleen Kennedy, head of the History Department, for their steadfast support. I am grateful to the staff of the Spencer Research Library at the University of Kansas for their help in sharing the Fike correspondence. A few months after that first visit to Lawrence, the COVID-19 pandemic threatened to upend further archival research. The patient help of librarians and archivists, however, made my return to reading rooms an especially welcome escape from months of isolation and lockdown. At the State Historical Society of Missouri's research center in Springfield, Erin Smither, Kathleen Seale, and Haley Frizzle-Green helped me access the diaries of Henry and Ellie Fike. I came to learn about Henry's Civil War comrades, thanks to the assistance of many people, including Will Shannon at the St. Clair Historical Society in Belleville, Illinois; Christopher Schnell at the Abraham

Lincoln Presidential Library in Springfield, Illinois; Deborah Houk, at McKendree University's Holman Library in Lebanon, Illinois; Dennis Northcott, at the Missouri History Museum in St. Louis; Dean Blackmar Krafft, who generously shared the Civil War papers of his ancestor, James Krafft; and the staff of the Lovejoy Library at Southern Illinois University in Edwardsville.

Getting to share research with students is one of the great joys of my job. Thank you to Trevor Martin, who helped dig into the Fike letters at an early stage of this project, and to Samuel Griffin, who tackled my research questions with diligence and good cheer. I also appreciate the graduate students whose discussions of the Fike papers helped me to see ways that this collection might prove useful to historians, as well as the undergraduates who endured my tangents about Union quartermasters with more patience than anyone deserves during an 8:00 a.m. lecture.

It has been a privilege to work with the University of Georgia Press, and I am humbled to see the Fikes join the fine collections within the New Perspectives on the Civil War Era series. I appreciate the wise counsel of editors Mick Gusinde-Duffy, Susanna Lee, and Judkin Browning, along with the thoughtful feedback of two anonymous readers. I am also indebted to Madison Mosely for her help in crafting the digital supplements for this book. All of these folks have made this a much sharper collection.

John Brenner, Kimberly Harper, and *Missouri Historical Review*, which previously published a version of chapter 5, kindly granted permission to reprint parts of that piece here. It was my good fortune to complete some of the revisions of this manuscript at the Dairy Hollow Writers Colony in Eureka Springs, Arkansas; I was even luckier to spend that time with friends and colleagues Chelsea Davis, Michelle Morgan, Yasmine Singh, and Julia Troche. I can only begin to express my appreciation for the innumerable kindnesses of family and friends who shared a meal, a drink, a laugh, or a word of encouragement over the course of this project. My heartfelt gratitude is with Kurt Neely, Christopher Phillips, Diane Mutti Burke, Heath Oates, Bryce Oates, Matt Bell, Darren Morrison, John Alan West, Trey Schillie, Dan Ferguson, Sam and Candi Brewster, Kevin and Cara Olson, Cristin and Jeremy Blunt, Kristen Epps, Shawn Cossins, Holly Holladay, Marlin Barber, Steve McIntyre, Tom Dicke, Murray Crawford, Mary Schnelle, Kristen Beerly, John Scott, Jim Scott, Luke Rader, Jamie Wackerman, Bach Hang, Chris Rees, Kristi Kelley, Grace Chang, Caitlin Antonopoulos, and Caleb Hearon. Huge thanks also go to Angie Whitesell, Joseph Vukcevich, Karen Whitesell, Dana Chambers, Bethany

Whitesell, Adam Whitesell, Kim Whitesell, and John Whitesell for their help in watching and hauling kids to piano lessons, sports practices, and after-school activities. A special note of gratitude goes to my parents, Kathy and Bob Neely, for all of the childcare, food, and boundless encouragement that they've provided during this project and all the years before it.

Mandy Kool believed in this project from the moment that I first described it. Her encouragement, enthusiasm, and love are gifts beyond measure and constant reminders of the power of words shared across the miles.

I also acknowledge the grudging contributions of my pets Apple, Bubs, and Lucy (named, yes, for Lucy Cimbaline Fike), who warmed my lap, sprawled across my keyboard, and sowed the kind of minor chaos that kept me from falling too completely into my work.

Finally, I dedicate this book to my children, Owen, Miles, Annie, and Ike, who thankfully have never known the terrors and trials of civil war but instead always provide me with the best of reasons—a game of catch, a batch of cookies in the kitchen, a bounce on the trampoline, a laugh in the car—to close my laptop and stay firmly rooted in the present.

A Union Tested

Introduction

The Epistolary Bridge

The Trans-Appalachian West
August 1862 to July 1865

The U.S. armed forces have depended on many materials to wage war. From bronze and iron to polymers and titanium, the vital stuff of battle has changed across centuries, but one unassuming item—paper—has remained ever indispensable. Never was this more true than during the Civil War. The *Official Records of the Union and Confederate Armies* testify to the ways that this bloodiest conflict in American history, a very real struggle of flesh and fire, played out across millions of written pages. That immense collection, spread across four series and seventy volumes, represents only a fraction of the paperwork that documented and animated the contest. Muster rolls organized men into companies and regiments; requisitions brought forth the staggering piles of food and materiel needed to sustain them; and casualty reports totaled the unprecedented number of dead and broken bodies. Legal tender buttressed governments sagging beneath the costs of war; newspapers yielded timely information and bursts of partisan ardor; and the tracts, novels, and printed matter that coursed through army encampments offered comforts sacred and profane.

On a most personal level, paper was the medium through which individuals tried to make sense of themselves and the troubled world they now inhabited. For the generation of people who poured themselves into letters, diaries, songs, and poems, the Civil War demonstrated that they were not only soldiers and civilians, husbands and wives, Unionists and Confederates, but also writers. Paper proved instrumental to the preservation of the republic and its families alike. Whether delivered by post or the kindness of a traveling friend, never before had so many private messages passed between the hands of Americans in such a compressed

Cimbaline Fike was an Illinois homemaker, wife, and mother whose Civil War letters captured her ardent unionism and struggles with chronic illness. Johnson County (Missouri) Historical Society

Henry Fike was a former schoolteacher and principal who served as lieutenant colonel and quartermaster in the 117th Illinois Volunteer Infantry. University of Kansas Kenneth Spencer Research Library

period of time.[1] Henry and Cimbaline Fike exemplified this truth, writing their way through a war that tested their nation and marriage.

The wartime exchanges between soldiers and their families have long been a key resource for understanding the people who endured the Civil War. Illuminating the social, cultural, and political cords that bound households to faraway forts and battlefields, the envelopes that traveled from every corner of the United States held more than the clippings and mementoes tucked within their trifold pages.[2] These parcels were an

---

1. The Fikes, like many people during the Civil War, came to prefer sending letters with traveling family members or friends, as they became aware of the disappointing vagaries of the mid-nineteenth-century postal system. Within weeks of Henry's departure from home, Cimbaline wrote, "I am very sorry that you have not heard from home sence you have been gon I have ritten 4 letters to you, one every day." Lucy Cimbaline Fike to Henry Clay Fike, August 29, 1862, Henry C. and Lucy Fike Papers (hereafter FP).

2. Frank and Whites, *Household War;* Roberts, "*This Infernal War*"; Keating, *Greatest Trials I Ever Had;* Berry and Elder, *Practical Strangers;* Donohoe, *Printer's Kiss;* Johannson, *Widows by the Thousand;* Christ, *Getting Used to Being Shot At;* Silber and Stevens, *Yankee Correspondence.* For the significance of letters exchanged between Civil War soldiers and their loved ones, see Wiley, *Life of Billy Yank,* 183–190, and *Life of Johnny Reb,* 192–216.

epistolary bridge that anchored civilians and soldiers across prolonged separations and the turbulent changes that suffused the distances between them. Letters became the arena in which the Fikes, like many Americans, attempted to maintain a flesh-and-blood relationship within the handwritten lines they delivered across time and space. Early missives bore the awkwardness of a new courtship, but their stilted formality, marked by Cimbaline's careful introductions ("It is with pleasure that I take my pen in hand") and signatures that dutifully noted Henry's rank and regiment, yielded to a familiarity that ranged from a gentle warmth to plainspoken bluntness. Messages of varying length and sophistication detailed the reconfigured contours of family and work, yet they frequently revealed much more than the familiar marrow of everyday life. Writing to one another prompted a remarkable degree of self-reflection and provided for each person the opportunity to learn anew about their partners, their communities, and themselves.

The Fikes' affectionate banter affirms what scholars have shown in tracing the rise of companionate marriages; Henry and Cimbaline, it quickly becomes clear, genuinely loved one another.[3] Yet marriage remained, in historian Nancy Cott's apt comparison, like a sphinx, both publicly conspicuous but full of private secrets.[4] The deeply personal exchanges kindled in wartime illuminate the intimate dimensions of ordinary Americans' lives that have too often eluded scholars. A combination of factors has deepened the shadows that obscured the private worlds of working people. Limited access to formal education denied many women and men the tools to document their thoughts and feelings, and many others, although literate, rarely found or made the time to write amid long days of wearying labor.

The Civil War, however, forced on people a protracted isolation from their loved ones and convinced untold numbers to take up their pens, some for the first time in their lives. Letters helped to lessen, though never collapse, the geographic distance. In an age of instant communication, the arrival of a note penned a week earlier might seem a poor substitute for the comforts of immediate connection and physical companionship, but in Civil War America such missives were a treasured lifeline, the vital (and sometimes only) means of spanning the chasms of

---

3. Mintz and Kellogg, *Domestic Revolutions*, 43–66; Rose, *Victorian America and the Civil War*, 148–161; Berry, *All That Makes a Man*; Rotundo, *American Manhood*, 130–157.

4. Cott, *Public Vows*; Fredette, *Marriage on the Border*; Hartog, *Man and Wife in America*; Grossberg, *Governing the Hearth*; Mintz, *Prison of Expectations*.

loneliness and uncertainty that separated households and army encampments. A distant correspondence could not reconstitute a marriage in all its fullness, but the comforts provided by its messages suggested that a relationship strained and nearly sundered by war might yet be sustained by words that fastened partners across many miles.

Readers can see in the Fikes' letters the many ways that the Civil War tested marriages and gender roles in the United States. As many historians have shown, much of antebellum society had clung to the notion that a woman's place was in the home, while men ventured into the rough-and-tumble public worlds of business and politics.[5] In farming communities, the boundaries between the home and the workplace had always blurred and overlapped, and with the coming of war, rural women now had to keep up with both their domestic responsibilities and the chores once handled by their male kinfolk. Women's responses to these challenges defied simple characterization.[6] Cimbaline Fike embraced such newfound independence and the chance to serve her family, community, and nation, yet she came to resent those who failed to appreciate her sacrifices both within and beyond her household.[7] The war likewise forced men to reckon with their altered standing as distant husbands and fathers. For Henry, soldiering challenged his manhood not only by testing his courage and prowess but also by exposing his limitations as a provider, far from home and sometimes unable to offer the stable income and emotional support that his family needed. Letters provided the medium through which Cimbaline and Henry confronted their struggles, distant but intertwined, and nurtured their hope for better days.[8]

Sitting near the confluence of the Mississippi, Missouri, and Ohio Rivers, the western Illinois country where the Fikes lived was a world in motion, but the Civil War marked the first time that they, like many other Americans, ventured far beyond the communities where they grew up. The youngest of eleven children, Henry was born in 1832 at the homestead that his parents had settled on Looking Glass Prairie. Within

---

5. McCurry, *Women's War*; Ginette Aley, "Inescapable Realities: Rural Midwestern Women and Families during the Civil War," in Aley and Anderson, *Union Heartland*, 125–147; Giesberg, *Army at Home*; Whites and Long, *Occupied Women*; Clinton and Silber, *Battle Scars*; Silber, *Daughters of the Union*; Lamphier, *Kate Chase and William Sprague*; Whites, *Civil War as a Crisis*; Clinton, *Other Civil War*; Clinton and Silber, *Divided Houses*.

6. Leonard, *Yankee Women*; Osterud, *Bonds of Community*; Faragher, *Sugar Creek*.

7. Sizer, *Political Work*, 109–121; Faust, *Mothers of Invention*; Bleser and Heath, "Impact of the Civil War."

8. Whites, *Civil War as a Crisis*; Mitchell, *Vacant Chair*.

a few years, other westering migrants established the nearby village of Mascoutah. Hemmed between Silver Creek and the rich, table-flat farmland that stretched to the nearby Kaskaskia River, the town grew quickly, fueled in part by the explosive development of St. Louis, Missouri, some thirty miles to the west. To the east of Mascoutah sat Clinton County, where Lucy Cimbaline Power, born in 1833, lived for her first two decades.

Cimbaline and Henry met at a religious camp meeting in the summer of 1853, but their courtship did not begin in earnest for another year. After marrying on Christmas Day in 1855, the Fikes purchased a home in Mascoutah, where Henry found work as a schoolteacher. The family's purchase of a farm just outside of town, which they leased for additional income, seemed further proof that they had attained financial security, becoming comfortable by outward appearances although certainly not wealthy. Their first child, a daughter named May, died in infancy. They rejoiced when a second child, Ellie, was born on January 16, 1861. Nineteen months later—more than a year after the Confederate attack on Fort Sumter marked the start of the Civil War—Henry mustered into the newly formed 117th Illinois Volunteer Infantry.[9]

Although born to the same region, the Fikes approached their wartime correspondence from strikingly different directions. By the time Henry enlisted in the Union army, he had spent much of his adult life within the written page, either studying or teaching others in rural schools and churches. A graduate of McKendree College, he frequently wrote for local newspapers and kept a diary that he would faithfully maintain for most of the next half-century. During the war Henry penned 314 letters to his wife, writing with the self-regard of an educated and, now, worldly man. Cimbaline, meanwhile, responded with 126 letters, most of them written from the family's home. The halting cadence, eccentric spelling, and haphazard punctuation of her early replies suggests that she, like most young women of her day, had fewer educational opportunities than her husband. Yet, in following Cimbaline across the full breadth of their exchanges, one sees how the war served as a most effective classroom, turning a once-reluctant correspondent into a confident, even forceful writer.[10]

---

9. Henry C. Fike Diaries (hereafter HFD), August 27, 1853; *History of St. Clair County*, 277–278.

10. Weir, "'An Oblique Place.'" For the reliance on phonetic spelling by other Civil War writers, see Private Voices, altchive.org, a digital project curated by Michael Ellis and Mi-

Cimbaline's literary evolution captures the strength needed to withstand the manifold crises that shook households in wartime. In particular, her letters remind readers that chronic pain and illness were not problems that only swept through battlefields and encampments. To be sure, the infectious diseases that plagued Union and Confederate soldiers were fatal horrors that prompted profound changes in medical science and procedure. Less studied, however, are the maladies that continued to afflict those at home, along with the ways that civilians struggled to recover their health in the midst of war. Cimbaline's letters detail a debilitating series of ailments: recurrent fevers and headaches, painful skin lesions, persistent melancholy, unspecified chronic illnesses that she described only as "my old diseases," and such sharp dental pain that she ultimately had most of her teeth removed. Ellie, too, endured repeated bouts of sickness so grave that Henry feared she would die before he could return home. To the Fikes' enormous relief, their daughter survived, but many other local parents mourned the losses of young children killed by smallpox, whooping cough, and outbreaks they felt helpless to stop. The treatments prescribed by physicians brought some relief, as did the comforts of prayer and family. Letters, too, offered to Cimbaline and other writers a kind of reflective solace, giving them the space in which to find meaning amid corporeal struggles they had to endure but perhaps would never win.

Henry was fortunate that serious illness did not incapacitate him until the final weeks of his enlistment. Until then, his correspondence detailed in remarkable breadth the world of a workaday Union regiment. Like most Civil War volunteers, he joined a company of men who lived only a short distance away. In addition to his neighbors from Mascoutah and St. Clair County, so many college classmates enlisted in the 117th Illinois that some came to describe the regiment as the "McKendree Boys."[11] These comrades elected Henry to the rank of lieutenant colonel, and his subsequent letters detailed with satisfaction how officers like himself enjoyed better lodging, richer fare, and other luxuries that enlisted men did not receive.[12] Henry also won appointment as the regiment's quar-

---

chael Montgomery, which has transcribed several thousand letters from common soldiers and their families. See also Ellis, *North Carolina English*.

11. For volunteers' motivations and the influence of community ties on Union soldiers, see Mitchell, *Vacant Chair*, 19–37, 151–160.

12. Cole, *Centennial History of Illinois*, 280. For the privilege of officers arranging for their kin to move with them into the South, see Bleser and Gordon, *Intimate Strategies*; Rose, *Victorian America*, 146–147.

termaster, the staff officer who shouldered the responsibility of feeding, clothing, and equipping his fellow troops.

As much as any cog within the Union war apparatus, his position was awash in paper. Each month he funneled to the War Department in Washington a flow of recordkeeping that detailed the quantities of men, mules, and money that passed his watchful eye.[13] In addition to documenting the on-the-ground workings of the Union's logistics operation, or what Henry dubbed "the machine," his private letters add color and texture to almost every phase of the regiment's service: the enthusiasm of mustering in, the tedium and diversions of prolonged garrison duty, interminable weeks of marching, the thrills and disappointments of combat, and the weary relief when peace returned at last.[14]

Henry's dispatches were also a vivid travelogue of the trans-Appalachian West, affording Cimbaline and readers today a stirring glimpse of the nation's vast scale and diverse landforms. The men of the 117th Illinois spent almost a year in the occupied city of Memphis, a point from which they warily observed the downstream siege at Vicksburg. They later ventured through the bayous of Louisiana, rocky Ozark hills, the piney woods of the Deep South, and finally the sparkling beaches of the Gulf Coast. Along the way, Henry steamed up and down the major tributaries of the Mississippi valley, describing with great interest the country along the Cumberland, Tennessee, Red, and Missouri Rivers. Letters from the field also captured with unsparing detail the destruction that followed the Union army's invasion of Confederate states. Henry alternated between expressions of compassion for the miseries of southern civilians and unrepentant anger at the treachery that justified such hardships. "I pity these people, for humanity's sake alone," he wrote to Cimbaline, before adding: "Most of them are rebels at heart, and deserve no mercy at our hands. What ought a rebel and traitor to expect from his country."[15]

Together the Fikes personified the active nationalism that linked loyal civilians and soldiers across the North. United by their willingness to sacrifice for a cause larger than themselves, Cimbaline and Henry scorned women and men who failed to match such devotion. Letters frequently

---

13. Historian Lenette S. Taylor writes, "Every quartermaster, regimental as well as federal, had to submit nine monthly reports and three quarterly returns. . . . The full set of reports required fifty-three separate forms." Taylor, "*Supply for Tomorrow*," 12–17, 203–208.

14. For the immense scale of "the machine," see H. Fike to C. Fike, December 6, 1862, FP.

15. H. Fike to C. Fike, December 26, 1864, FP.

affirmed their congruent views of manhood and civic duty.[16] A person who would not shoulder arms on behalf of his country, they maintained, was neither a true patriot nor a man worthy of respect. As draft calls in Illinois increased through the fall of 1864, many men sought to avoid conscription by finding substitutes to take their place. Henry mocked those who refused to accept "prizes drawn in Uncle Sam's lottery." Cimbaline, who established the town's Union League, wrote that neighbors who hired substitutes "dont show much love for there country," and added, "I wish they would not alow any one to pay monney to git out."[17] Even Ellie, their mischievous toddler, was proud to tell visitors that her father had gone off to fight the rebels. "Every good man goes," she explained. "My pa is good."[18]

While celebrating their mutual unionism, many of the Fikes' letters lamented the widening schisms that fissured their community. On multiple occasions, Cimbaline derided the men who would not enlist and threatened violence against those whose dubious patriotism, she thought, verged on treason.[19] "For my part I feel like puting on briches now, and fiting some of the copperheads in Mascoutah," she wrote in the summer of 1863.[20] Such exclamations were not merely rhetorical. As hundreds

---

16. For loyal northerners whose primary motivation remained the preservation of the Union, see Gallagher, *The Union War*; McPherson, *For Cause and Comrades*, 90–116; Hess, *Liberty, Virtue, and Progress*. For nationalism and loyalty in the North, see William Blair, "We Are Coming, Father Abraham–Eventually: The Problem of Northern Nationalism in the Pennsylvania Recruiting Drives of 1862," in Cashin, *War Was You and Me*; Gallman, *Defining Duty*; Silber, *Daughters of the Union*. For manhood and duty in the Civil War era, see Berry, *All That Makes a Man*; Brian Craig Miller, "Manhood," in Sheehan-Dean, *Companion to the U.S. Civil War*, 795–810; Grasso, *Teacher, Preacher, Soldier, Spy*; Mitchell, *Vacant Chair*.

17. H. Fike to C. Fike, September 24, 1864, FP; C. Fike to H. Fike, September 25, 1864, FP. For draft resistance in the North, see Joan Cashin, "Deserters, Civilians, and Draft Resistance," in Cashin, *War Was You and Me*, 262–285.

18. C. Fike to H. Fike, September 16, 1863, FP. Few scholars have studied the experiences of children during the Civil War. A notable exception is Marten, *Children's Civil War*, 68–81. For the moral absolutism that shaped children's understandings of the war, see Peter Bardaglio, "On the Border: White Children and the Politics of War," in Cashin, *War Was You and Me*, 315–331.

19. For understandings of duty in the Civil War era, see Gallman, *Defining Duty*, 188–222; McPherson, *For Cause and Comrades*, 22–29.

20. C. Fike to H. Fike, June 25, 1863, FP. For women who took up arms as Civil War soldiers, see Blanton and Cook, *They Fought Like Demons*. For "the garb of gender" in the Confederate South, see Faust, *Mothers of Invention*, 220–233. Historian Jennifer Weber's history of antiwar dissent in the North devotes only a few paragraphs to the wartime politicization of women, but she suggests that outspoken women like Cimbaline were not alone, noting "Women, who were not allowed to vote and many of whom had been political agnostics, grew more vocal about the matters of the day." Weber, *Copperheads*, 47. See also Silber,

of volunteers left Mascoutah to serve in the Union army, anxieties grew about the shadowy figures who prowled the town's streets at night.[21] Cimbaline resolved to arm herself after learning of the break-ins and threats of sexual violence made against her neighbors. Weeks later, waking to the rustle of a potential burglar, she threw open a window and fired her pistol wildly into the night, scaring away the would-be intruder.[22] The "war widows" who struggled with worry, privation, and illness could find vital support from nearby family and friends, but as the war dragged on, these webs of connection often frayed into what Cimbaline called "a big fuss" of ideological strife and personal acrimony.[23] "The worst is the women fight," she wrote. "I thought it was enought to have wore [war] aroung us, let a lone having it among us."[24]

The Fike papers, in their frequent depictions of the social and political tensions that shook one rural Illinois community, join a deepening scholarship on the Border West that explores the complexity of a fractious middle ground where North bled into South. Much of this recent work shows how the sharply drawn lines of a political map that separated free and slave states belied the messy realities of places where households divided by loyalty and ideology remained tied by culture, kinship, and commerce.[25] Several studies have considered how Abraham Lincoln's turn toward emancipation alienated many white Unionists in the loyal states of Kentucky, Missouri, and Illinois.[26] The Fikes, however, evinced the determined resolve that kept many border households solidly behind

---

Daughters of the Union; Giesberg, *Army at Home*, 119–142; Blair, "We Are Coming, Father Abraham–Eventually," in Cashin, *War Was You and Me*, 184–191; Jimerson, *Private Civil War*, 27–49; Mitchell, *Civil War Soldiers*, 56–84.

21. Muster rolls show that 338 men who enlisted in various Illinois regiments claimed Mascoutah as their hometown. Fred Delap, Illinois Civil War Muster and Descriptive Rolls Database, Illinois State Archives, Office of the Illinois Secretary of State, https://www.ilsos.gov/isaveterans/civilMusterSearch.do (hereafter Delap, ICWMDR).

22. C. Fike to H. Fike, September 13, 1863, FP.

23. Relatively few studies of the northern home front have focused on rural communities. Instead, they typically look at more populous urban areas. Exceptions to this trend are Etcheson, *A Generation at War*; Raus, *Banners South*; Doyle, *Social Order*.

24. C. Fike to H. Fike, October 19, 1864, FP.

25. Phillips, *Rivers Ran Backward*; Epps, *Slavery on the Periphery*; Robinson, *A Union Indivisible*; Earle and Burke, *Bleeding Kansas, Bleeding Missouri*; Oertel, *Bleeding Borders*; Amy Murrell Taylor, *Divided Family*; Jeremy Neely, *Border between Them*; Anderson, "Fulton County War."

26. Phillips, *Rivers Ran Backward*; Stanley, *Loyal West*; Astor, *Rebels on the Border*; Marshall, *Creating a Confederate Kentucky*.

the Union cause, along with the ways that the war kindled shifts in racial attitudes among white Unionists.[27]

The Fikes have largely gone unnoticed by historians, but one rare exception identifies Henry as an example of the pervasive anti-Black racism that prevailed among white Union soldiers, including those who came to accept emancipation as a key war objective.[28] Although fair in its broad contours, such an assessment overlooks the fuller context of his evolving ideas on race and freedom. Unlike the white Union troops whose deployments brought their first exposure to African Americans, Henry had moved among people of color, both free and enslaved, in Mascoutah and nearby St. Louis.[29] His travels into the South sparked a dawning empathy for African Americans and the injustices that enslavement had inflicted upon them. Like many of his peers and the Union army more generally, Lieutenant Colonel Fike depended on the labor of the formerly enslaved people who served his meals, cleaned his quarters, cared for his horse, and performed myriad tasks around Fort Pickering, but it was the men who volunteered to fight in the United States Colored Troops that garnered, in his estimation, something closer to genuine respect.[30] There were clear limits to such changes, however. By war's end, Henry could marvel at emancipation's revolutionary implications for southern society, but he remained just as comfortable using racist language to describe the Black people within his orbit.[31]

The seven chapters that follow trace the Fikes' wartime exchanges in chronological order, beginning with the dusty afternoon in August 1862 when Henry mustered into service and concluding with the summer day almost three years later when he returned to Mascoutah for good. The chapters are organized by the different western points where the 117th

---

27. Manning, *What This Cruel War*. For the need to examine the Border North within the wider regional permutations of Civil War loyalties, see Clinton and Silber, *Battle Scars*, 11.

28. Historian Chandra Manning notes, with some accuracy, "Henry Fike ... was anything but a radical abolitionist." Manning, *What This Cruel War*, 123.

29. See HFD, January 12, 1851; April 10, 1852; and July 18, 1853. Although the 1860 federal census reported that Mascoutah had a Black population of only 15 individuals (out of 2,076 inhabitants of the town), one of those individuals was Griff, the longtime farmhand employed by Henry's parents. St. Louis, where the Fikes frequently traded, had a free Black population of 1,865, along with an enslaved population of 4,346. Kennedy, *Population of the United States*, 99, 279, 283.

30. Glatthaar, "Duty, Country," in Cashin, *War Was You and Me*, 332–357; Mitchell, *Civil War Soldiers*, 126–131.

31. For the persistence of racist language even among antislavery northerners, see Rael, *Black Identity and Black Protest*, 82–117.

Illinois moved over the course of the war. Aside from Cimbaline and Ellie's lengthy visits with Henry during the regiment's stay in Memphis, they otherwise spent the war in western Illinois. An array of primary sources help flesh out the people and places mentioned in the Fikes' letters. These corroborating sources include Henry's diary, military records, historical newspapers, census manuscripts, and the diaries and letters produced by his fellow McKendree Boys.

The opening chapter illustrates how the divergent emotions triggered by the Civil War cleaved a single household. Henry, like many of the men who volunteered to fight, eagerly embraced the opportunity and resolved, as "a true patriot to his country," to endure whatever hardships his three-year enlistment might bring.[32] As he joined the army, the war seemed to him a communal enterprise, perhaps the greatest adventure that he and his fellows would ever undertake. They mustered into service at Camp Butler, just a few miles outside of Springfield, Illinois, and by November 1862 several weeks of training transformed these young farmers and other raw recruits into passable soldiers.

Their encampment sat only ninety miles north of Mascoutah, but for Cimbaline it was too often a world apart. She faced her husband's absence with barely concealed apprehension. Poor health and the frictions that unsettled her community were familiar burdens that loneliness rendered even heavier. Yet both Fikes were buoyed by their developing correspondence and a shared belief in their conjoined duties, knowing that theirs was a struggle worth fighting. "This wor is a horble thing," Cimbaline wrote. "Wod to god that this rebelion could be put downg in one day."[33] They recognized, however, that a civil war deep into its second year was not likely to end anytime soon. As the miles between the couple grew wider, their letters assumed greater significance, each reply a relational cord capable of spanning whatever distance lay between them.

Within three months of their initial separation, the Fikes found themselves fully engaged by the challenges of wartime, as chapter 2 reveals. In addition to the nonstop efforts of caring for their spirited daughter, Cimbaline took up volunteer work and the necessary chores of managing the family's finances. Henry's arrival in Memphis on November 16, 1862, represented his first exposure to the Confederate South, and he quickly noted the danger posed by guerrillas who prowled the woods outside the

---

32. H. Fike to C. Fike, October 14, 1862, FP.
33. C. Fike to H. Fike, October 12, 1862, FP.

city. Fort Pickering, the blufftop garrison where the 117th Illinois was billeted, offered a safe vantage from which to undertake the hands-on work of an army quartermaster. Preparations to seize the downstream city of Vicksburg, the final rebel stronghold on the Mississippi River, brought a thrum of activity to occupied Memphis, which bustled with soldiers, cotton traders, and a teeming surge of war refugees.

After January 1, 1863, when the Emancipation Proclamation took effect and the Union began to muster Black volunteers into Federal service, Henry looked upon the organization of the United States Colored Troops with great interest. He hoped to secure an appointment to lead one such regiment, but that ambition remained yet unfulfilled. Although a shared melancholy dimmed the couple's first Christmas and anniversary apart, they soon arranged a months-long sojourn to Tennessee for Cimbaline and Ellie. The family's stay, however temporary, was a precious gift available to officers but not to their enlisted comrades, whose loved ones remained back in Illinois.

Victories at Gettysburg and Vicksburg in July signaled a shift in momentum toward the Union cause, and Cimbaline's loyalist ardor, as chapter 3 shows, burned more brightly than ever. She was actively involved in the separate Union Leagues established by the men and women of Mascoutah, not only sewing the flag of the male group but also organizing the Independence Day fundraiser for her own association.[34] The rapid growth of each league worried neighbors who feared that such fervor might unleash a violent backlash against antiwar dissenters. Cimbaline reported that Mr. Nellson, one local Copperhead, "wos gitting sceard. he wos afraid tha would send him to dixey and burn his property." Another, Mr. Scharp, "is very much friten. His wife said she nose wose afraid to go to sleep at night for fear she would wake up and find thare hous on fire."[35] A burst of vigilantism several weeks later showed ample reason to be fearful.[36]

Aside from a brief furlough to Illinois, Henry remained near Memphis, where the sweep of martial law and other transformations sparked by the Federal occupation proved a constant curiosity. Few topics drew more

---

34. In contrast to the male-dominated home guards and volunteer militias organized in eastern cities, the Union Leagues in Illinois were grassroots organizations that included both men and women as members. See Paul Taylor, "*Most Complete Political Machine*," 157–177. For the significance of such handmade flags within a context of increasingly commodified patriotism, see Cohen, "'You Have No Flag.'"

35. C. Fike to H. Fike, June 5, 1863, FP.

36. C. Fike to H. Fike, August 16, 1863, FP.

attention in his letters than the surging population of Black refugees who sought freedom behind Union lines but found themselves less secure than they might have expected. Not unlike the vigilantes in Mascoutah, members of the 117th Illinois accused one Black boy of theft, tied him to a tree, and flogged the youth. Such denial of due process, Henry wrote, provoked sharp disagreements within the regiment: "Some say, if the 117" Regiment is going to turn out to tieing up negroes to trees, without trial or jury, and beating them with a horse whip, they beg permission to hand over their commissions, and to be 'excused.'"[37]

The Fike family happily reunited in Memphis in October and remained together through the first month of 1864, when the extended garrison duty of the 117th Illinois finally came to an end. On January 28, Henry sailed down the Mississippi River as part of the 16th Army Corps toward a destination unknown to himself or his enlisted comrades. His first real experiences as a soldier on the march—the focus of chapter 4—turned out to be a pair of expeditions into the Deep South, first across central Mississippi and then along the Red River of Louisiana. After a full year spent following the movements of other Union armies through newspapers and regimental gossip, Lieutenant Colonel Fike now relished "soldiering it in earnest."[38] The Federals who marched east from Vicksburg in February saw limited fighting but caused tremendous damage en route to Meridian, destroying railroads, burning farms, and helping to free more than two thousand enslaved people. The Red River expedition, which began a month later, proved to be a dismal failure. Despite the verve of accounts that detailed the battles of Pleasant Hill and Mansfield, a disappointed Henry was eager to return northward.

In his absence, Cimbaline boarded at the Memphis home occupied by the family of Nathan Land, a fellow officer and Mascoutah resident. Newspapers provided a sporadic, occasionally accurate source of information about the 117th Illinois and its movements further south, but personal correspondence remained the most direct and dependable lifeline between loved ones. Even though Cimbaline wrote fewer letters from Memphis, her weariness, too, was evident: "This wore is a very croul an weaked [wicked] one. Making some very unhappy famlys. For my parte I am very tired of it, and wish it wos over with."[39] Henry's safe return to Memphis brought some comfort, as the Fikes would remain

---

37. H. Fike to C. Fike, June 21, 1863, FP.
38. H. Fike to C. Fike, April 12, 1864, FP.
39. C. Fike to H. Fike, May 10, 1864, FP.

together through the end of summer, but sobering realities, including the inconclusive military developments in the East and the full year that remained of his enlistment, loomed over their reunion.

Events in the final months of 1864, detailed in chapter 5, suggest how their post–Civil War lives seemed both tantalizingly close and unbearably distant. Although the Fikes each steamed upriver from Tennessee, only Cimbaline came back to the family home. Henry instead landed on the west bank of the Mississippi and moved with the 117th Illinois to Jefferson Barracks, the army post south of St. Louis where Federal troops massed in anticipation of a Confederate attack. The double-edged meaning of the regiment's arrival just across the river from Mascoutah was plain to see. On one hand, its members were closer to home than ever, and crowds of local visitors made the camp look, in Henry's words, more like a county fair than a military installation. Yet on the other hand, the rebel forces who advanced north from Arkansas brought the war dangerously close to home, fueling wild rumors and setting off alarm bells in the town. Invading troops, however, did not arrive but instead veered toward Jefferson City, Missouri, where U.S. forces had ensconced a loyal provisional government in the first months of the war. With Union soldiers, including Henry, now in pursuit, the Confederates raced west to the Kansas border, where another Federal army waited and ultimately dealt the rebels a smashing defeat.

The improving prospects for Lincoln's reelection further lifted the Fikes' confidence, in spite of widening draft calls and the shirking men who still avoided conscription. Yet the fall exchanges also revealed acute stresses on their marriage, and Cimbaline, again wracked by pain and illness, confronted the startling debts that Henry had amassed but not disclosed to her. These obligations, coupled with her unhappiness in Mascoutah and an exodus of friends and neighbors, brought forth a kind of marital reckoning. Although the letters that once trussed their marriage now groaned with suspicion, the correspondence of that autumn managed to hold their marriage together. The Fikes began to imagine a different kind of postwar life, if only they could survive the war to pursue it.

After a miserable trek across the snow and mud of Missouri, Henry savored the respite of a Thanksgiving spent at home. On November 28, his regiment again departed Illinois for Tennessee and began a season of campaigning, documented in chapter 6, which saw military victories but even greater physical challenges than the grueling marches of the past year. In December 1864 the 117th Illinois took part in the Union victory at the battle of Nashville. From there, Henry and his comrades marched southwest across a forlorn landscape, passing through towns that had been nearly obliterated. South of Pittsburg Landing, Henry wrote, "Nearly all that is now left, is the naked chimneys, which seem to stand as monuments of the desolating effects of war."[40] Cold, hungry, and footsore, the Union soldiers finally established winter quarters at Eastport, Mississippi, but weeks later Lieutenant Colonel Fike managed to secure another three-week furlough home. Cimbaline's correspondence during this campaign had been more sporadic, likely the result of her painful coughing fits and debilitating headaches. As smallpox swept through Mascoutah that winter, killing several people, she took comfort in the prospect of moving with Ellie to the country home of her brother-in-law, writing "I think it will do me mor gud than meddison."[41]

The conclusion of that February visit marked the beginning of the Fikes' final wartime separation. Chapter 7, unlike those before it, includes only letters from Henry since those from Cimbaline have not survived. His dispatches from the Deep South follow the 117th Illinois from New Orleans to Mobile Bay, where the Federals laid siege to the Confederates' last major garrison on the Gulf Coast. After Union forces captured Mobile, the 117th Illinois marched north into central Alabama. In Montgomery, the original capital of the Confederacy, they at last received word of the official surrenders of enemy armies under Robert E. Lee and Joseph Johnston. Union forces rejoiced, believing that this long-anticipated news meant their swift return northward.

Weeks of interminable waiting punctured their jubilation. Despite the boredom and illness that gripped Henry and many comrades throughout that enervating summer, they also witnessed scenes of wonder, none greater than the massive crowd of formerly enslaved people who thronged city streets to herald the triumphant arrival of a fleet carrying hundreds of uniformed Black troops. Most white Unionists were nonetheless in no mood to celebrate, even on Independence Day. "Our boys don't care much about celebrating the 4" in the army. All they think of is getting home," Henry wrote.[42]

The Fikes' Civil War had been a story of perseverance and adaptation, but by the summer of 1865 their flagging endurance neared its limit. Buffeted by loneliness, pain, and mounting financial worries, Cimba-

---

40. H. Fike to C. Fike, January 2, 1865, FP. For descriptions of the fighting in Nashville, see H. Fike to C. Fike, December 19, 1864, FP.
41. C. Fike to H. Fike, January 3, 1865, FP.
42. H. Fike to C. Fike, July 4, 1865, FP.

line's letters repeatedly pressed Henry to resign and return home as soon as possible, some three months before his enlistment was set to expire. He initially demurred but eventually embraced the idea. An epistolary bridge, that vital connection to his wife and daughter, had sustained him through his service; now, with the war won, that same lifeline called him home. "I am bound to get out of this hot country," he declared on July 9, his final dispatch from the Deep South. "You'll not catch me here again soon."[43] The arrival of his discharge papers three days later signaled that he was at last homeward bound. A litany of fitful delays stretched his trip across two weeks, but by August 1865 he finally returned home, ill and exhausted but profoundly relieved.

---

43. H. Fike to C. Fike, July 9, 1865, FP.

Editorial Note

The documents presented in this collection make up roughly one-half of the extant wartime correspondence between Cimbaline and Henry Fike, who exchanged more than four hundred letters between August 1862 and July 1865. A few dozen messages have not survived, and others do not appear in the following chapters for various reasons. Some replies are quite short, consisting only of a few sentences or noting the enclosure of mementoes, and many more are extraordinarily long, dwelling on the people, occurrences, and thoughts that surface more succinctly in the excerpts that follow. A handful of letters, such as the first reply from Cimbaline, appear in full, but most have been edited for the sake of redundancy or brevity, omitting information that is extraneous (describing, say, the weather in a distant town), unclear (referring to people and past events whose relevance to the Fikes remains ambiguous), or repetitive. During the summer of 1863, for example, Henry often cut the boredom of his prolonged stint at Fort Pickering by writing multiple letters per day, many of which reiterated the same points. Both Fikes were also incorrigible scolds, forever reproaching the other for not writing more often. Such comments, which sometimes stretched across entire pages, have largely been omitted.

These transcriptions try to maintain as much fidelity as possible to the Fikes' handwritten correspondence. The original spelling and punctuation are mostly unchanged, and editorial notations such as [sic] appear sparingly in order to retain the substance, tone, and color of each author's unique voice. Although exasperating to modern eyes, the peculiar spelling used by Cimbaline exhibits the phonetic consistency of a person who drew on spoken language to guide her transition to written communication. Readers who struggle to make sense of her passages should try reading them out loud. In the cases where even that might not eliminate confusion, explanatory brackets appear to suggest her intended meaning. Many of Henry's letters, whether complaining about *musquitoes* or wishing to get *payd*, likewise reveal that spellings in nineteenth-century America were more variegated than today's readers might expect.

The primary material in this book is accompanied by a digital component, a website that allows students and scholars to interact with the volume's content. Search for this book on www.ugapress.org for links to the bonus material.

CHAPTER 1
"Do My Duty"

Camp Butler, Illinois
and
Mascoutah, Illinois
August 1862 to November 1862

On August 25, 1862, Cimbaline and Henry Fike began their Civil War in a swirl of conflicting emotions. Henry, like most army volunteers, had scant military experience. He did not enlist until the second year of the war, a fact that his letters did not explain, but mustered into the 117th Illinois Volunteer Infantry eager to help put down "this accursed rebellion" and willing to accept whatever sacrifices his service might entail. The motivations that inspired soldiers to volunteer varied and often overlapped. Some joined out of principle, committed to the defense of the federal Union and republican self-rule; others, mustering into a unit of neighbors and other men they knew, responded to pressures, unspoken or not, to defend and uphold the honor of their towns. By joining Company K, made up largely of men from Mascoutah and St. Clair County, Henry was joining a war with and for his community.[1]

Alone, weakened by poor health, and worried about the illness of their young daughter, Cimbaline faced the unknown prospects of war with less enthusiasm. The departure of her husband, like hundreds of others in Mascoutah, threatened to destabilize her household. With the loss of Henry's teaching salary, she welcomed boarders into the family home, but these young women proved to be a bother greater than the meager income they provided. The unreliability of male kinfolk, whom Henry had asked to manage tenants and pay creditors in his absence, deepened Cimbaline's concern about the family's finances.[2] The competition to

---

1. Duerkes, "I For One Am Ready"; Murdock, *Patriotism Limited*, 16–41; Hicken, *Illinois in the Civil War*, 2–5.
2. For the response of rural women in the North and West to wartime challenges, see Joseph L. Anderson, "The Vacant Chair on the Farm: Soldier Husbands, Farm Wives, and

replace Henry at school unleashed jealous rivalries, and the appointment of a new minister widened rifts within the church and community. The piercing gossip of neighbors sharpened Cimbaline's loneliness, stirred thoughts of moving, and even challenged her marriage. What's more, nighttime marauders now prowled the town with apparent impunity, demonstrating that even though the nearest battlefields were many miles away, another war loomed on Cimbaline's doorstep.[3]

The Fikes' first letters upend expectations that military life would prove more unpleasant than the supposed comforts of home. The stature and popularity that came from years spent working in the schoolhouse helped Henry win election as the regiment's lieutenant colonel and appointment as its quartermaster. He clearly valued the confidence placed in him by friends and neighbors. The privileges that his rank conferred likewise proved a source of growing appreciation. Not only did Henry, as an officer, receive higher pay, better housing, and a horse of his own, but he also enjoyed a surprisingly sumptuous diet, a luxury that he came to document by noting his gradual increase in weight. Soldiering, he found, might prove to be an adventure more exciting and comfortable than he had expected.

August 25, 1862, 10 o'clock p.m.
Chinery Hotel, Springfield, Illinois

Dear Cimbaline,
We had a warm dusty trip. The boys seem in the very highest spirits. Our company and the O'Fallon company filled two cars 'chuck full.'[4] The conductor on the train from St. Louis up locked each company up in its car in order to keep other persons from getting in and passing them-

---

the Iowa Home Front, 1861-1865," and Ginette Aley, "Inescapable Realities: Rural Midwestern Women and Families during the Civil War," in Aley and Anderson, *Union Heartland*, 48–168. See also McElligott, "'A Monotony Full of Sadness.'"

3. For violence on the Illinois home front, see Miller, "To Stop These Wolves' Forays"; Buck, "'Contest in Which Blood Must Flow'"; Anderson, "Fulton County War at Home."

4. The "O'Fallon company" likely referred to the men of Company I; of that unit's one hundred members, the largest number (forty-four) came from the railroad town of O'Fallon. Fred Delap, Illinois Civil War Muster and Descriptive Rolls Database, Illinois State Archives, Office of the Illinois Secretary of State, https://www.ilsos.gov/isaveterans/civilMusterSearch.do (hereafter Delap, ICWMDR).

selves off as soldiers and thus travel free. Notwithstanding the windows were all up, the cars soon became excessively warm and the boys forced the doors open—the conductor fixed them and locked them again. But pretty soon the boys broke them open again. The conductor shut them again; then the O'Fallon company tore down and smashed to pieces both doors of their car—tore out the stove-pipe and threw it over board, and broke out several side windows, and swore they intended to have air. It is useless to say that a good breeze floated through the car all the rest of the way up. Our boys had their door open but did not act so rudely. One reason why the boys cut up so, was because they got a hint that the conductor was a little secesh [secessionist].[5] Some fellow paid the conductor a good joke for his smartness. . . . I want you to read my letters to mother[6] and then keep them all filed away.

Your loving husband,
H. C. Fike

August 26, 1862, 9 o'clock p.m.

Camp Butler, Illinois

Dear Cimbaline,
I seat myself on the ground this evening to drop you a few more lines. This morning after breakfast, Col. Moore[7] and I went to work, and by noon I had secured my position as Regimental Quarter Master in Col. Moore's Regiment, which is No. 117. After dinner I went to work. I proceeded out to Camp Butler where I found seven companies on hand.[8]

---

5. Although a Union state and home of Republican president Abraham Lincoln, Illinois also included many antiwar Democrats and Confederate sympathizers. See Phillips, *Rivers Ran Backward*, 127–128, 211–235; Barry, "Colonel Mitchell's Wars"; Allardice, "'Illinois Is Rotten with Traitors!'"

6. Here Henry refers to his seventy-year-old, twice-widowed mother, Nancy Fike, who lived near his home with Cimbaline and Ellie. His father, Abel, who was Nancy's second husband, had passed away in 1852. United States Federal Census (hereafter USFC), 1860, Town of Mascoutah, St. Clair County, Illinois, 545–546; *History of St. Clair County*, 276–277; Abel Abraham Fike, https://www.findagrave.com/memorial/27843166/abel-abraham-fike, accessed December 9, 2023. For the relationships between soldiers' wives and their in-laws, see Nicole Etcheson, "No Fit Wife: Soldiers' Wives and Their In-Laws on the Indiana Home Front," in Aley and Anderson, *Union Heartland*, 97–124.

7. A schoolteacher from Lebanon, Risdon M. Moore, thirty-five, was elected colonel of the 117th Illinois. Delap, ICWMDR.

8. Established in the summer of 1861, Camp Butler first sat on the banks of the spring-fed Clear Lake, six miles east of Springfield. Peterson, "History of Camp Butler."

Located just south of Springfield, Illinois, Camp Butler was where the 117th Illinois and many other Union regiments mustered into service. It also held a large number of Confederate prisoners of war. Sangamon County (Illinois) Historical Society

The first thing I did was to go to headquarters and make requisition for about 400 blankets, which I drew and distributed to the Regiment.[9] I got through just about one hour ago. I was, of course, mustered in to-day and consequently am now one of Uncle Sam's boys. I have received my appointment from Gov Yates.[10] There are several thousand men here now. There are about 2000 secesh prisoners here in custody. 200 of them took

---

9. Unlike quartermasters a year earlier, who suffered frustrating delays as northern mills shifted to the production of coarser and heavy woolens demanded by the army, Henry Fike was able to fulfill his request with remarkable dispatch. Risch, *Quartermaster Support of the Army*, 351–359.

10. Governor Richard Yates, a Republican, served from 1861 to 1865. See Bohn, "Richard Yates."

the oath of allegiance to-day, and will consequently be released. . . . The boys are all in good spirits and are singing and cheering.[11]

I will write soon again. I feel very anxious about Ellie. Take good care of her.

Your affectionate husband,
H. C. Fike
Regiment Q. R. 117 Ills.

Wednesday, August 27, 1862, 3 o'clock in the morning

Mascoutah, Illinois

Dear Henry accorden to your request I now write you a few lines—Ellie is not so well as she was when you left home she seen quite well all day Monday—Monday night she was taken somthing like she was at first—Tusday she lay all day without noticen any thing with a hot fever this morning she seems better—her fever is not so high—The Dr. thinkes she is not daingors—I know she is very sick I hope she will bee better soon I received a letter from Webb[12] Monday evening wich I will send you—I heard to day that tha was a great meney at Springfield without Blanketes or any thing to sleep on I would like to know if you want anything & I want you to come home as soon as you can. I do feel so lonely sence you left am out of heart about Ellie. I hope she will be better before I write again write soon and offten for I want to hear from you all—Yours truley
  Lucy C. Fike

---

11. Union victory at Fort Donelson, Tennessee, in February 1862 resulted in fifteen thousand rebel prisoners being transferred to a makeshift prison established at this new location, and prisoner escapes became a nightly problem. Colonel William Hoffman, the commissary-general of prisoners, observed: "The camp is not inclosed and the detention of prisoners there depends more on their willingness to remain than upon any restraint upon them by the guard." United States War Department, *War of the Rebellion* (hereafter OR), ser. 2, vol. 3, 367. See Peterson, "A History of Camp Butler," 78–80.

12. Henry received a letter from "L Webb," written at Fort Snelling, Minnesota, just days before Fike traveled to Camp Butler. This is likely Loren Webb, a Methodist minister who, in the spring of 1861, volunteered for a three-month enlistment in the 9th Illinois Infantry, from which he resigned as captain on July 10, 1862, only to reenlist in the 11th Minnesota Infantry. L. Webb to H. Fike, August 19, 1862, FP; Delap, ICWMDR; Civil War Soldiers and Sailors System database, National Park Service, https://www.nps.gov/civilwar/soldiers-and-sailors-database.htm, accessed December 9, 2023 (hereafter CWSS).

August 29, 1862, 10 o'clock p.m.
Camp Butler, Illinois

Dear Cimbaline,
I received a letter from your hand to-day I was becoming very anxious to hear from home. I am exceedingly sorry to hear that Ellie is still so ill. I hope she will get better and soon recover. I hope you will console yourself as much as possible in your loneliness, and let me know immediately, by telegraph if Ellie gets dangerous. If you attempt to telegraph me, have the person who telegraphs from Lebanon to St. Louis, to find out from the telegraph operator if the dispatch is immediately sent from St. Louis to Springfield. . . . If you can not telegraph immediately through to me, send a special messenger on the Rail Road to me.
   Your affectionate husband.
   H. C. Fike
   Reg. Q. M. 117 Ills. Vols.

August 29, 1862
Mascoutah, Illinois

Dear Henry
It is with pleasure this evening I set down to write or to anser you letter that I just received. The second one I have received from you I am very sorry that you have not heard from home sence you have been gon I have ritten 4 letters to you, one every day & Ellie is some better to day she has been verry sick sence you left. She hasn't walked but a few steps sence Monday—I have been sick myself sence you left. I hope we both will be well soon I am very glad that you have obtain your office but I would be much gladder if you could be at home. I will stop riten to night it is late an I do not feel very much like riten When I hear that you have heard from me I will write you a long letter
   Yours truley
   Lucy C Fike

Sunday afternoon, August 31, 1862
Camp Butler, Illinois

Dear Cimbaline:—

Our regiment have only got under plank sheds which afford a pretty good shelter, from the night air, but if a hard beating rain should come, the boys would undoubtedly get wet. It has showered a little to-day, but wet nobody. I have a good 'Wall' tent, which will keep me dry, let come what may, so you need entertain no uneasiness. You wrote me you heard that we had no blankets. We did hear that in Lebanon but we drew blankets the first day I arrived. I drew blankets within two hours after I got in. . . .[13]

We have a good many men here in camp; about six thousand—all come in within a few days. The government is clothing and arming them as fast as it can. I do not know how long we will remain here—some think we will only stay here until we get fully outfitted and then remove to some other camp for drilling and instruction. I do not pretend to know. One regiment has already left, and the talk is that another one will leave on Wednesday. I will give you a list of what we eat: We have wheat bread and crackers, pickled pork, fresh beef, Irish potatoes, rice, hominy, peas, coffee and sugar—you may depend upon it I have my coffee sweetened 'all right.' . . . We had a sermon this morning at 11 o'clock from Rev. Gregg,[14] a minister present. The shower of rain that came up interrupted the service, but the minister will resume it again this afternoon. He seems to be a splendid preacher. His text was 'God is love.' From present indications we have a good moral regiment. Every night can be heard the singing of church songs in the various camps. This indicates that the soldiers, if not moral and religious themselves, have been blessed with moral instruction, and been brought up in communities where religion is known and taught.

Your affectionate husband,
H. C. Fike
R.Q.M. 117 Ills. Vols.
P.S. Do not forget to write.

---

13. Army regulations stated that soldiers were to receive a pair of gray, all-wool blankets every five years, with one to be issued in the first year and another two years later. See Risch, *Quartermaster Support of the Army*, 351–359.
14. This is likely the Reverend Martin B. Gregg, pastor of the Presbyterian Church of East St. Louis, Illinois. *History of St. Clair County*, 178.

September 2, 1862
Camp Butler, Illinois

Dear Cimbaline:—
I sit down and just snatch a moment to write you a word or two. I have been hard at work all morning, having lumber hauled to make barracks. The cars on the Rail Road landed with about 75 thousand feet of lumber & I had to superintend the hauling of the most of it about one half mile to where we are making our barracks. There is a great demand for lumber, and the Quarter Masters are all on the lookout for their own regiments. You may depend that I watch out for our own. . . . Tell all the folks, that I am trying to do my duty and not to be uneasy on my account.
   Your affectionate husband,
   H. C. Fike

September 2, 1862

Dear Cimbaline:—
I want you to read my letters to mother, and she can then get all the news you derive from my letters I saw a few secesh prisoners released to-day. They were let out at the gate of the enclosures in which they have been confined since the battle of Ft. Donelson.[15] They were provided with their dismissal papers, and had provision to do them several days in the haversacks. The manner of releasing prisoners generally is to afford them means of transportation to some point near home. But those released to-day preferred striking out on 'their own hook,' to going in the usual way. They said they had relatives down in Franklin county this state, where they would aim to go too at first. I talked with some secesh prisoners to-day who were detailed to dig a well, (they had guards with them.) and they seem to think we can never whip them out They seem to have great confidence in Jeff. Davis.[16]
   Your affectionate husband,
   H. C. Fike

---

15. Brigadier General Ulysses S. Grant's capture of Fort Donelson on February 16, 1862, aided the Union army's advance up the Cumberland River into central and western Tennessee.

16. Franklin County sat in the portion of southern Illinois known as "Little Egypt," above the confluence of the Ohio and Mississippi Rivers at the town of Cairo. For the political conservatism of this region, see Burke, "Egyptian Darkness."

September 23, 1862
Mascoutah, Illinois

Dear Henry

It is with pleasure I take my pen in hand to inform you that we erived at home to day. I feeld very tired after my jurney. It is very tirsom to travel with a child and espesley with as cross a one as I have. I feeld as tho, I would never want to see Camp Butler again, I dont think I ever was so glad to see home in my life as I was to day I am well axcept a sore throught Ellie is not very well her little joy is stolen she has some fever an is very cross to day.
  Affectionate wife
  Lucy C. Fike

September 28, 1862
Mascoutah, Illinois

Dear Henry

After Ellie an I tock a long play an she has gon to sleap I thought I would rite you a few lines tow send by John Moser[17] to you to let you know how we wer gitten along & When I arived at home I wos quit tired an all most give out, after resten a day or tow I felt much better. And Ellie to was quit unwell but she has improved sence an seems quit playfull to day. I hope she will git along now. When I come home I wos vext and made to see how thinges was. every was tore upside downg. It was 10 o clock when I got home and the Brexvis [breakfast] dishes was not wash my roomes below I lock up when I come home tha was open an durty an some little thinges misen which I didnot like very well. Tha didnot do anything while I was gon only eat and sleep an fuss. Elen wanted to boss, an Miney didnot like to be best [bossed] so Miney told on Elen in Elen told on Miney.[18]

---

  17. John Mosar, a twenty-year-old private in Company K, was also from Mascoutah. Delap, ICWMDR.
  18. According to the 1860 census, three young women—Mary Warner, Hannah Matthews, and Martha Ritter—lived as boarders with the Fikes. As subsequent letters will reveal, Cimbaline cycled through several boarders during the war. Here she may be referring to Ellen Barth and Minna Schiermeier, who in the recent census appeared as the unmarried daughters of local women who were listed as the heads of their respective households. USFC, 1860.

I told tham when I hearde ther storeys that I was at home now an I intended to boss an have thinges to my nosen [notion] an if tha didnot like it tha could leave that was the worde with the bark on.[19]

Monday, September 29, 1862

Camp Butler, Illinois

Dear Cimbaline,

I do not pretend to know how long we will remain here in this camp. Some think we will leave in the course of a couple of weeks, and others think not so soon. I cannot say how that may be, but I want us all to be ready when the order comes for us to move, so that we can obey it immediately and thus do our duty. This is what I enlisted in the war for—to do my duty, and so to perform that duty that it may be some help towards putting down this accursed rebellion. Before I left home, I was fully aware that the soldiers had to undergo many hardships and deprivations but then I went into the service fully determined to endure these hardships; so I will not in the least be disappointed if they come. If they do come, which I expect will be the case if we remain long in the service, this determination of mine, I know, will help me to endure them with more fortitude. I want you to give yourself no uneasiness on my account whatever, for I warrant you that I will fare as good as any in our regiment will. I have no fears the least that I will suffer for anything to eat or to wear, inasmuch as everything of that kind for our regiment has to pass through my hands. So you may rest assured that I shall take care of No. 1.—[20]

Your affectionate husband,
H. C. Fike

---

19. One dictionary explains that to take the "bark off" was "to give one a hiding." Mathews, *Dictionary of Americanisms*, 77.

20. The quartermaster's peculiar station, in which nearly all regimental supplies passed through his hands, meant not only that could he easily satisfy his own needs but also that such a privileged position might draw the suspicion and ire of his comrades. See Lenette Taylor, "*Supply for Tomorrow*," 14–15; Keating, *Greatest Trials I Ever Had*, 35.

September 29, 1862
Mascoutah, Illinois

Henry
Today I have made you twelve dollars wich I will send to you. You cand use than if you think you will like than if not send that home—If tha is anything more you want send word an I will try to send it to you Mary Curtis is to start for Camp tomorrow—If she has such a time as Mrs. Land[21] an I did she will be glad when she gites home. I dont intend to tell anyone let that go and sadisfi thamselves. . . . Helen Rahill has got the school out hear Frank Risley applied for it but she could not git it Mrs. Gibbes an Mary Curtis felt very much disopointed.[22] This evenning becous tha did not git some letters I left an told tham I knew I would git one for you was somuch better to write then there man was. Tha wished that I would not git one be like tham. But I got one an stop and told tham. I will stop writen for fear I will not have aneything to write next time. It is bed time so good night
Lucy C Fike

October 8, 1862
Mascoutah, Illinois

Dear Henry
I take my seat to night to fulfill your request I felt worse this time to part with you then I every did. Befor when you left you could say when you could come back. This time you could not say when perhaps never in this world I did not sleep much after you left. I lay along time thinking if we should never meet again what a miserable place you would leve mee

---

21. Mary Curtis was the wife of James Curtis, a lieutenant in Company K. In this case "Mrs. Land" could refer to three women whose husbands also served in Company K: Minerva Land (wife of Captain Nathan Land), Mary Land (Private John H. Land), or Sarah Land (Corporal James Land). Delap, ICWMDR; USFC, 1860.

22. As Henry's niece, seventeen-year-old Helen Rayhill was well positioned to secure this opening at the school where he had recently worked as teacher and principal. Her apparent rivals were Frank Risley, a former clerk from the nearby town of Lebanon who served as a sergeant in Company C, and Calvin Gibbs, who had worked as a teacher before mustering into Company K as a private. Census manuscripts do not indicate whether the latter's wife, Celia Gibbs, worked as a teacher as well. *History of St. Clair County*, 277–278; Delap, ICWMDR; USFC, 1860.

now happyness for mee to see in Mascoutah. Oh that I could bee with you, how much happery I would bee.... Ellie woke up in the morning I ask her wher her Pa was she look over behind on the beed and said Oh oh *gon gon* she was quit buisey all day helpen us with thinges. I think I must have a horse off my owen. Then I can go when I want to what do you think about it. Mother came home last eveng she felt very much disopointed not seeing you she did not heare that you wos at home untell Sunday evening.... I must stop writen—it is late an raining very heard and I feel very tired after my trip—I hope that I shall hear from you soon and very offten

   from your wife
   Lucy C Fike

October 9, 1862

Camp Butler, Illinois

Dear Cimbaline:
I arrived here safe and sound to-day about four o'clock p.m. Our regiment is still here, and probably will be for a few days yet. The reason it is detained is because the government has not yet paid off all the advance pay and bounty.[23] We may remain here all the remainder of the present week, but I do not know for certain.

I will give you a short account of my trip up. We arrived in Belleville at sunrise, took breakfast, and there Ausby[24] and I took cars for St. Louis—Don[25] rode my horse down to St. Louis from Belleville. I went over into the city and telegraphed up here to see if our regiment was about to move—found out they had not gone. I then bought myself a sword, two pistols, a sash, India Rubber blanket & leggings, and a valise (or handtruck) and army saddle. In the afternoon I shipped my horse ('Selim' is his name.) to Alton on a boat, and I took the cars up....[26]

---

23. Cole, *Centennial History of Illinois*, 277–278.
24. When the war broke out, Ausby Fike was forty-eight years old—nearly twice the age of Henry, the youngest of the Fike siblings. Ausby was a merchant and former county judge to whom Cimbaline turned for aid in managing the farm's affairs during the early months of Henry's enlistment. USFC, 1860, 547; *History of St. Clair County*, 78, 278.
25. Doniphan Fike, sixteen, was Ausby's second-youngest son. He mustered into Company K of the 117th Illinois as a musician. *History of St. Clair County*, 278; Delap, ICWMDR.
26. Selim was the name of a thoroughbred racehorse that had been owned by the Prince of Wales and had won several major prizes from 1806 to 1808. Taunton, *Portraits of Celebrated Racehorses*, 49–53.

I sent back $30 by Ausby to you. The things I bought cost so, that I could not spare any more. If you need any more before I can send you some call upon Ausby and you can get it. If you need any at anytime let me know too in time and I can, no doubt, help you. I will write a letter to William Slade[27] in a day or two about that little note. I don't want you to stand in need of any thing necessary for your comfort, and will help you anytime to the very last cent I have. Some of those notes of mine that you have will be due in a month or two, and you can get the money on them. If that German renter does not come up and sign those two notes in a few days, have Riley Edwards[28] go and see him, sometime when he is down in that settlement.

From
your affectionate husband,
H. C. Fike

October 12, 1862

Camp Butler, Illinois

Dear Cimbaline,
The boys generally are getting tired of this place, and are becoming more and more anxious to leave here and be removed to some point further south than this. It seems that the only thing that detains us here is the want of money to pay off the men their first month's pay in advance. As soon as that is paid, I guess we will go—I cann't say and don't know where.

I want you to cheer up and be in as good spirits as you can, while I am

---

27. William Slade, an unmarried twenty-one-year-old farmer, was not among the St. Clair County men who volunteered to enlist in the summer of 1862, but a year later he mustered into the 26th Illinois Infantry. USFC, 1860, 257; Illinois Adjutant General, Regimental and Unit Histories, 76; Index to Compiled Service Records of Volunteer Union Soldiers, RG 94,M539, National Archives, https://www.fold3.com/image/293777712, accessed December 9, 2023.

28. The identity of this tenant is unclear. Census returns from Mascoutah reveal more than two dozen households with inhabitants who had been born in Prussia, Saxony, Hessia, or other German-speaking areas in Europe. The concentration of German immigrants was particularly high in the nearby town of New Baden. Riley Edwards was a farmer who lived in Madison County, just to the north of Mascoutah. USFC, 1860; Illinois State Marriage Index, Madison County, July 18, 1861, Volume 6, Page 175, License 11, https://www.ilsos.gov/isavital/marriageSearch.do, accessed December 9, 2023.

away. I hope I will not be separated from my dear family more than a few months at furthest. You will feel lonesome sometimes undoubtedly, but cheer up, and remember there is a better time coming. Go around and visit among the neighbors and you will thus pass a great deal of your lonesomeness until I come home to stay. You wrote that Mr. Carr had vacated the house he had rented from me, and wanted to know how long he had been in it. He went into the house on the 21 day of August and was therefore in it nearly two months. I want you to charge him for two months, at $5 per month, which will make him owe you $10. He may not want to pay for two full months; but that is the custom to count pieces of a month, the same as a full month.

Your affectionate husband,
H. C. Fike

October 12, 1862

Mascoutah, Illinois

Dear Henry

I received a letter from you last evening staten that you wos well allow your trip to Camp wich I was very happy to hear. I did not hear as soon as I expected to & This has been a very lonsom sabath. Now Church to day town seems quit still. . . . We have heard bad nuse from Cornth sence the last battle Mrs Britt has come home. James is wounded in the back of the nake [neck] Mr Britt wos killd in the first of the Battle lay on the feel two days before his wife found him and when she found him his hole fase wos shot off an was stript of all of his clothes.[29] . . . I didnot sleep but alittle for thinking about you and the poor solgers—to think off the many thousenes that wos out in camp that stormey night. Yes and mit say thousenes out without campes or even nothen to lay on. Hundreds out on guard in the rain an cold with out aney thing to ceep tham warm and

---

29. Mary Britt was the widow of Captain William Britt, a member of Company F in the 9th Illinois Infantry, who was killed at the Battle of Corinth in Mississippi on October 3, 1862. James A. Fike, a corporal in the 9th Illinois and the only son of Henry's older brother Nathan, was wounded in the neck at Corinth but returned to service, finally mustering out at the end of his three-year enlistment in August 1864. Application WC39430, RG 15, Case Files of Approved Pension Applications of Widows and Other Dependents of Civil War Veterans, National Archives and Records Administration, https://www.fold3.com/image/297517763, accessed December 9, 2023; Delap, ICWMDR; *History of St. Clair County*, 135.

tow think off hundreds of power women and children at home sufren while thinking of ther freandes for away from tham This wor is a horble thing, wod to god that this rebelion could be put downg in one day & and . . . I feele quit lonely all so still. Ellie is asleep. She beates all for michief that I ever saw I cannot leave her one minit She gites up in a char an croles on the beed or on the table in the window pules out the fire tares up the carpet turned over the chares dables in the watter gites in the cubbred pules of her shoes and stockens and then if slapes her she will git up in my lap and huges and kisses me and then go sen do the same thing over. . . . rite often yours in love L.C. F

9 Oclock 44 1/2 minutes

When I would like to see you on you big fine black hors in full dress. Now and then I hear you spoken of as a fine looken Offerses and rother the best one in the Regment I would like to see for myself. Mother wos hear when I reveiwd you tow last letters and heard tham red. She ses mine has not come yet I guess he has forgot he has a Mother no body cares for me. Ellie offten ses my Pa my pa is gon when we ask her wher you are. Now she is standing behind me pulling at the map. . . . I would not take the world for her. When we go to beed she will fold her little armes aroung my neck an kiss me When go to sleep. Then I allways think of you I must stop riten. I feel very bad. Lucy Fike

October 14, 1862

Camp Butler, Illinois

Dear Cimbaline,

You wrote considerably in your letter concerning the exposure and deprivations of our soldiers. I know that a soldier's life is one made up of hardships and many times of wants and even sufferings. But then, who is there, that is a true patriot to his country, that would not be willing to undergo these things in behalf of his needy country? To-night, since dark has set in, two fellows in the tent next east of mine, have been playing for an hour or so upon the guitar and violin. Among other airs performed, they played the good old tune of 'Home, sweet home.' I thought I never heard any music as sweet in my life as it was. I had to stop writing a while and listen; and while thus listening my mind naturally ran back to home, and I sat a long time musing upon things and affairs of our own happy fireside. It seems to me now, that if I ever live to get back home again to stay that I shall enjoy it better than I ever have before. I don't mean by this that I am any ways homesick now; far from it. To be sure, nothing would afford me greater satisfaction than to be with you, but then, I feel that I am here to do my duty, and *I must do it,* and when I come home to stay, I will feel much better by it. I have written to you already about renting our house. If you have any more chances to rent it, ask $5 per month, if the person wants it only a few months or by the month, and make them pay monthly. If they want it by the year take $50 for the whole year.

Your affectionate husband,
H. C. Fike

October 18, 1862

Camp Butler, Illinois

Dear Cimbaline,
Amos Day[30] promised me he would see to having your wood and coal hauled. I will write him a letter some of these days, and keep his memory refreshed in that way. If you need corn or the like, have Ausby to speak to some of our renters to haul and fill up our corn crib. They ought to fill it up before bad weather. You should have some hay, if you keep a cow. You might get this, perhaps, from the renter on my old home place. As soon as I get hold of some money I shall remember you without fail. I want you and myself both to live as economically as we can until we get free from debt. But still I want you to have all the money need to keep you well and independent, and you shall have it, if it takes all I can earn to do it, while I am away. However, you need anticipate no fears on that score.

Your affectionate husband,
H. C. Fike

October 19, 1862

Mascoutah, Illinois

Dear Henry
Our new Preacher has mooved and live in Andersons[31] hous north of us he preach to day in our church to day tha wos quit a good crowd out to

---

30. Amos Day, thirty-three, was a Mascoutah farmer. USFC, 1860.
31. This likely referred to Anderson Fike, thirty, the oldest son of Ausby. USFC, 1860; *History of St. Clair County,* 278.

hear him. People genrley think his femley will be liked better then Risleys is. most every body is out with tham now. Thav have thoudout good meney steres [stories] and hintes about peeple in Mascoutah. I dont know but one famley hear that calls in to see tham offen. That is Uncle Tomey Rainforth.[32] The people will be glad when tha are gon. Frank espesley. I wos about turnen Miney of last week she didnot want to go. She told me if I would cep her she would stay for $3 a month an come home every sunday night at 10 clock Mortha Blacker wantes to come and stay withe me for the same prise but I donot want to take her from Mrs Ross[33] for fear of heard feelenes & Mother got a letter from James Thursday evening. he is at the hospitle near Caro Mouncitty [Cairo Mound City][34] he is quite unwell with his wound has the fever with it. He wantes some one to come and see him an wanted Mother to send him $5.

Sunday evening.

This has been a lonely day to me. I went to Church this afternoon at 3 Oclock to hear Rev. Brown preach. He preach his sermon an give out his hame asked some Brother to rase the tune. No one did so he ask some sister to lead in singing. After a while tha squeld it out. Then he ask some Brother to lead in prayer. all was silent. Then he ask Mother to pray. She prayd a pretty good prayer preyed for the Union for the sick solgers for the well ones for the Offersers then for our enimons [enemies]. after all she prayd for our quartley meeting & After meeting some of tham concluded that we had better git up a singing class.

October 29, 1862

Camp Butler, Illinois

Dear Cimbaline,

This afternoon a great many of our regiment, and I among them, went to town and heard Parson Brownlow[35] speak. There was an immense throng

---

32. Thomas and Nancy Rainforth lived a few houses away from the Fikes. USFC, 1860.
33. Mrs. Ross was likely Aledy Ross, thirty-two, who in the 1860 census lived in Mascoutah with three young people identified as servants. Martha Blake, only seven years old at the time of that enumeration, still lived with her parents. USFC, 1860.
34. Cairo sits at the far southern tip of Illinois, at the mouth of the Ohio River; Mound City is located about five miles upstream.
35. The "Fighting Parson," William G. Brownlow was a Methodist minister and newspaper publisher from eastern Tennessee whose fierce denunciations of slavery and secession earned him many enemies in the South. After being expelled from the Confederacy,

assembled to hear him. He spoke in the rotunda of the State House, standing upon the first platform above the lower floor.... Parson Brownlow spoke nearly two hours, and such speaking I never heard or saw. The immense, vast crowd, at times, when he would be dwelling upon some cruel, horrid scene he had witnessed in Tennessee, would be still as the hall of death, and the tears would be flowing in torrents from hundreds and hundreds of eyes, and in a moment afterward, his speech would bring forth the loudest cheering and stamping, and clapping of hands and yelling that I ever heard. Taking it altogether, I never witnessed such a scene. It was well worth my trouble to go to see him, and hear him. He is anything else than easy upon the southern traitors and their Northern sympathizers.

Friday morning, October 31, 1862

I feel as well as I ever felt in my life. I now 'pull down' 161 pounds, which is 11 1/2 pounds more than I weighed when I first left home in August last.[36] I have had no good opportunity yet of getting my picture taken. The first chance I have, I will get it, and send you. Since we officers, having been messing together, we have fared quite well indeed. We have as good to eat as we desire. A man does our cooking.

Your affectionate husband,

H. C. Fike

November 2, 1862

Mascoutah, Illinois

Dear Henry

This is sunday I donot feel very much like going to church to day At home and feel very lonsom and all most like I had lived longe enuf in this trubleson world. I feel sometimes like I could not cepe hous any

---

Brownlow embarked on a widely celebrated six-month speaking tour across the North. Said one Springfield paper, "Suffice it to say that his speech was such a one as no one other individual living, perhaps, could make, and its effect was correspondingly great." "Great Mass Meeting," *Illinois Daily State Journal*, October 31, 1862, 2; Coulter, *William G. Brownlow*, 208–234.

36. A postwar study published by the U.S. Sanitary Commission reported that the average weight of Civil War soldiers was 141 pounds. Henry, at five feet eleven inches, was three inches taller than the volunteers of the same age, and the weight gain that he will describe during his service says perhaps more about the relative comfort in which Union officers lived than it does his peculiar stature. Gould, *Investigations in the Military*, 403.

longer I onley wish that I could sell every thing we have got and I wos a thousen miles from hear. Eney how out of Mascoutah It gites worse every day. Seenes like every thing is tore up side downg Nothen goes on rite. It is heardley safe for a deasent women to be on street after dark. The men has nearley all gon crasey about the wemen. some you would not think off[37]

November 6, 1862

Camp Butler, Illinois

Dear Cimbaline,
The Colonel told me this morning that we will go as soon as cars can be had for our transportation—he thought perhaps we might get off by Saturday or Sunday. We are to go to Alton, and there take a boat, and proceed down the river, by Cairo, on to Columbus in Kentucky. If you will look on the map hanging up on the wall, you can see that Columbus is about twenty miles below Cairo on the east bank of the Mississippi River. When we get there we will be about as far from Mascoutah as we are now. . . . I was glad to hear that you all seem to be so well and hearty. I hope you will take good care of little mischievous Ellie while I am absent. Give her plenty of playthings to amuse herself with & thus keep her out of mischief. As soon as she can say a few words get her a little primer, and by the time she can talk good, she will know her alphabet. It would be a great comfort to me if I could be home ever evening and spend the pleasant hours with you and have a 'big play' with Ellie. No doubt it would be a source of comfort to you also. But since we are necessarily so parted, we must cheer up and keep in lively spirits. I feel very cheerful myself, and I hope you will do so too. If some of your neighbors do not do what is exactly right, you never mind it, and keep straight forward on in the discharge of your Christian duties. . . . If you have not already done it, you had better give those accounts to Philip Postel[38] to collect as soon as you can. When you write tell me how Amos Day keeps you furnished with the

---

37. Few Civil War newspapers from St. Clair County survive, but the local news in one Springfield paper suggests that Mascoutah was hardly alone in its struggles with crime. Days before Lucy's letter, a piece titled "Another Burglary" noted, "There are evidences of the presence of skillful burglars in our city, which should place our citizens upon their guard." *Illinois Daily State Journal*, October 31, 1862, 3.

38. Philip H. Postel, forty-three, was a wealthy mill owner in Mascoutah. USFC, 1860; *History of St. Clair County*, 354–355.

necessaries for housekeeping. If any of my renters come at any time and pay you any money let me know, and I will tell you how to appropriate it, after you have taken out what you need. If that man on my farm west of Fayetteville, does not come and sign those notes in a week or so, have Philip Postel to attend to it for you.[39]

Your affectionate husband,

H. C. Fike

Sunday, November 9, 1862, 6 o'clock p.m.

Camp Butler, Illinois

Dear Cimbaline,

Tomorrow afternoon we purpose to leave. We expect the train here at twelve o'clock. We can load up in the course of an hour or two and then we will be off for Alton, where we take a boat for *Memphis*, in Tennessee, instead of Columbus, Kentucky, as I before wrote. . . . Memphis is a good ways from home, I know, but people don't all die that go down there immediately. I want you to keep cheerful and visit around a good deal, and grow to be a hearty, robust, stout good looking cheerful 'duck of a wife'—just the kind I want to find you when I come home. Bless Ellie's little soul, I would like to see her often, and have a play with her. I know she will be a great deal of company to you. I am glad you find her so mischievous as she is. I think it a good sign for her. I always found my mischievous scholars, as a general thing, were the smartest and quickest to learn. . . . Do not forget, if I am not at home when Ellie is two years old, to mark her height on the door that opens into the kitchen, right above where I marked her height at one year old and weigh her and set it down in the back the Testament. . . . I must stop for to-night and sow [sew] a button on my pants. You may know I am fattening, for I am bursting off all the buttons, nearly every day. You would have laughed if you could have seen me early the other morning, sitting up on top a box by the stove, sewing up my pants before I could put them on. But such is camp life, and I take it in the very best of spirits—and always will.

H. C. Fike

---

39. Fayetteville lies eight miles due south of Mascoutah, on the banks of the Kaskaskia River.

November 12, 1862
On board the *Empress,* On Mississippi River,

Dear Cimbaline,

I am seated in the steamboat cabin this evening, and shall endeavor to give you a slight sketch of our journey since my last letter, which I wrote on board the boat coming from Alton to St. Louis. . . . The boys seem to keep in very good spirits. They have poor accommodations about sleeping, having to occupy the outer decks of the boat, which is rather unpleasant, it being quite cool. They nearly all have good shelter overhead, but it is open all around only when canvass is hung up. They have pretty cool sleeping of nights. The officers all have good rooms, and warm comfortable quarters, and beds to sleep in. Our mess, consisting of the Colonel, Lt. Colonel, Chaplain, Adjutant, Quarter Master's Sergeant, and myself, have our mess-chess along, and have our cook provided our own meals; we think fifty cents a meal a little too steep, when they furnish but very little better than we ourselves have. The boat we are on is a very large and nice one. It is loaded very heavily with freight, and has a good many passengers on board, and besides all this, all our regiment about 850 men, and then still besides about three hundred head of beef cattle, which they are taking down to Columbus, Kentucky for our army. So you may judge that we have somewhat of a crowded time. Our regiment has a brass band, and a string band, and a lot of us have got up a kind of singing club, and among us all, we manage to keep the crowd entertained with music. Besides this there are belonging to the regiment as regular musicians, twelve drummers, three fifers, & ten buglers, making one and all about fifty musicians. We officers, who had revolvers, had considerable sport to-day, as we came along, practicing shooting at ducks, snags, and everything we could see. I killed a duck in the operation. As we passed any body on the shore of the river the boys would send up a shout. And I tell you the way they would make the welkin ring when we would pass by a town. At a town called Liberty, we stopped, for the crew of the boat to take on wood. Quite a crowd of citizens collected on shore to look at the soldiers on the boat. There was a young lady among them who had a quantity of apples, which she threw in among the boys, and such other scrambling and shouting you never saw. The men are not allowed to go on shore at any of the landings.

November 13, 1862

Mascoutah, Illinois

Dear Henry
I set myself downg this evening after returning from Church. to write you a few lines to let you know we are in resible [reasonable] health. . . . Nothen very strange a going on in Towen as I know off. We have been truble with some on among the hous for two or three nighths. Nocken on the windowes and through one the window and crack it. One night while I was gon some one came and nock on the window and told Miney to open the door she ask who it wos. He ses you know who I am open the door she would not. he went off. Another night some one come and tryed to git in. Three nights some one tryed to come in the hous. I intend to git a revolver an truble som of tham if tha truble me a gain. Miney is agoing to leave hear next Monday—Mortha Blacker is coming to stay with me Miney does not want to go a way. I thought Mortha would bee company to me at nights Just now Miney told me that Match [?] abuths girl ask her the other day if you did whip me some times she said she heard so. That you wos so meen to me. I should like to know how you and anderson settle up about the Buggy Miller came and paid me $29.50 rent What shall I do with it

   I received two letters from you last evening. I read the one you rote at Camp Butler. then I redd the one you rote at Allten I feel very sorry that I rote anything to you about the nuse I had heard I wish now I had not said any thing about it untell you come home again. you seem to feel so bad about it. But I will tell you I wos told this nuse. I plege my word that I never would tell you who told me. befor tha would tell me whot it wos. I have been sorry sence that I ever made such a promis. I told the person then that I wos sorry that I ever made such a promis. If I even thought such a thing of you I never could live happy. I will tell you one thing. the person wos a man that told me this nuse. a bout you comeing from Charty [?] Otenes with a women The other part a bout you stopen at Risleys Mrs. Risley told it her self at Mrs. Matheuse and Miss Addy Mathews told me she told about Anney and I she said she supose Anne an I had quit a battle. but she wis sure of one thing that Anne gave me what I meeded. spoke very slitely of me in every respect. Her and tha girels

gave tham the hole histry of Rayhills[40] folkes and me. Tha told tham that I did not know much. that you never went about with me very much. You never come in their house but once with me then you acted as tho you wos asshamed of me and tha belived you wos you after came in at night and set tell ten oclock with tham tha supose I did not know it sence we had wordes with each other you seen frenleyer then you and did you did not care for me. Tha knowd you wos asshame of me Anne said one day when tha wos speaken a bout the school. . about heaen a Exibission she said she entended not to have any this year. Tha said if you wos hear tha would have one. No she ses we woudent for I would not let him. I have manege him and ruld him. and I can a gain. I never would be ruld by him like Hanher was that one thing serten. Frank said when I went to Springfield an Camp Butler I saw more then I ever seen in my life. This is onley and interduction to what tha have said a bout us It seemes a little heard to have tham to go aroung and talk so after we have gone than so much and been so good to tham I allaways told you tha wos such a famley. But you would not belive me. You allways seem to think the sun rose and set in there hous. And when I told you tha tolk about me you seem to think I wos to blame. Tha wos all right and go thare as often as ever you did. Now tha have this to through up that you seem frenleyer after this happen then you did before that you knew that i wos to blame. I think I have reten enufe a bout this. It allways makes me mad. when I think of it.
. . . I wish you would write Amos Day a letter to sture him up to his duty
  L C Fike

Saturday, November 16, 1862.

On board Steamer *Empress* about 100 miles above Memphis

Dear Cimbaline,
We have passed several nice looking places. We have seen on the shore a good many negro plantations. The proprietors seemed to have good nice houses to live in, surrounded by about fifteen or twenty nigger shanties—looking like a small village. We passed, this afternoon, Ft. Wright or

---

40. Charity (Henry's older sister) and Charles Rayhill lived on a farm three miles east of Mascoutah. *History of St. Clair County,* 113, 278.

Fort Pillow, on the Tennessee shore.[41] It is situated on a very high bluff. A small force is stationed here. A great many boats are now running the river, carrying troops down to Memphis, and other places below here. While we were stopped this forenoon, I took a little stroll out into the Arkansas woods. There is a great deal of mistletoe growing here on the trees. It is an evergreen that grows in large bunches all over a tree. I expect mother can describe it to you. I climbed up a large sycamore tree about fifty feet high, and got some. I will send you a small twig of it in this letter. I will also send a small twig of a cotton-wood tree, as little mementoes of the productions of Arkansas soil.

From the inhabitants, who live along here, we learn that the rebels are taking steps to press in every man immediately. Every night we stop, we put out a strong picket guard. Last night there were three regiments of us together, and we had out a pretty large line of guards, and then sent a company or two out scouting to see if there were any of the rebels to be seen hereabouts. Some reported to us this morning that the rebels are at work through here. One man and wife came to the shore where we were landed and had a small lot of furniture. They said they wanted to go north the first opportunity they could get. This country, along the river, generally looks very shabby.

Your affectionate husband,
H. C. Fike

---

41. Through the summer of 1861, Fort Wright, Tennessee, had been the rebels' forwardmost defensive position on the Mississippi River, but by the time that Henry passed, the post was occupied only irregularly. Confederates had abandoned nearby Fort Pillow on June 4, 1862.

CHAPTER 2

"I Never Had Such Thinges to Attend to Before"

Fort Pickering, Tennessee
and
Mascoutah, Illinois
November 1862 to May 1863

After three months of drilling at Camp Butler, the men of the 117th Illinois Volunteers eagerly disgorged from the crowded steamboat they had shared with hundreds of bawling cattle. Henry stepped upon the Mississippi River landing and marveled at the changes that the Union army was bringing to the "enemy's country." Federal troops had captured Memphis on June 6, 1862, and initiated a military occupation that imposed a new order on the city, its people, and the surrounding landscape.[1] Soldiers felled broad stretches of timber to construct a blufftop garrison, Fort Pickering, and to feed the thousands of Union campfires that blazed along the river. Within the city, officers razed dozens of houses abandoned by rebels and repurposed some of the finest homes left standing into temporary quarters for themselves. As regimental quartermaster, Henry could rejoice in the comforts that left him "well, hearty, fat, and saucy," in contrast to the cotton tents and hastily erected barracks in which common soldiers would face a cold, wet winter. His duties included the seizure of whatever wagons and mules he could find, and he provided first-hand knowledge of the hardships that an invading army inflicted on an enemy's population and economy. Only rarely did he express regret for such "evils and consequences of war." Confederates, he noted, "should have considered this matter before they commenced this wicked rebellion."[2]

---

1. Union forces had captured Memphis on June 6, 1862. See Hess, *Civil War in the West*, 59–60; Tomblin, *Civil War on the Mississippi*, 109–122.
2. Both quotations come from H. Fike to C. Fike, November 26, 1862, Henry C. and Lucy C. Fike Papers (hereafter FP). For the Union occupation of southern cities, see Ash,

Henry's regiment reached Memphis almost two months after President Lincoln issued his preliminary Emancipation Proclamation, which announced that all people held within bondage in the rebellious states would be forever free on the coming New Year's Day. Although the order exempted Tennessee, Henry's letters reveal how the erosion of slavery followed the Union army's movement into the middle Mississippi Valley. The organization of the United States Colored Troops starting in January 1863 marked a turning point in the war and in Henry's views of African Americans. The epithets that littered his correspondence bespoke a deeply rooted bigotry, but within a few months he observed of formerly enslaved men, "There is no doubt but that they will make *good* and efficient soldiers." Soon thereafter Henry expressed interest in pursuing a commission to lead a regiment of Black troops.[3]

Uncertainty pierced many of the letters that the Fikes shared after Henry left Illinois. Although his wide-eyed descriptions of military service once rang with the enthusiasm of a grand adventure, months spent waiting—for the regiment's next movement, for a rebel attack, for encouraging news from campaigns elsewhere—brought a dull acceptance that he might remain near Memphis indefinitely. The confused war news did little to relieve the couple's loneliness. Despite the company of neighbors and the antics of young Ellie, Cimbaline quailed at her realization that this first winter apart would likely not be their last. Picking lint, to be fashioned into bandages for wounded soldiers, alleviated her isolation but proved a solemn reminder that her husband and his comrades might return home broken men, or perhaps not at all. As her burdens of financial vulnerability and lingering illness grew heavier, Henry proposed that his wife and daughter come stay with him near Memphis. The discussion, planning, and anticipation of such a visit carried the Fikes through January, when the family was at last reunited in Tennessee, where they remained together until April.

After Cimbaline returned to Mascoutah, she and Henry confronted the most intimate strains on their relationship. Their correspondence continued a dialogue apparently commenced during their brief reunion, but its exact substance can appear inscrutable to readers outside of the Fikes' marriage. The affection and earthy humor that leavened their

---

When the Yankees Came; Hess, *Civil War in the West,* 62–74.

3. H. Fike to C. Fike, May 25, 1863, FP. For the attitudes of other white Illinois volunteers toward emancipation and African American soldiers, see Girardi, "'I am for the President's Proclamation'"; Harris, *History of Negro Servitude,* 226–244.

springtime exchanges suggested that their love would endure. Facing whispers that she had returned home pregnant, Cimbaline joked, "The peple are all such fools that tha think a woman can not sleep with a man unless she must be knock up the first pop," to which an amused Henry replied, "Tell them they will have to wait till I come home."[4]

November 18, 1862

2 1/2 Miles South East of Memphis, Tenn.

Dear Cimbaline,
We are now, emphatically in the enemy's country. They are in pretty strong force, within about twenty miles of here. Our pickets are stationed out a couple of miles beyond our encampment. The guerrillas are prowling around through these woods in small squads, shooting or capturing our straggling men as they can get a chance. Only a day or two ago, a couple of soldiers from the Wisconsin 32d were out squirrel hunting, some two miles from camp, and were captured by some guerrillas. They were paroled and released. It is evident that a man can not be too careful here.

You would laugh if you could see our encampment. The boys have what are called shelter tents. They consist of two pieces of cotton cloth about five feet square—buttoned together on one side, and then stretched across a ridge pole, and then open at both ends. They have buttons on all sides, so that you can fasten together as many as you please.... Try and write often. I have not heard from home since the 8" inst. I won't really expect a letter for a day or two. Give Ellie a hug and kiss for her pa and
Your affectionate husband,
H. C. Fike

November 19, 1862

Memphis, Tennessee

Dear Cimbaline,
To-day our regimental officers have moved into and occupied a nice large two-story house by the side of our encampment.... It is a right new frame

---

4. C. Fike to H. Fike, May 1, 1863, FP; H. Fike to C. Fike, May 10, 1863, FP.

building, larger than your father's house, where Gundlach[5] now lives. It contained about twelve or fifteen *very* large rooms. The house is splendidly furnished inside and out—large windows & blinds. I have to myself a nice large room eighteen feet square, three large windows, a large door into the hall, a nice cast iron grate for coal, all set in a cast iron fireplace, a good fender in front. We found plenty of coal, just in the door yard, and to-night I have a large fine blazing fire in the grate, casting light all over the room, and I am sitting by my desk writing you this letter. . . . Taking it all, round and round, we are fixed as comfortably as we want to be. All I lack to make my room as happy as any on earth is the presence of you and my little darling Ellie. If there should seem to be prospect of our remaining here long after a while, I might want you folks to come down and pay us a 'flying visit' in our Southern home. We can get all the darkies we want. You can see them around town in any quantities to suit customers. We had not been here an hour in camp before one or two of the captains had 'confiscated' a nigger. . . .[6] The amount and beauty of shrubbery in Memphis exceeds by far, anything of the kind I ever saw. In fact I would be very favorably impressed with Memphis, if I had not found many of the splendid residences unoccupied—occasioned by the proprietors leaving for parts unknown. . . I was up in the city to-day, flying around on 'Selim,' I am endeavoring to get things about right as soon as I can. We will get our government teams to-morrow, I think. I went and saw the Quarter Master about it today. I will get seven wagons and forty-four mules—six mules to a wagon, and one each for the commissary sergeant and Quarter Master's Sergeant to ride.[7] There is a great deal of cotton brought in here to sell. To-day, as I was passing along a street I saw a good many wagons from the country loaded with cotton. I asked a darkey on one of the wagons to hand me a bunch. He pulled out a handful and gave

---

5. This was likely John G. Gunlock, a German-born distiller. United States Federal Census (hereafter USFC), 1860.

6. The U.S. Congress passed the First and Second Confiscation Acts in August 1861 and July 1862, which enabled Union forces to seize enslaved people held by rebel owners. Syrett, *Civil War Confiscation Acts*, 1–34.

7. Mules, like horses, were crucial to the Union war effort, and as regimental quartermaster, Henry was responsible for the acquisition and care of draft animals. A recent environmental history estimates that the United States procured more than three hundred thousand mules during the Civil War. Browning and Silver, *Environmental History*, 109.

me. I send you a small tuft of it in this letter. The nigger said the cotton was raised in Fayette County Tennessee.[8]

Your affectionate husband,

H. C. Fike

November 20, 1862

Mascoutah, Illinois

Dear Henry

A nother sabath day hes past and the downg of night has made it apperents. We are all well. . . . Wos Church to night. Charley—McDonel[9] from Lebanon preach I wos out and tock Ellie. You would have laft if you had been thear and seen her. I never saw a child cutup so in my life. She run the hous oer and at last she went up in the stand wher the preacher wos and look out of the stand at me and said peep Mo peep Mo at last she went to our Minester and comence playing with him. he gave her his knife. she came runing to me, and said see Mome see Mome. Then she went to Mother and took over the banch at her said Granma peep Granma at that the peeple commence lafen at her. So I had to take her out an spank her be for I could make her bee still. . . . I have not had a letter from you sence last Wendesday evening. . . . It just seem to me you are dead now. You have got so far off from me. I dont hear from you half so offten as I did when you wos at Camp Butler. Why is it have you frogoten home and mee.

L C Fike

November 25, 1862

Mascoutah, Illinois

Dear Henry

I cannot think of much to write, as I donot go out much to git the nuse. The health is very good in towen. . . . Anderson has refused to pay Mother

---

8. Fayette County sat just east of Memphis, which was located in Shelby County. Barely two months later, Charles A. Dana, a former journalist and now an assistant secretary of war, observed that the cotton trade that passed through Memphis threatened to ensnare Union soldiers within a profitable illicit trade. He wrote: "Every colonel, captain, or quartermaster is in secret partnership with some operator in cotton; every soldier dreams of adding a bale of cotton to his monthly pay." United States War Department, *War of the Rebellion* (hereafter OR), ser. 1, vol. 51, pt. 1, 331.

9. Charles McDonald, fifty-six, was a Methodist minister. USFC, 1860.

that deat he ode her. The suit went on in Coart and she got jugement a gainst him. I wish you would tell me how you and him settle tha has been som dispute about it. Mr Stocke[10] has suid you for twenty dlers. he said you oid one hondred more wich he thinkes he will not git. I wish our detes wos paid If it takes the last cent we have I must stop writen it is 10 oclock Ellie is a saying to go to sleep she thinkes she cannot go to sleep unless I rock her. So good by to night

Wendesday night 10 oclock

We are all quite well to night. We have just had a lint picken at our hous tha have all gon home except Mary Jane Fike.[11] she entendes to stay all night. Ther wos ten laddyes hear and not one young man. That lookes like poor sho for Mascoutah dont it Last night some one open the window at Dr Landes hous and wos about giten in when his wife woke up and call the Dr she call him three times before she awoke him then the man wos about in: he howled at him. When he run and left the window up and the gait open. Night before last some one tryed to brake in Mr Garrett[12] hous, and another hous in towen Tha has been seen tow or three persones standen in our yeard an porch sence you left. I began to feel affraid to say hear now I never felt so untell latley. I never go to beed untell ten eleven or twelve some times one oclock Then I dont sleep much. I forget to tell you. I received tow letters from you this evening. wos glad to hear you was well and so well provided for. I onley wish I was with you to ceep your room in order insted Mr Beath.[13] I would like to come downg and see Memphes when all gites quite If you cannot come home. . . . This is 4 letters I have reten to you write often. I would like to hear ever day

From your affection wif L C Fike

---

10. This is likely tenant farmer Jacob Stock, age forty-three. USFC, 1860.

11. Mary Jane Fike, eighteen, was Henry's niece and the second-oldest daughter of Ausby Fike. USFC, 1860. One Civil War newspaper noted, "If a lady can do nothing else for her country, let her pray to God and pick lint." *Gallipolis Journal*, September 25, 1862, 4. See also *Alton Telegraph*, September 12, 1862, 3.

12. This is likely John Garredt, fifty-three, a teamster whose household appears a few pages away from the Fikes in the 1860 enumeration. USFC, 1860.

13. Charles Beath, a thirty-two-year-old Maine native, served as a quartermaster sergeant in the 117th Illinois. Although most members of the regiment hailed from St. Clair and nearby counties, Beath worked as a carpenter in McLean County, about 140 miles north of Mascoutah. Fred Delap, Illinois Civil War Muster and Descriptive Rolls Database, Illinois State Archives, Office of the Illinois Secretary of State, https://www.ilsos.gov/isaveterans/civilMusterSearch.do (hereafter Delap, ICWMDR); USFC, 1860.

Memphis, Tennessee

Dear Cimbaline,

Hurrah! for me! Hurrah! I say. I feel like turning seven summersets in rapid succession. Clear the track, you scamps, who don't get any letters from home, and let me have room to open my letter. Yes, my own letter from my wife. I presume that is enough, to let you know that I received a letter from you to-day, and something of my state of feelings on the reception of it. It was the first I have received from you since I received the one Lieut. Fike[14] brought to me. I was very much rejoiced to hear of the good health of you all. You cannot begin to imagine the anxious state of my mind, when I am *over two weeks* without any word from you. *I do hope you will write to me oftener than you have done lately.* . . . I have heard and read a good deal about the doings and sayings &c. of the secesh; but I have learnt a great deal more, even in the short time we have been in Memphis. They are wonderfully deceitful and cunning. Only four miles from our encampments, out on the road, they burnt two or three bridges to hinder the movement of our troops to-day. The other day while I was up in town, there was a steamboat load of Confederate prisoners just ready to start down too Vicksburg to be exchanged. About a dozen or fifteen secesh ladies (?) [parenthetical question mark in the original] assembled on the bank, with cakes, apples, pies, &c. which they wished to get to take on board and give to the prisoners. But the officers would not allow them to go on board, nor to send anything whatever on. So you may believe that they did not compliment the officers very much in what they said. They stayed about an hour. It would take four pages to describe the whole scene to you; and I will not undertake it here I shall mark it down as *one* of the circumstances that I will *tell* you, when I come home. If you laugh over it, as I did, your sides will be sore for a week. Men come to Col. Moore, here, every day, with complaints on account of depredations committed by the soldiers. 'Tis true, that a good deal of stuff has been destroyed, houses burnt, and other meanness perpetrated in this region. But then, it is hard to find out who does it. However, this is one of the evils and consequences of war; and they should have considered this matter before they commenced this wicked rebellion. Some of these scenes, where persons come and ask for protection, are truly heartrend-

---

14. Lieutenant John W. Fike, twenty-six, was Henry's nephew and a member of Company K. Delap, ICWMDR; *History of St. Clair County*, 278.

ing. Old men will come, and talk, while the tears will run down their cheeks in torrents. Little children will come and represent their mothers as widows, and ask for help. There appear to be more widows down here than I ever saw. Nearly every buggy driven into from the country is driven by a widow. We generally know about what kind of *widows* they are. They are not exactly grass-widows but what we call war-widows. I presume you understand what I mean by a war widow.

Your affectionate husband,

H. C. Fike

November 28, 1862

Fort Pickering, Memphis, Tennessee

Dear Cimbaline,

We are now in Fort Pickering, which is at the lower or south side of Memphis, immediately on the bank of the Mississippi river. The fort contains something like one hundred acres or more—I can't tell the exact contents. It is about one mile long and lies right along on the bank of the river. There are three other regiments in here with us: the 120 Illinois, 130 Illinois, and the 48" Ohio. The fort has a great many large guns in it. Some that throw balls weighing 32, 64, 84, and more pounds.[15] Our regiment has been assigned to the management of these large guns. The men will commence the practice of handling and maneuvering these guns immediately. They will have an experienced gunner in the business to command them in these exercises. His name is Capt. Silverspar. Besides this exercise, they will be drilled as they formerly have been, in the use of muskets. The army that left here two or three days ago took all the government wagons with them, and pressed a great many private teams into the service; so teams, and the like are rather scarce hereabouts just now; but we will have plenty in a few days. We had considerable sport and amusement in moving our regiment into the fort. As long as we could get no government teams to bring our things in, the Colonel authorized me

---

15. These projectiles may have been the 32-pound Hotchkiss Type II Case Shot, fired from a 4.5-inch siege rifle; the 64-pound Britten shell, fired from a 7-inch Blakely rifle; and the 84-pound Hotchkiss Bottle Top Bolt, fired from a 6.4-inch Parrot Rifle. Bell, *Civil War Heavy Explosive Ordnance*, 152, 242, 252.

to 'press in' some teams. I called to my aid the Wagon Master, Mr. Hoit,[16] and Mr. Beath, and we went to work. We proceeded into town, and just took every thing we came across in the shape of wagons, drays and carts. We had considerable of time at it. Some would come along willingly and others would not. A good many men were hauling along the streets, and we made them unload right where they were, and come along. It was no use to commence to listen to their complaints and excuses; for they had a thousand to give of every kind. We just made them dry up and come along. To-day, to carry out the joke, we went to the livery stables and 'pressed in' a lot of fine carriages to bring in our sick from our recent camp.

Your affectionate husband,

H. C. Fike

November 29, 1862

Mascoutah, Illinois

Tha seemes to be quite excitement about some one trublen [troubling] fokeses houses in towen. The first of this week some one went to Nancy Tegermen hous and open the window and got most in when she heard the nois and got up and told him if he come that she would split his braines out with the ax. he said not to be to sasey or he would come in and do as he pleaset with her he told her he had lived hear six mounths and behaves him self like a gentleman now he entended to let him self lose and do all the mischief he could. The same night some one wos at Dock Otenes wife hous and acted about the same. I belive I said somting about some one trublen Dr Landes and Mr Garett hous in my first writen. I oneley want you to furnich me with a good—Pistol. Then I will use it if any one attemptes to truble me. I heve not any thing that I could defend my self with Amos Day has got your Gun

I want to know how much you ow Gim Padfeel. Elisebeth has been blowen about that you ode Him six hundred dollers that she dont expect tha will ever git it. You are gon and liven fine riden your one hundred an seventy five do horse. I am at home spenden all the money you send to me. for fine clothes and for a hired Girel to wait on me. while I am cutten spuges [sponges]. She is not the oneley one that ses that. Mascoutah is

---

16. At age forty-four, John Hoit, the wagoner of the 117th Illinois, was one of the oldest members of the regiment. Delap, ICWMDR.

the most miserble plase I ever lived in. It is fifty times worse then it ever was. It is fild up with more widdowes from aroung in the Country. every little hous has got a famley of that charker in it. some of tha tounges is a foot long Milt McPonles wife came home from Camp Butler when your Regment came to st louis. she raised quit a fuss among the wor widdowes about ther husbanes. I heard Mary Curtis give her fites one evening about her tellen that Cap Landes companey said tha all tha wanted wos git him in Dixey then tha would schept him an come home. she said he wos the menest cap in the hole Regment. Some of the boys came very near shuten him before tha left Camp Butler & I shall bring this letter to a close by hopen I shall hear from you to night. I have dreamp of you every night sence you left camp Butler I dremt last night I saw you riden Selem with your head tide up with a white henkerchief I thought when I meet you. You would not speak to me. I shall feel very uneasy untell I hear from you again write after from your affectionate wife

L C Fike

December 1, 1862
Fort Pickering, Memphis, Tennessee

Dear Cimbaline,
I want you to write to me *immediately*, if you have not, already done it, what you think about coming down to Memphis and spending a few weeks. The regimental officers and myself had another talk to-night about it. We do not want to send you all, word to come until we get better fixed up, which will be a week or two. In the meantime, if you intend to come, I want you to begin to get ready. I want you to come if you can consistently with your feelings. You would see many things that would be great curiosities to you. I want you to try and have some money on hand *ready* to come when we send for you. Look over those notes, and see what ones are due. I think you will find some of them came due to-day. Send word to them immediately to pay you. Do not leave home with less than fifty or sixty dollars. See Ausby, and maybe he will come with you. If all come, that are talked of, there will be some eight or ten ladies come.[17]

---

17. Having their wives and children stay with them while in the field was a privilege available only to officers and not the entire regiment. Such distinctions did not escape the notice of enlisted men and their families. As regimental officers retreated to more comfortable lodging in Memphis, Monroe Joshua Miller, a private from Company I, wrote to his

Your affectionate husband,
H. C. Fike

December 1, 1862
Mascoutah, Illinois

To night I feel quite lonley I have been picken some lint that work all ways makes me feel solem. I all ways feel that it mite b use for some of my friendes for all I know.
L C Fike

December 4, 1862
Fort Pickering, Memphis, Tennessee

Dear Cimbaline,
I was really glad to hear that you all were enjoying good health when you wrote your letter—There is no news that you could send that would be more acceptable to me, than to always tell me you are all well—What a blessing real good health is. How highly we should always prize it, and take care of it. I never enjoyed better health, and felt better in my life, than I have experienced this fall so far. If during my absence from you I can be always blessed with the same I shall consider myself as highly favored. I expect you will begin to think that I will be a 'rouser' soon, when I tell you that I am still 'on the mend.' I now weigh one hundred and sixty-six—pounds. I do not know when I will stop growing. I always was like a rabbit—get fat in the winter. I hope when I return home to find you weighing a little more than usual.

You spoke in your letter of being desirous to visit the land of Dixie in the coming spring. I would be glad to see you down here before that time. . . . We will be apt to remain here all winter, and we can, I think, make arrangements to very comfortably entertain our families here, as long as you may wish to remain. There are a great many houses here, which people have left, and they are being filled with the officers of various regiments here. It will cost some more to board here than it does

---

wife, Linda: "I don't wonder that you feel badly when you see others able to go to their husbands and stay with them while you are deprived of that privilege." Monroe Joshua Miller to Linda Miller, November 17, 1862, Monroe Joshua Miller Papers (hereafter MJMP).

at home, so we must expect to have to spend a little money. But when I spend my money in adding to my social comfort, I feel like it is well spent. You must prepare to lay up a little for that occasion. Do not start with less than about sixty dollars. If I knew when we would be paid off, you might not have to bring any money. But that is an uncertain event, and can not be relied on with any certainty. . . .

I would like for you to tell me: who *that man* was, who told you that *story* about me, that you spoke of in a former letter. *I will know* sometime, if I live, and it would add greatly to my comfort and ease of mind to know *soon.* I think you can give me no *good* reasons for withholding his name from me, if you respect my feelings in the case, and are desirous of enabling me to defend myself from any such charges. I now request you to give me the name, for the reasons I have given. And as for the subject, I expect never to mention anything about it again to you by letter, unless something new of the kind occurs again.

Your affectionate husband,

H. C. Fike

December 6, 1862

Fort Pickering, Memphis, Tennessee

Dear Cimbaline,

The 'old scratch' must have got into some of those mean men who are sneaking around houses in the night time. Some of them should be shot. I think it would be well for you to procure a revolver, and have some one instruct you how to load and shoot it; and then you can practice in the use of it, and be able to defend yourself. . . . The Wagon Master and I have been busy hauling wood to-day. We pressed in 22 teams out of the city, and hauled about 50 cords. It requires an immense amount of money to carry on this war. As an idea of it, I will state that it takes about $120 to *feed* our regiment *one day.* The troops around Memphis, I guess, burn about 150 cords of wood per day.[18] Everything works on a big scale.

---

18. A cord of firewood requires felling four trees of twelve-inch diameter. Henry's estimate suggests that the Union troops in Memphis consumed the equivalent of roughly six hundred trees per day, just for heating. Mercker and Taylor, "Firewood Harvesting," 9. For the vast quantities of wood that Civil War armies harvested from southern forests and woodlots, see Browning and Silver, *Environmental History,* 175–179; Nelson, *Ruin Nation,* 103–159.

It would require too much space in this letter to give a full description of how the machine works. I will defer that matter until I get to see you.

Your affectionate husband,

Henry C. Fike

December 7, 1862

Fort Pickering, Memphis, Tennessee

Dear Cimbaline,

I want you to get away from 'old hateful Mascoutah,' as you call it, awhile, and come and see me. You will enjoy yourself here very well I think with the wives of the other officers that are coming. And, besides, you will see a great many things that are new and interesting. . . . I can not think of much to write to-night, so I will close. I have not yet, met with an accident sufficiently injurious, to cause me to wrap my head in a white handkerchief; and I hope I never may. The health of our regiment is as good as usual. I was vaccinated to-day by Dr. Wiley, as a preventitive against the small-pox.[19]

Your affectionate husband,

H. C. Fike

December 7, 1862

Mascoutah, Illinois

Dear Henry,

This letter leves us in tolerble health. To day I wos at church. Babtis Church. The funrel surmon of that little girel Mr Brown reased. This after noon I wos at class meeting. for the first time sence you left. To night Martha has gon to church. I and Ellie is a lone. she has gon to sleep I feeling quit lonley thinking orer things that are past and gon present and futer. it onley makes my heart ake within me. And to attemp to discribe my feelenes to you I cannot. It would bee usless for me to attempt it at the present time. So I will refrain from it. . . . The nuse in Mascoutah is about as usuel. onley some off the peeple talkes a bout ar some of the lades a

---

19. A year earlier, the Union's Army of the Potomac had attempted to vaccinate all of its soldiers, but the practice was less common in the Mississippi Valley. Browning and Silver, *Environmental History*, 35–37.

bout trying to git up some kind of amusementes about Chrismas something like tabloes [tableaus] and singing. To git money to carrey on our aid socity. I dont know wher we will successeed or not. Tha is someney contrary ones hear. . . . Anderson wos hear yesterday. he enform me that he had traided your hors again and giv twenty dolers to boot. he thinkes he has got a pretty good one now. He is a going to St Louis next week. I told him to git me a pistle I think I shall have use for it if times dont git better hear soon You spoke in your letters about mee coming downg to Memphis this winter to see you. Mother is not willen for me to try it now. she thinkes she can not stand it for Ellie and I to go or to start now while it is so cool and the river so low. She thinkes we would never live to git thair The nuse is now that the small pox is in St Louis and Bellbille.[20] I would like to go on a visit to Memphis very much endeed but I think I would reather go in the spring when the wether is warmer then it is now. I will think it over and see Mrs Land and see what she thinkes of it. . . . Mother just came in and told me that Mr Reeves and two others have returnd to towen from St Louis. Tha say that tha could not git pasege to Memphes and all so said that tha did not entend to go and fite to free the negroes. Tha dont entend to go a tall. I wish you would send some one after tham and mak tham go. He is no good hear onley createn a great tolk a bout himself and some off the wimen I feel vext about it and espesley about him not caren my letter to you.

Respectfully yours Lucy Fike

December 11, 1862

Fort Pickering, Memphis, Tennessee

Dear Cimbaline,
I will name over the principal rations we draw in ten days: Two Thousand seven hundred pounds bacon; Four Thousand six hundred pounds fresh beef; Ten thousand, one hundred pounds of flour, (which is 52 barrels); one thousand one hundred pounds of beans; seven hundred pounds rice; six hundred pounds coffee; eleven hundred pounds of sugar; and other things according But the fun comes in, when I get to dividing this

---

20. By the end of November, the St. Louis Board of Health had ordered that notices be posted "in the most conspicuous manner" outside the homes of people infected with smallpox. "Proceedings of the Board," *Daily Missouri Republican*, December 1, 1862, 3.

all out among the ten companies. I worked at it to night till nine o'clock. I am getting somewhat used to it, and it does not tire me so much.

Your affectionate husband,

H. C. Fike

December 13, 1862
Fort Pickering, Memphis, Tennessee

Dear Cimbaline,

I feel more than ever disappointed this evening. . . . This evening a *very* large mail came—some two or three hundred letters—*but none for me.* What is the matter? I have written about *seven letters to you* since I have received any *from you.* I think I have good reasons for feeling somewhat hurt at you, for neglecting to write to me. A great many letters came this evening from Mascoutah. Capt. Land received three letters, Lt. James Curtis, three, and a host of others got some, too, from Mascoutah. But 'poor me' had to stand back in the cold and take it. . . . Dr. Whitaker, Chaplain Gillham, Capt. Land[21] and I were the four who agreed to send for our wives to come together. We also agreed to write as many as *three or four* letters, one after another telling you of the fact, and giving you the directions of our plans in the case. We talked it over with as much earnestness and deliberation, as if we were concocting a plan of attack, for capturing Vicksburg. If you have received all my former letters, written about it, within the past week, this letter will, undoubtedly, seem like a foolish repetition.

Your affectionate husband,

H. C. Fike

December 14, 1862
Mascoutah, Illinois

Dear Henry,

To day is another raney Sunday. I dont think I ever saw more water on the groun then tha is at the present time. The streetes is full off watter.

---

21. Captain Nathan Land, also an officer from Company K, was Henry's first cousin. Delap, ICWMDR; *History of St. Clair County,* 277. This first person may be twenty-four-year-old William Whittaker, the only person with that surname in the muster rolls of the 117th Illinois, but those records and the federal census alike identify him as a farmer, not a physician. John D. Gillham, twenty-eight, served as a regimental chaplain. Delap, ICWMDR.

Mascoutah looks like a see of watter. It has raind so hard tha has not been any sabath school nor church to day. It is one of the lonsomes dayes I ever saw. You know I all ways disliked raney sundays for it seem so lonson to me. You may amagen I dislike tham mor now then I ever did befor. Time pases very slow with me. It seemes to me you have been gon a year when I think you may be gon three years and perhapes never to see you again It fills my eyes with tears, my heart all most sesces to beet. Ow whot a world of truble. It seemes to much for me to bear when I think how I am left hear and wher I am, and the kind off peeple I am laft with to live and git a gong with. With all of my others trobles. It is to much for any one to bear. Tha is som good peeple hear after all. some I like as well as any of my freandes I have any wher. But tha is so maney off the other charker [character] hear. That it makes it very disagreable living. . . . I have been truble more lattley with my old diseases than I have been for some time. I thinke I better send to Dr Fitch for mor meddason. What do you think a bout it. I have not had a letter sence last tusday evening from you. I think I can say the same to you as you have to me I would like for you to write little offtener some times I do not git a letter from you for a week. Then I will git tow or three in a day or tow. Then i half to weat a nother week. I have retten tow you this last week. One to you on buisness, about Cox what shall I do about it. I think I better give hime some of those notes is due if he will take tham and try to borrow the rest of the money if I can. Those notes White has got, he tells me he can not git the money without suing tham. The paper I gave to Mr. Postle he ses he canot coleck but a little of the money I can not colect aney of those notes myself. I have not received any money from any one sence you left home ecept Mr Miller you said in your letter that I must not leave home with less then fifty or sixty dollars when I started to Dixie. I donot know wher I will git it, for it is all I can do to ceep a nufe for famley use. I try to live as saven as I can to live comferble. You know that I allways tryed to live saven an git a long with as little as possible & About comen downg to see you this winter. I think I btter wait untell spring. I think I would enjoy it btter then I would now in the cold and mud. Mother and Osbay is not willen for me to leve now when the smallpox is about. Tha think the trip is to grate one for me in the winter. That I am not able to stand it. I better go in the spring. . . . I want to know what you think about me renten tha hous out in the spring to some good famley, and bord with tham. If tha is not any prospect of you comen home It would be great deal cheeper for me to live. In fact it would be cheper for me to sell off every thing we have and shut up the house and bord, then to ceep hous. It cost me about twelve or fifteen dolers a month ceep house the very best I can do. I have to pay for every little thing I git don. It is a great deal of truble for me to run a roung and git some body to hold coail wood chopt, corn and hay hold. This thing and the other don. Some times I am out and cannot git it don when I meed it. When I do a big price to pay. . . . I never had such thinges to attend to before. I did not know the truble of it. . . . I guess you hav not received the letter I sent by him or started to you. I heard yesterday it wos at his hous. Old rip he ought to be shot You wanted that I should tell you what that man was that told me that nuse a bout you. You said that I could not give no good reson for withholding his name from you. I think I can I know he has been a good friend to you and is a firend to you now. I know if I should tell his name to you tha would be a fuss more then this I would not bee ceepen my word and promis to him At first I did not belive it and I told him so. I thought I never would mensen it to you. but it bore upon my mine so strong with some other thinges I had heard. I could not healp it. I found my love was failen for you, and I know if it wos so or if I ever found it to be so I never would live with you a gain, never have any love for you. I allways said if I had such a man and knew it. I never could love him, or I never would live with him if he wos the richest man on earth I would rather live on bread and watter and live happy. If I ever find out what I want to find out then I will tell the hold secret not the name

4 oclock in the afternoon

I hope I shall hear from you offtener then I have in time past. And I do hope and pray that we will for git thinges that has past and our love may grow stronger for each other and if we are permited to live to gether a gain as man and wife that we may live happer then we ever have lived before. And if we are not permited that pleasure on earth again, may we live hear on earth so we may meet in heaven to peart nomore, wher pain and misure trubles are not felt and feard no more. May this be our prayer.

Lucy C. Fike

December 16, 1862

Mascoutah, Illinois

You will receive my letter in this envelip. I started to you by Reeves the first day of this month. He left hear and went to St Louis stayed a day or tow an returend. He said he wos put in prisen becous he wos a solger I think this is not so. He is very sick now. I dont cear much if he dies. Any one is so fraid of a bulit as he is out [ought] to be dead.[22]

Respactfuley yours

Lucy C. Fike

December 23, 1862
Fort Pickering, Memphis, Tennessee

Dear Cimbaline,
I was as glad as usual to hear of your good health generally, though I was sorry to hear of the returning symptoms of your old complaint. You also spoke of your lonesomeness, and the weary hours you were compelled to wear away, at home, in the bad rainy weather you have had lately. I expect that you have lonesome times indeed. I can assure you that we have anything else but lonesome times here. Every thing is exactly the reverse. But, before I commence to speak further about affairs here, I will revert to a few things you referred to in your last letter. But before I even do this, I will say, that I was very *much disappointed* indeed, on reading my letters to-day, to find that you did not intend to visit me at the time I have previously spoken of.

Now a word or two about affairs here. There has been a good deal of excitement here during yesterday and to-day. Pretty strong apprehensions of our being attacked by the rebels have been felt by our men. The Secesh have lately taken Holly-springs, in Mississippi, and burnt part of the town and captured some thousand or two prisoners.[23] The rumor now is, that they are advancing this way. The forces in our fort, are wide awake, and on the watch out. Every man is at his post. The rebels seem to think that they can now do something here, since so many troops have gone down the river. But if they attack us, they will find that there are several thousand of us here yet, ready to give them a warm reception. Our men are all sleeping on their arms. Our regiment has become very well skilled in the handling of the heavy artillery, and could, in an engagement, do *some execution.*

---

22. Evidence suggests that Reeves returned to the regiment and served most of his remaining enlistment, until being discharged for disability on October 16, 1864. Delap, ICWMDR.

23. Earl Van Dorn's Confederate forces captured Holly Springs, Mississippi, on December 20. Grant, *Personal Memoirs,* 291–301.

Your affectionate husband,
H. C. Fike

December 25, 1862
Mascoutah, Illinois
[Marginal comment at top: Married 1855]

Dear Henry,
To day is Chrismis. A very lonsome one to me Tha was Church at 11 oclock to day. And a ball at the Fike hous to night. After all it is very quite in towen. I onley wish I was in Memphis to spend my Chrismis with you To day we have been marred seven years, and this is the first Chrismis we have spent sepret from each other. I hope it will be the last one while we live.
Lucy C Fike

December 27, 1862
Fort Pickering, Memphis, Tennessee

Dear Cimbaline,
We have not very late news from up or down the river, or out in the country. We still feel prepared to meet any emergency. The authorities here are taking steps to guard against any dangers which they can prevent. At the upper end of the fort they have had holes pierced through the brick walls. Outside the fort they commenced today to tear down the houses close by, which would render a shelter to an attacking enemy. An officer told me they calculated to tear down about sixty houses. Many of these are splendid residences, with the nicest kind of yards filled with evergreens &c. The whole ground covered, and the buildings to be destroyed, are about as much as that part of Mascoutah east of Scheve's[24] store—only the houses are generally finer. It will be a big job, but will be accomplished in a few days. We have plenty of work hands down here, and you know plenty hands make light work. These houses are to be removed so as to give us a chance to see any enemy that may come through town.

---

24. Merchant Julius Scheve appears in the Illinois state census conducted in July 1855 but not in the 1860 federal enumeration. Illinois State Census, 1855.

Your affectionate husband,
H. C. Fike

December 30, 1862
Fort Pickering, Memphis, Tennessee

Dear Cimbaline,

I want to the renter on the Dupuy[25] farm to haul all my corn to the distillery, if they are buying corn. That, I think, would be the best way to dispose of it. As for the rails needed on the farm, I told him plainly, and thought he seemed willing to it, to make the rails himself, and have them hauled and do all the necessary repairing, and I would allow him all that it was worth when we settled for the rent. This, I think, is a fair bargain. He will have opportunity of doing this during the winter. As for the potatoes, they had better be sold, if possible, to some of the stores. I do not know what particular advice to write to you, more than I have already sent, about renting out our house. Ask Ausby what he thinks about it. I would not know what to say, unless I could see the person who might take it. About the mortgage you spoke of in your last letter, that is all not so.—just gas.

I will close. Now, about bringing Ellie when you come to Memphis, *if you don't bring her along.* I don't want you to come at all. You understand that—don't you? I am hearty and well.

Your affectionate husband,
H. C. Fike

December 31, 1862
Mascoutah, Illinois

Dear Henry

I do feel so lonley to set hear alone, thinken over thinges that has past within the last year, And to think one yeare ago we wos both at home. now so for apart. Alltho I wos sick in beed but it wos a happer new year. Then this one will be We are for apart, tho may it bee to night. That we

---

25. This is likely Edwin Sackett, twenty-two, or Andrew Ford, twenty-two, whom the 1860 census listed as living with farmer Justice Dupey. Corn that was distilled into liquor was less expensive to transport than corn hauled in bulk. USFC, 1860.

both may bow our selves befor god in humbleness and thank him for his goodness and merces duren the last year. May we pray—earnsley for him to spar us a nother year and that we may live nearerunto him and be permitted to see each other again hear on earth

From your wife,
L.C F

January 3, 1863
Fort Pickering, Memphis, Tennessee

Dear Cimbaline,
Since Mr. [John] Curtis left, times around here have been very quiet and peaceful, until last night, when a little 'scare' got up. About 10 o'clock the reports of four or five muskets were heard outside the fort, in the direction of a nigger town containing some thousand darkies. A slight alarm sprung up immediately in the lower end of the fort, next to the nigger quarters. Some infantry were sent out to investigate the cause of the shooting. The word soon came back that the guerrillas had made a dash in among the darkies and had captured some twenty or thirty of them.[26] One or two companies of cavalry and three or four companies of infantry were sent out forthwith, and scoured the woods around, but found no secesh. The whole affair turned out to be nothing. The shooting was caused by the guards firing at some fellows trying to run through their lines. This took place close to the nigger town, and scared them, and made them think the secesh were among them. The fright did not extend throughout the whole fort; so you may imagine that the fort is pretty extensive.

We are all anxiously awaiting the final decision of the Vicksburg fight.[27] From accounts received here from below, for the last day or two, we learn that fighting has been going on there for several days. I think our forces will surely turn out victorious.... If you come, I apprehend no danger....

---

26. This raid occurred just two days after President Lincoln's Emancipation Proclamation had taken effect and declared free nearly all enslaved people living in Confederate states. Raiders likely intended to enslave the Black victims they abducted.

27. Heavy rains and the difficult, swampy terrain to the west and north of Vicksburg thwarted the campaign to take that city, which Grant commenced in the winter of 1863. One Wisconsin officer reflected on these failures in the lower Mississippi Valley and concluded, "This winter is, indeed, the Valley Forge of the War." McPherson, *Battle Cry of Freedom*, 590.

We are making arrangements to lodge all of our wives inside the fort. We can not get very nice houses; but they are comfortable. We have hired a negro man and his wife to cook for us, &c. Besides these, we have a nigger to take care of our horses. Come along, and I have no doubt you will be satisfied.

Your affectionate husband,
H. C. Fike

January 9, 1863
Mascoutah, Illinois

Dear Henry
To night I set downg to write you a few lines, we are all well in good spiretes, *Our Cow had* a caff to day & & To night Mrs Land came up and we had a long tock about our visit to dixey, We have come to the conclusen that we will make a effert to leave Mascoutah next Tusday the 13 I beleve and go to St Louis and git on the first boat that leaves for Memphis I want you to be on the lookout and be redy to meet us at the landen. I want you to be the first man I see after we land, I want you to git some good plase for me to stop at when I git thare, untell we can make our one arangementes. . . . I will stop writen to night and clos my letter, I will tell you all the nuse when I see you so good by tonight

from your affectionate wife
Lucy C Fike

April 21, 1863
Fort Pickering, Memphis, Tennessee

Dear Cimbaline,
I expect I shall feel very lonesome now. Everything seems so still about the house. We all feel that Ellie's little prattling tongue and pattering feet will be missed. Although she was, at times the cause of trouble, yet the pleasure of her presence—more than amply repaid all.

Your affectionate husband,
Henry

April 22, 1863
Aboard the *Empress*, Mississippi River

We are past Island No 10 about one half hour ago, sence we left thear this boat an the Empres has been runing races. She past us at last, and all the ladys are glad of it. . . . Ella cried so heard when you left I tock her to my room an sed to her if she did not hush I would whip her, she said I told papa and crid the hearder She is now standin in a chear at the window looing out and call to ask Pa I will stop cribling for I cannot write and tell you all about it when I git home.
 Cimbaline

April 26, 1863
Mascoutah, Illinois

Dear Henry
I got home Friday evening about 4 olock. Tha wos not looking for me We rode up to the gait and got out, and went to go in the hous. Mother came out, but she did not know who I was untill I spok and laft. Then she look at me a moment, Then she tock holt of my hand and said, Why Cimbaline is this you, Then she hug me and cryed and said, I am so glad, Then she tock Ellie in her armes and kiss her prety near all over. . . . As soon as the peeple heard I had com Tha begin to flock in to hear all the nuse, and to git letters, I don nothen but receve company Friday evening and saduray, I got very tired anseren qustions.
 Respectfuly yours
 Cimbaline

May 1, 1863

This morning finds us as usual. Yesterday wos fast day. We had church. . . . All the peple had quit a tail on me when I come home. The nuse wos that I wos as big as I could walk and I said I didnot entend to come home untell I went to Corinth, so tha all begin to run to see me as soon as I come, Tha wos all so disopointed that tha had to tell whot tha had heard, The peple are all such fools that tha think a woman can not sleep with a man unless she must be knock up the first pop.
 I will close this letter and mail it this evening.
 Cimbaline

May 6, 1863

Fort Pickering, Memphis, Tennessee

Dear Cimbaline,
We like our new quarters very well; they are near town. I saw Capt. Hawes[28] up in the city to-day. He looks well. To-day, a deserter while trying to escape from the guardhouse, was shot dead by the guard. The guard ordered him to halt, which he refused to do, when the guard fired—the ball going entirely through him and he fell dead. Lt. Wallis was within a few steps of him at the time. He was shot about 2 o'clock this afternoon, and buried about 5 o'clock. How short a time between his walking around, and lying in the cold grave.

Sunday Evening, May 10, 1863

I was much amuzed at the stories you said were awaiting you at home. They surely must think that you have a patent way of getting *fat* in three months. Tell them they will have to wait *till I come home.* Don't read this to any one, or let them see it. . . . Give Ellie a kiss for her 'papa'—Be sure to inform me when the *little stranger,* the people expected, 'comes to town.' I should like to see the little 'feller'—Write soon and often.

Your affectionate husband,
Henry

May 15, 1863

Fort Pickering, Memphis, Tennessee

Dear Cimbaline,
The *Belle Memphis* arrived here last night from St. Louis. She had on board 13 men and 11 women who have been ordered south of our lines by Gen. Curtis of St. Louis.[29] They are secesh sympathizers. This morning's *Bulletin* says that Jeff. Davis has issued a statement that such persons will not be received inside their lines, unless they can give security for

---

28. This is likely Captain Alexander G. Hawes, twenty-seven, a publisher Belleville, also in St. Clair County. Second Lieutenant William Wallis, twenty-six, was a native of Ireland and a member of Company C. Delap, ICWMDR.

29. Major General Samuel R. Curtis served as Union commander of the Department of the Missouri. Gerteis, *Civil War St. Louis,* 276.

their own support and maintainance. This will place these 'Copperheads' in a close place. That is good enough for all such traitors.[30]

Your affectionate husband,
Henry

May 16, 1863
Fort Pickering, Memphis, Tennessee

Dear Cimbaline,

This is Saturday evening, and everything is quiet in camp. The health of the regiment is good. This afternoon I took a good swim in the 'mighty Mississippi' for the first time in my life.[31] After my physical ablution I feel much better. . . . Everything is now going on smoothly in camp. We have no news of any interest in town. The news, from the vicinity of Vicksburg, indicates that we may expect to hear of some stirring events in that quarter. I think surely our armies will do accomplish something within a month or so, if they ever expect to do anything.

Sunday Evening. May 17, 1863.

Col. Merriam[32] was 'officer of the day' in the fort to-day. This afternoon I rode around with him, as he went around on his duty visiting the guards who are stationed along the breastworks. At the lower end of the fort, near those two mounds is the negro regiment encampment.[33] We went through their camp. It is just as clean as nice as any encampment of white soldiers—The drakes have just received their new uniforms this morning. They are the proudest set of fellows you ever saw. They look

---

30. Historian Jennifer Weber writes that most Copperheads were not traitors, but self-described conservatives, concerned about the nation's welfare, who wished to see a restoration of the status quo ante bellum: "The vast majority were loyal to the Union. They were sincere in their belief that the Lincoln administration and the Republican Congress were overstepping their constitutional bounds." Weber, *Copperheads*, 6–7. For Unionists' perceptions of treason among antiwar neighbors, see Lawson, *Patriot Fires*, 82–88.

31. Modern readers may struggle to imagine bathing or swimming safely in the deep, turbid, and fast-moving Mississippi of the present, but during the Civil War, long before a system of levees, locks, and dams narrowed and deepened its channel, the river was considerably slower and shallower.

32. Jonathan Merriam, the Vermont-born lieutenant colonel of the 117th Illinois, stood at six feet two-and-a-half inches tall, making him one of the tallest members of the regiment. Delap, ICWMDR.

33. Secretary of War Edwin Stanton sent Adjutant General Lorenzo Thomas west to organize regiments of Black troops in the Mississippi Valley in March 1863. Cornish, *Sable Arm*, 112–113.

quite well indeed—and I believe will make good soldiers. At any rate, time will test the matter.

Your affectionate husband,
Henry

May 19, 1863
Fort Pickering, Memphis, Tennessee

Dear Cimbaline,
There is now another 'scare' here. Rumors say Gen. Grant has whipped the rebels in the country east of Vicksburg, and it is thought, if that is true, that the Confederates will make a dash up in this direction. The rebel General Chalmers is reported only some twenty miles east of here with a pretty strong force.[34] We have got a good many more large cannons mounted and ready for use than when you left. I guess we are prepared for them if they come.

Your affectionate husband,
Henry

May 23, 1863
Fort Pickering, Memphis, Tennessee

Dear Cimbaline,
The Marine Brigade all went below this forenoon. 'Tis said they are going to the vicinity of Vicksburg. We received good news from the region of Vicksburg to-day. The report is that Gen. Sherman has captured Haine's Bluff with some eight thousand prisoners, and near a hundred cannons &c.[35] I suppose we shall have to wait a few days for the news to be corrected and revised, before we get the correct information about the whole affair. We have no doubt of the fact that the victory has been won by our side, and that it has been a most glorious achievement. We must wait and see.

Yesterday afternoon, Adjutant General Thomas, who is in the west

---

34. James Ronald Chalmers began the war as a colonel in the 9th Mississippi Infantry and was promoted to brigadier general in February 1862. James Ronald Chalmers, National Park Service, https://www.nps.gov/people/james-ronald-chalmers.htm, accessed December 9, 2023.

35. Hess, *Storming Vicksburg*, 81–85.

planning and organizing negro regiments, was out in the negro town, below the fort, and addressed the 'darkies' on the war questions of the day. He pleased them wonderfully and made them show their 'ivory' and hollow and cheer most enthusiastically. I was present, and saw the performance.

Your affectionate husband,
Henry

May 24, 1863

Mascoutah, Illinois

Dear Henry
Our school is not doing much good for its self. I have heard sence I came home that you said if you could git a onerble discharge this summer you would come home and take charge of the school next year. Tha has been a great meny asked me about it Mother gave Osbay money while I was at Memphis to pay our texes. He went up to pay it when he got thear he paid for the 180 ac. The rest he did not pay, but tock the money to stop some of his excusions so the scheriff told Mother, your hous and tow lots and the little brick is advrtised for sail Osbay has not treated me right. I will tell you all about it when I see you.
From your affectionate wife Cimbaline

May 25, 1863

Fort Pickering, Memphis, Tennessee

Dear Cimbaline,
The organizing of negroes into military companies, and arming and equipping them for service, is progressing finely. I presume you remember that there was a regiment under headway when you left here. This is getting along finely; and several companies have already received their guns and accouterments, and uniforms, and present a *very* soldierly appearance indeed. There is no doubt but that they will make *good* and efficient soldiers. There is a great demand for positions in this and other negro regiments forming in this region. The regiment organizing here in the fort, it is understood, is to remain in the fort, and take charge of the heavy guns. Thomas Curtis expects a Captains commission in this

regiment, and I guess he is pretty sure of getting it.[36] He has worked *very* faithfully indeed, in the cause and deserves a *good* position. What would you think if I should get a good position in that regiment? If I see a good chance to better my condition in the way of getting *up*, I intend to embrace the opportunity. I don't know that I have any prospects just now; but I intend to keep on the look-out.

Your *affectionate* husband,
Henry

May 26, 1863
Mascoutah, Illinois

Dear Henry
Ellie is standen in a cheer at the window up stares in the north west room looking out at the little pigs in the street That roome is my bead room now, Marth has the little room the south west one. We try to git in the most publick plase in the hous so we wont be lonsom Ellie oftens tolks of her. Pa she ses papa will come some time I ask her whot I should write to her pa, she ses me is papa baby he is gon to the wor. Pa is gon he shoot the rebles. She stays at Mothers more then half of her time. Mother lets her do as she pleses. I want you to come home this summer, so Ellie will not forgit you all together she tolks of you so mush, In her dreames she will hallow out pa pa. She often wakes me in the night by saying Pa then she will lafed I want you to come home tow I am afraid you will forgit how home looks and I and Ellie.

From
Cimbaline

May 28, 1863
Fort Pickering, Memphis, Tennessee

Dear Cimbaline,
Here's at it again. What in the world will I write to fill up this letter. I have nothing new to write. I don't know what I shall do, unless I do as I advised you to do in my last—put in a little nonsense to fill up. . . . Mr.

---

36. Thomas Curtis, thirty-two, was a private in Company K.

Appleby, who had been home on a furlough of twenty days, brought us down lots of good things.[37] When he left us, we placed in his hands money sufficient to bring us a good supply of butter and eggs. He did so, and we intend to live while we do live. He brought us some excellent butter—some Illinois butter—fresh butter, good butter—loyal butter—none of your Northern Copperheadism in this butter. It is not mulatto butter, if it is *yellow* butter. . . . No news in the regiment. So I will wind up this silly letter, hoping after all, that you will ever remember I am

Your affectionate husband,

Henry

---

37. John Appleby, forty-four, was a private in Company D and one of the oldest enlisted men in the 117th Illinois. Delap, ICWMDR.

CHAPTER 3
"Makes Me Feel like Fiting"

Fort Pickering, Tennessee
and
Mascoutah, Illinois
May 1863 to October 1863

Cimbaline was in no mood to suffer fools as Independence Day neared in 1863. Two years of bloody civil war had yielded only fitful progress for the United States, and troubling developments revealed how ideological divisions continued to roil St. Clair County. After the alarming surge of crime in the months since Henry and more than three hundred of the town's men had marched off to war, the impudence of local Copperheads finally brought Cimbaline to her breaking point. Upon hearing that some men had taken to the nighttime streets and bellowed their support for the Confederate president, she wrote, "If ever I hear any one call Jeffs Davis name in or about my house, I entend to take a stick and brake theare head and let the copper rune out," adding "I have a stick layde up for that purpis."[1]

A rumor that someone in the neighboring town of Fayetteville planned to run up a "secesh" flag on July 4 was even more galling. Weeks earlier Cimbaline and other women in her neighborhood founded a Union League, the kind of patriotic organization established in communities across the North to help raise money and supply comforts of home to soldiers in the field.[2] Local men soon founded a league of their own. Despite another bout of poor health, Cimbaline assumed responsibility for helping to organize an Independence Day fundraiser and for sewing the Union Leagues' flags, even as a bitter struggle for control of the women's group nearly spelled its undoing. The mere suggestion that an enemy flag might fly on that most sacred of civic observances was unconscionable. "The verry thought of one makes me feel like fiting," she declared.

---

1. C. Fike to H. Fike, June 25, 1863, Henry C. and Lucy C. Fike Papers (hereafter FP).
2. Bahde, "'Our Cause'"; Lawson, "'A Profound National Devotion.'"

As if to make good on her threat, she noted her willingness to visit Fayetteville, axe in hand, to destroy any pole that dare fly such a banner.[3]

At Fort Pickering, the 117th Illinois Volunteers continued to perform garrison duty. After interminable months of patrols, pickets, and guarding prisoners, many men longed to join the mass of Union troops that Ulysses Grant was assembling at Vicksburg.[4] Henry thought that the long-expected capture of that city, which would give the Union control of the entire Mississippi River, portended an end to heavy fighting in the West. The coming months would also heighten the contradictions he observed in occupied Memphis. Some quarters of the city saw a renewed flourish of commercial activity, much of it fueled by an illicit cotton trade; elsewhere, railroads disgorged a heartrending cargo of bedraggled refugees, most of them children. He cheered the loyalty oath that inspired an apparent change of heart among many southern civilians, and his developing ties with "respectable secesh" families raised hopes for a peaceable postwar world.[5]

More than ever, Henry expressed a growing fascination with the formerly enslaved African Americans who streamed into Memphis by the hundreds. His letters revealed the army's dependence on the labors of Black men and women and the racial prejudice that permeated the military. He applauded the growing number of volunteers who filled the regiment of United States Colored Troops organized at Fort Pickering, noting how the presence of these troops cheered the city's Black population and unnerved its whites in nearly equal measure. Yet, in contrast to the respect that Henry paid to the "soldiers of color" in the "negro regiment," he still used demeaning language to describe the other Black people he encountered around Memphis. The brutal punishment that white soldiers inflicted on a Black youth accused of theft, tying him to a tree and beating him with a horse whip, underscored the vulnerability of formerly enslaved people, many of whom had fled to the city seeking the protection of Union forces. A great many freed people lived in the flood-prone bottoms beneath the blufftop fort, and hundreds more lived at the "contraband" settlement that the army established on President's Island, in the channel of the Mississippi River. Henry endorsed efforts to establish self-sufficient farms that Black refugees would work to earn

---

3. C. Fike to H. Fike, June 30, 1863, FP.
4. For garrison duty during the Civil War era, see Lang, *In the Wake of War*, 38–181.
5. H. Fike to C. Fike, August 16, 1863, FP. For Union soldiers' perceptions of white Southerners, see Jimerson, *Private Civil War*, 124–179.

their keep, lest the government "have to feed them, and get nothing out of them for it."[6] Those who could fight, he believed, should enlist; all others had a responsibility to support themselves.

Cimbaline was no stranger to the challenges of sudden independence. When Ausby failed yet again to pay her family's taxes and settle its accounts, as Henry had requested, she confronted her brother-in-law about his negligence and resolved to handle such affairs herself. Weeks after a mob lynched a German-speaking burglar, she foiled an attempted break-in by throwing open her bedroom window and firing her pistol into the Illinois night. Cimbaline also despaired about never finding relief from carbuncles, chronic pain, and unspecified ailments. Financial strain made certain treatments nearly unaffordable, and a September visit to the dentist, who removed all of her upper teeth, saddled her with guilt about its expense. Even in rare moments of good health, smallpox was still an ever-present danger; one grim letter noted the deaths of several Mascoutah children, likely from whooping cough. Her efforts in tending to the sick infant of a neighbor, like her work within the Union League, revealed a woman enmeshed within her rural community, but too often Cimbaline felt alienated and regarded herself an undeserving victim of small-town gossip. Little did she know that her outspokenness won her admirers among the 117th Illinois. Monroe Joshua Miller, who assisted Henry with his quartermaster papers, confided to his wife, "Mrs. F. is independent and fearless enough to tell any one to her face what she has to tell."[7]

---

6. H. Fike to C. Fike, August 21, 1863, FP. The term *contraband* generally meant any property captured from an enemy that an army could put to use, but in the early months of the Civil War it came to refer frequently to formerly enslaved people. Henry's usage in 1863, many months after the Emancipation Proclamation, reflects the economic lens through which many white soldiers continued to view African Americans. For the ways that this term (and others) emphasized property over personhood, see Amy Murrell Taylor, *Embattled Freedom*, 9–10.

7. Monroe Joshua Miller to Linda Miller, December 16, 1863, Monroe Joshua Miller Papers (hereafter MJMP).

May 30, 1863
Mascoutah, Illinois

Dear Henry

We formed our Union Liugh [League] last evening in Mr White office I thinke we will have quite a large socity in a little time... Ellie tolks of you so much. She ses Pa will come and see us some time. She is the worst child you ever saw for mischeiviouness. I dare not leave her alone in a room, if I do she will tare eney thing upside downg.

May the 31

If I am well enufe, I entend to go up to Belleville next week and do alittle traden and pay our taxes and git those deeds recorded, I gave tham to Osbay last fall, but he neglected to attend to it, As he does every thing else, I never entend to ask him to attend to anything for me again, unless he emproves in attending to his one buisenes better.

I will close this letter and mail it this evening, Ritten by, Cimbaline Fike

May 30, 1863
Fort Pickering, Memphis, Tennessee

Dear Cimbaline,

A boat arrived from below this evening, and states, when she left Vicksburg, fighting was still going on. Our army has the city and fortifications entirely surrounded. They are fighting there every day, more or less. Every one who comes from there, says that we are *bound to succeed*. Accounts differ somewhat as to the amount of supplies the rebels have in there. Some say they have enough to do a good while, and other accounts say they are now on quarter rations.[8]

Your affectionate husband,
Henry

---

8. Historian Earl Hess notes that by late June the Union siege of Vicksburg pushed the rebel garrison there to a crisis point; he wrote, "The Confederates were down to a biscuit and a couple of mouthfuls of bacon each day." Hess, *Civil War in the West*, 157.

June 1, 1863
Fort Pickering, Memphis, Tennessee

Dear Cimbaline,
You have some idea of the labor required to make up my usual monthly reports. I used to think making out a Common School Schedule was a monstrous job; but that isn't anywhere now, compared with my present reports.[9]

Your affectionate husband,
Henry

June 2, 1863
Fort Pickering, Memphis, Tennessee

Dear Cimbaline,
It is now just dark, and I have lighted my candle and seated myself for the purpose of penning a few lines to you. I have just had a good swim in the river with the Chaplain and about twenty or thirty of the boys; and I feel first rate. One or two hundred of our regiment go in swimming every day. The river is literally alive with them from sunrise to sunset. The soldiers have also gone, pretty extensively, into the fishing business. There are any amount of lines and hooks all over the river. Garrett Land and I have commenced the business to-day.[10] We have set out a 'trot-line' four hundred feet long, with about one hundred hooks on it. We expect to haul them in—in amounts and quantities to suit. The boys catch them every day weighing from five to fifty pounds. Fish are plenty, in camp.

You said in your last letter, that you wanted me to come home, for fear I will forget you and Ellie, and how home looks. You need not fear anything of that kind. I shall never forget you—no never—I am really glad to hear that the ladies of Mascoutah are going to organize a Union

---

9. Each month regimental quartermasters submitted nine reports to the office of Quartermaster General Montgomery Meigs, in addition to the returns they completed every quarter. A full set of monthly reports consisted of fifty-three forms detailing receipts and expenditures of property and funds, plus a thorough accounting of everything that the regiment had on hand. Lenette Taylor, *"Supply for Tomorrow,"* 203–204.

10. Garrett C. Land served as a sergeant in Company C of the independent Alton Battalion. Fred Delap, Illinois Civil War Muster and Descriptive Rolls Database, Illinois State Archives, Office of the Illinois Secretary of State, https://www.ilsos.gov/isaveterans/civilMusterSearch.do (hereafter Delap, ICWMDR); *History of St. Clair County*, 151.

League. I hope you will put the thing through, and see who is true blue. If it grinds any of the secesh sympathizers, just 'let it grind'; who cares?
  Your affectionate husband,
  Henry

June 4, 1863
Mascoutah, Illinois

Dear Henry
We are all tolerble well I have not time to write you a long letter to day. Under the present circumstances I hope you will excuse me. Now I will give you the reson. Mr Whites baby has been very sick ever sence sunday, and i have been thare conciderble of my time with it. I donot think it ever will git well. In fact I know it cannot. The Doctor has given it up some days ago. Mr White is sick himself not able to see to the baby. Yesterday I wos with it all day and untell eleven Oclock last night, This morning I went downg and stayde untell twelve olock, and promist to go back after dner, but I have not gon yet, it is now four. I had the oner [honor] this after noon finichen the Union Leuige flag of the gentlemens on my soeing mechine. The first worek I have done sence I wos sick. . . . I must say before I close I am realy glad you all have plenty of butter and eggs downg to your house. I think you officers mite send up and invitasion for some of us to come downg and eat butter and eggs with you, I must close this letter and go and see that babe as I promist to. I hope you will excuse me for not writing more this time I will write in a few days and give you all the nuse as fare as I know
  From your affectionate wife
  Cimbaline

June 5, 1863
Fort Pickering, Memphis, Tennessee

Dear Cimbaline,
I was pleased to hear that your Union League has been organized, and put under headway. I wish you all unbounded success and prosperity. Give my respects to every lady that joins in with you. . . . In our ride around town I saw one sight at the Charleston depot, which exceeded anything of the kind I ever saw, in all my life. It was a lot of refugees, to

about the number of two hundred, who came in from the east, last night, on the railroad. They are from northern Alabama and Mississippi, some two hundred and fifty miles from here. The company or crowd consisted of twenty-five men, fifty or sixty women and large girls, and over one hundred children from six months old up—every size and age you ever saw. There were several *old* men and women, who looked to me to be anyhow eighty years old. And, now, this large group was all out-doors under the railroad depot-shed, which is merely a projection of the roof of the building, some two hundred feet long. They were on the bare ground; some standing, some walking around, some setting on old chairs, some setting on the ground, others lying on the ground, others on a quilt pallet. I saw one old woman, anyhow eighty years old, lying on a quilt, and another quilt over her. One or two children, and a young man were very sick. I don't think they were suffering for anything to eat. Their clothes were quite shabby, and mostly homespun, except in a few instances. The children appeared to be the only cheerful ones in the crowd. Some of them acted so funny I almost felt like smiling; but the whole scene presented such a pitiful and heartrending appearance that I could not help feeling exceedingly sad over the sight. The most peculiar thing of the whole affair, was the great proportion of children among them. And notwithstanding this fact, if there is any truth in the old adage that 'coming events cast their shadows before,' there was plenty of evidence that the number would be considerably increased, before long. Taking it all and all, it was indescribable, and I shall not attempt it any further; but merely add that I learn they are all to be sent North, as soon as possible, and provision made for their comfort, &c. . . .[11]

Your affectionate husband,
Henry

June 5, 1863
Mascoutah, Illinois

Deare Henry
This evening finds us as well as usul. White baby is dead, it dyed last night about eleven oclock. Tha have gon to the funerel this afternoon. I think

---

11. The southern refugees who migrated northward, many of them recently liberated from bondage, faced hostility from many of the inhabitants in their adopted homeland. See Schwalm, *Emancipation's Diaspora.*

I shall go to Belleville tomorrow and attend to paying our taxes and git those deeds recorded.... The gentlemen has a very larg socity about the same as the ladys. Some of the seses [secesh] hear are giting friten Mr Nellson asked one of our union men whot it ment.[12] That tha wos giting such clubs. The said he wos gitting sceard. he wos afraid tha would send him to dixey and burn his property. Mr Scharp is very much friten. His wife said she nose wose afraid to go to sleep at night for fear she would wake up and find thare hous on fire I hope we will friten soe of our cessess [secesh] ladys so tha will not be quit so bold as tha have been, some of tham have openly declared tha was Copperheads. If tha speak such lanuage to me I will tell tham I think thare are soft heeds two.
    Cimbaline

June 7, 1863
Mascoutah, Illinois

Dear Henry
To day finds us all quit unwell. Ellie is not well. She has had some fever, and has quit a large bile on her little hip, wich makes her very fretful. I am very unwell myself I supose I have exposed myself two much during the last week attendend to Whites child and going up to Belleville yesterday. It wos very late when we got home. When Osbay found out my buisness, he proposed to to go with me and take me up himself. So I concented and went up with him in his buggy. We settle up our taxes, and left those deeds to be recorded. I tole Osbay I entended to have that buiseness attended to if I had to attend to it myself I told him I wose one of those kind of women to have every thing done in its proper time. He appoligised and said he out to had it attended two long ago, but he had neglected to do so.
    From your affectionate wife
    Cimbaline Fike

---

12. It's unclear whether this Mr. Nelson is William or B. M. Nelson.

June 7, 1863
Fort Pickering, Memphis, Tennessee

Dear Cimbaline,
I believe they are 'pressing in' all the boats here, to run the river below here. I don't know what it is for. The proceeding, I presume, has something to do with the fighting at Vicksburg. The great celebration came off in the city of Memphis yesterday, according to previous announcement.[13] The day was very fine and pleasant, and every thing passed off well. . . . At one house close by 'court-square' a small rebel flag was seen by the window. Our men immediately arrested the male inmates of the house, and placed them in the 'Irving Block,' and, I understand, placed them in irons.[14]

Give Ellie another big hug and sweet kiss for her papa.
Your affectionate husband,
Henry

June 8, 1863
Mascoutah, Illinois

Dear Henry,
You wanted that I should promis to write a letter every other day to you. I am afraid to promis that I will for fear I will neglect it some time. so I will promis to write as offten as I can You can write every day better then I can every other or every three days, you are writing most every day. You can scrach of a few lines most eny time, I have evry thing to attend two at home and ceep house, and everything to see if it is in its proper plase, and done in its proper time One half of the time I am not able to see to every thing. No one knous what a trile it is to git along under such circumstances. I donot feel disposed to mumer at my trubles, as I know

---

13. Preparations for the June 6 celebration, which marked the one-year anniversary of Union gunboats overwhelming rebel forces and taking possession of Memphis, had been underway for at least two weeks. See H. Fike to C. Fike, May 24, 1863, FP.

14. Soon after capturing Memphis, Union forces converted a four-story office building that Confederates had used as a hospital into a military prison. *Memphis Daily Union Appeal*, July 22, 1862, 2; L. Galbraith and W. Galbraith, *Lost Heroine*, 93n12. See also *Harper's Weekly* 8, no. 402(1864): 588, https://archive.org/details/harpersweeklyv8bonn/page/588/mode/2upf, accessed December 9, 2023.

it will make you feel unhapy. I shall try to git along the best I can. I hope you will write as often as you can. I have not any thing more to write of any emportents Ellie is very cross to day, and not very well. Good by this time
   Respectfully yours, Cimbaline

June 12, 1863
Fort Pickering, Memphis, Tennessee

Dear Cimbaline,
Yesterday morning, in company with John Mosar, I walked up town. The sidewalks wer perfectly thronged with 'blue coats.' I met with, and talked with some of the *real* 'live Yankees.' They seem to entertain a very high opinion of the 'Western boys.' And well they may; for the Western boys have accomplished four fifths of what has been successfully accomplished, thus far, in this war. As I came in from town, I bought a 'good fat hen'—paid half dollar for it—and had 'Jim' make me some good chicken soup. You know that is a medicine I generally use, when I am 'unfit for duty.'

It does me a great deal of good to hear of the success attending your Union League Society. I received a letter from Dr. Ross[15] to-day, in which he states the men's Union League, is in a very prosperous condition, and exerting a very salutary effect upon those tinctured with the doctrine of Copperheadism. I am glad to hear that some of them are beginning to 'quake in their boots.'
   Your aff. husband,
   Henry.

June 13, 1863
Fort Pickering, Memphis, Tennessee

Dear Cimbaline,
There is quite a sensible difference in the appearance and demeanor of the citizens now, to what it was previous to the issuing of Gen. Hurlbut's

---

15. Alexander Ross, fifty, was a Mascoutah physician. United States Federal Census (hereafter USFC), 1860.

late order.[16] It is wonderful how the taste of the softer sex has changed in favor of *blue*. It is blue trimmings now from head to foot;—little and big have taken up with the fashion. However, I am satisfied that this change is the result of hypocrisy and deceit.[17]

Your affectionate husband,
Henry

June 14, 1863

Mascoutah, Illinois

Dear Henry
Our Union Leigue is a bout to go under. We have had to many boses. The Risleys girels and White wos boses. The magarty of our leigue wos not in faver of it Tha tock every thing in to theare hands. We had no use of a Presadent or a vise presadent tha had privet meetings and made pass words and the sinds for our Liegue. So our President resind. . . . Few of us has meet sence our last meeting. We have concluded to start a new liegue and elect our offersers over after tha are gon. . . . I like the prosedings of the Memphis Celabrasion very much. I wish I could have been tharer. I wos rather sureprised to see such a Union feeling in that city. I have a better opinion of Memphis or the citisons of that plase then I ever had befor sence this wor commenced. I hope by the time I git redy to visit that plase again, that I will not meet with theare snearls and frounds as I did last winter.

From your affectionate wife
Cimbaline Fike

June 21, 1863

Fort Pickering, Memphis, Tennessee

Dear Cimbaline,
We have heard nothing more of the cavalry engagement that occurred out east a day or two ago. Things have subsided some. Yesterday a 'nig-

---

16. Stephen A. Hurlbut, at that moment a brigadier general. Lash, "'Federal Tyrant at Memphis.'"

17. Another Union soldier in Memphis also noted that "secesh ladies" had begun to change their behavior: "Their noses have been turned up for some time, but a late order has been issued, requiring all to take the oath or move beyond the federal lines, this turns their noses down." David McFarland to Dear Wife, June 16, 1863, David McFarland Papers.

ger' boy stole about $15. from a man in company 'B.' This morning they 'walloped' him some, and he forked over $4;—he had spent the balance. They then set him adrift, and told him to skedaddle, which he did in good earnest.

For several days we have been receiving news of the rebels advancing from Virginia, up through Maryland into Pennsylvania. But we feel that our army is able to attend to the case. I think the people of Pennsylvania will arise *en masse*, and defend their rights and homes.[18]

Your aff. husband.,
Henry.

June 21, 1863
Fort Pickering, Memphis, Tennessee

Dear Cimbaline,

There has been considerable talk in the regiment to-day, about whipping the 'nigger' this morning. All think the boy should have been punished in some way, for stealing the money, but do not approve the manner in which the whipping took place. Lieut. Gillmore was at the head of the whipping operation.[19] There is considerable of feeling in reference to the matter. Some say, if the 117" Regiment is going to turn out to tieing up negroes to trees, without trial or jury, and beating them with a horse whip, they beg permission to hand over their commissions, and to be 'excused.'[20]

I am sorry to hear that you 'Union League is about to go under.' You

---

18. For the northward advance of Confederate forces during this stage of Robert E. Lee's campaign into Pennsylvania, see Guelzo, *Gettysburg*, 64–79.

19. First Lieutenant Frank H. Gilmore, a twenty-nine-year-old printer from Company B, apparently faced few consequences for his part in the whipping, as he was later promoted to captain. Delap, ICWMDR. Weeks earlier, Hurlbut wrote to President Lincoln that the challenge of soldiers administering justice for the two thousand Black refugees in Memphis, "not supported by the Government [and] crowded into all vacant sheds and houses living by begging or vice," posed a burden for the army. "Pilfering & small crimes are of daily occurrence among them & I see nothing before them but disease and death." S. Hurlbut to A. Lincoln, March 27, 1863, in Berlin et al., *Freedom*, ser. I, vol. I, 304–306.

20. The flogging was only one example of the brutal violence that white soldiers meted upon Black residents of Memphis. Humphrey Hood, a surgeon in the 117th Illinois, reported that on June 16 three Union soldiers shot and murdered a young Black man who had stolen an orderly's horse. Humphrey Hood to Benjamin S. Hood, June 17, 1863, Humphrey H. Hood Papers.

said you thought you had too many 'bosses.' I should think, out of so many bosses, you surely could get one boss, that would boss the concern straight along.

Tell Martha Blaker to hold on untill the war is over, and I'll bring her a nice young man from the war, to marry. She must never marry a young man, who is too big a coward to shoulder a musket; or afraid to sleep in a tent, and endure the hardships of a true genuine soldier. I am in earnest. The man who can't, if necessary, wrap himself up in a blanket and lie down on the naked mother earth, without any other covering, isn't fit to lie in a nice warm bed, with a neat good wife. What do you think of that doctrine? Am I 'right on the goose?'

Your affectionate husband,
Henry.

June 23, 1863
Fort Pickering, Memphis, Tennessee

Dear Cimbaline,
I should like very much to be at Mascoutah, the approaching Fourth of July. If I am not there, I want you to remember me especially on that day. If I can not be present with you, and my friends on that occasion, and mingle with you in the festivities of the glorious old Fourth, I trust you all will remember me, though hundreds of miles from your presence;—and that I am endeavoring to discharge my duty, in my humble capacity, towards putting down this wicked rebellion, which has caused so much bloodshed,—broken up so many once happy families,—rendered mournful so many parents, wives and children. May our army be rewarded with victory and success, such as will enable the right to prevail, harmony once more to be restored, and peace and prosperity again flourish in our land and country.

I trust your Union League will prosper and do much good. You have but a faint idea of the encouragement and stimulation it affords the soldier in the field, to hear that his mother, sisters, and *wife* are also engaged actively in behalf of the same common cause.

Your affectionate husband,
Henry.

June 25, 1863
Mascoutah, Illinois

Dear Henry
It seemes that I will never git entirely well again I have given up allmost all hopes of any cure in my case. When I take meddison, it seemes to realeave me to some exsten, but does not cure me I feel out of heart, of every enjoyen any health again. It has been two months to day sence I arived at home. It seemes like six months more then tow. If every women thinkes the time as long as I do that has a husban and friends in the wore, I think tha would be willing to enlist and go and healp settle or fite untell peace is obtain, and our goverment restored to peace. For my part I feel like puting on briches now, and fiting some of the copperheads in Mascoutah, that is horowing for Jeff Davis on the streets in the dark. Tha seeme to be out with the dogs. . . . If ever I hear any one call Jeffs Davis name in or about my house, I entend to take a stick and brake theare head and let the copper rune out. I have a stick layde up for that purpis, One half of it is ropt with theare one collers. Being I would not like to have ours staind with theare haitful blood.
 Yours respectfuly, Cimbaline

June 30, 1863
Mascoutah, Illinois

Dear Henry
Dr Ross told me to day he heard that some one entended to rais a ceseese [secesh] flag at Foyettville on the fourth of July. I told him if I knew that any person would do such a thing I would go all the way downg thare, and bee redy when tha hoisted it on the pole, To teake a ax and cut it downg, and cut it all to peases, I would go an do that very thing. If I knew what I heard was so. If tha wos ten thousen coperheads standen by It makes me mad to hear anyone tolke of a coperhead. The verry thought of one makes me feel like fiting. . . . I hope to see you soon. So good night
 Respectfuly yours
 Cimbaline

July 29, 1863
Fort Pickering, Memphis, Tennessee

Dear Cimbaline,
I want you to tell me how you feel every letter you write. If there is anything you want; any kind of medicine you think would help you, I want you to get it, I don't care what it costs. I want you to get perfectly well and stout again, & I don't care what it costs to procure the proper medical treatment or means, I am willing to foot the bill. I don't want you to think or feel that I am not willing for you to get anything you want. . . . There is one conclusion that I have come to, in reference to your case. If your health does not become good by this fall or winter, I shall endeavor to come home in the spring and start to travelling with you, up north somewhere. I think that will cure you sound and well. That is what I shall try to do, if the trip down here this fall does not restore your health. I want you to write to me on that subject, and give me your views in reference to the matter. You may depend, that, if I live, *I will do what I have said, if you are willing.* Depend on that.
  Your affectionate husband,
  Henry

August 7, 1863
Mascoutah, Illinois

Dear Henry
My health is a bout as good as when you was hear. I cannot *tell* any difference onley my eyes are very weak again. I cannot see to work much. I fear tha is but little hope of me ever recovering my health again. I have given up all most all hopes of ever thinking of enjoyen health again. Some of Dr Fitchs meddisons I think has healpt me more then anything I have taken. I have thought of sending for more of his meddison when i have money to spair. I cannot at the present time. I onley have 10 do [dollars] now. White told me sence you left, that you said for me to pay him 5 do for that map, and for him to hand it to the man you bout it from Then I will not have but 5 do left at the last of this month I will half to pay Martha some three Do

About our trip up north, next spring. I can-not say anything about. I donot see how you can go with me, while you are engage in the armey. I will never ask you to resine and leave the armey for that purpis, or any other while I can ceep up. Or as long as your health continues to be good. I think myself if I onley could leave Mascoutah. My health would be better. You know your self I never wos sedisfide to live hear in good health, and when you wos at home. How could you expect me to be sadisfide now in poore health and you gon. Me left hear allmost alone, from all my peple Now way of going ay plase, and mite say no one lives hear that cears [cares] for any one but theare selvels. Now plase of amusement now parttyes to go to, to pass of the lonsom hours. Nor not meny plesent plases to visit. . . . Stay at home take care of the hous. Occasenly a newscaryer comes a long and delivers the nuse of the town. Occasenly tells me somthing that does not please me very well then I will study over it untells it coses me to see truble, then I have no one to go tow that I can trust to tell my trubles tow. So you can see that I stay at home and greeve it out untell it allmost makes me sick. Some times I allmost wish I could fine a plase wher I never could see any one again I will stop hear and change the subject

Yours. from Cimbaline

August 11, 1863

Mascoutah, Illinois

Dear Henry

Tha is conciderble of sickness among the childeren aroung now. Some tow or three barred [buried] day. I think the bell has toned to day four or five times. . . . Ellie ses for me to write to you, that she is a good girel, and loves her Granma, and that she loves to go and see her, and eat meat. And that she loves Dr Land for he gives her canday. Uncl Jime for he gives her aples to eat. While her Pa gon to the wore to shoot the debles. My pa is a good man. If he has gon and left my Ma at home. By and by Moma and I will go to Dixey and see my papa. Then I will git more candy.

Write offten. Remember you have got a wife and a child at home, as well as a great maney other men in the armey, who would love to hear from you as often as covenent. No more at present. From you

Affectionate wife. *Cimbaline*

August 16, 1863
Mascoutah, Illinois

Dear Henry

Tha were a very sad axident hapent hear last Thursday night, a bout midnight Tha were a strange person came hear some time during the day, lounge aroung untell night. Then he broke in to Mr Belces store hous.[21] Wos taken downg such goods as he wanted, when Mr Belce woke up, and asked whot he wanted Thinking it wos his son after something The rober made at him and struck him a cross the fore head, and one eye with a very large chilzel [chisel], nock him downd. By this time his son, and one ore tow more ran in to his assistance so tha cought the rober. The rober being a German. It raised ther temper so tha tock the man downg to the woods and hung him the same night. I forgot to mention in the scufel, that his son got shot thrue the hand, by the rober.

You better beleive, we ceep close wach over our locks and boltes. And ceep a lite aberning all night tow. I expect you think that is foolish, but we dont care, so we are sadisfide. . . . This is the last letter I entend to write to you, untell I receive one from you I donot see why you cant write offtener than you do. Being you are allways writing That is your buisness in the armey

From Cimbaline

August 20, 1863
Fort Pickering, Memphis Tennessee

Dear Cimbaline,

As I have written, it seems to me, almost hundreds of times, I have the same old story to repeat of 'no news.' Every thing, these hot and dreary days, passes along very slowly, and in a monotonous way. . . . From many accounts given by the Southern papers, there is a strong feeling springing up in several of the states, to disclaim their disloyal actions, and try to reinstate themselves in the old Union. They seem to be growing sick of the war. May they become sicker and sicker, is my prayer.

  Your aff. Husband,
  Henry

---

21. This is perhaps James M. Bale, the only merchant identified in the 1860 census with a surname that begins with B. USFC, 1860.

August 21, 1863
Fort Pickering, Memphis, Tennessee

Dear Cimbaline,
This afternoon, after I had finished your letter, I sent it up to the P.O. by 'Lindsey' our new darkey. Then Mr. Cavell, Lt. Wallis and I took a good long walk down to the nigger town, below the fort, and then we crossed over to 'President's Island,' where there is another nigger town of some two thousand inhabitants. . . .[22] The contrabands on that Island, are engaged in cultivating three farms, and building huts for themselves to live in. The government is trying to arrange it so that negro refugees, who come here that are not able to serve in some of the negro regiments, can be placed in a situation to produce or earn their own support. I think the idea a good one; at any rate, a better plan, than to have to feed them, and get nothing out of them for it.
   Your affectionate husband,
   Henry.

Aug 24, 1863
Mascoutah, Illinois

Dear Henry
To day is another lonsom day. No church in town. . . Tha seem to bee conciderble of sickness aroung now. Espesley among the children. The hooping couff is ragen among the children hear I supose you have heard before this time of the big fire we had in Mascoutah. It is quit a loss, to Mr Postle, he seem to take it very cooly. Ses shuch things will happen sometimes.
   Respectfuly yours, Cimbaline

August 28, 1863
Mascoutah, Illinois

Dear Henry
I heard some great nuse a bout the 117 Regmentle Quarter Master Few days ago. Tha wos a man come home on a furlow, who wehn at home

---

22. For the U.S. Army's policy of isolating Black refugees on islands in the Mississippi River, see Amy Murrell Taylor, *Embattled Freedom*, 87–92.

lived at John Pittes fothers or with one of his brothers. I do not know witch. John Pittes saw him, and enqurred a bout some of the boys, among the others, he asked a bout John and you Well he said John wos a good fellow—all the boys liked him—But for Henry Fike, he wos the meanest man in the Reg. The porest Q M that he ever saw. Said you allmost starved the boys. When you was at home they had plenty to eat. But as soon as you returned, it wos the same old thing he said non of the boys liked you and tha entended to put you out of office, and git some one that would not ceep all the best for him self

Yours with respect
Cimbaline

August 28, 1863

Fort Pickering, Memphis, Tennessee

Dear Cimbaline,

As [Capt. Whittaker] and I started up town this afternoon, two companies of the negro regiment came along, going up to the railroad depot, in the city, to receive and escort into the fort, some three hundred of their 'cullud brudders,' who were coming in on the evening train, from towards Corinth, to join the negro regiment in the fort. The Captain and I 'kinder' fell into the crowd, as these went from the fort. They created an intense amount of curiosity in the minds of many of the citizens, to have a peep at the 'soldiers of color' The niggers along the streets, through which they marched, flocked together, on the sidewalks, to see the sight. I heard one little boy hollow out, 'La! look at the nigger soldiers,' and away he bolted full-tilt, into the house, to tell the rest of the folks, I guess. I saw white women peep out and look up the street, and, when they discovered who was coming 'curl up their proboscis,' and retreat back within-doors, in disgust, I suppose. I saw one 'she-cesh' come round the house, into the front yard, and take the young ones of her tribe, into the back yard. I suppose this was done to keep them out of danger (?) [in original] What do you think about it? The negro troops are doing finely. Those who came in this evening, will fill up the regiment inside, to eight full companies. Thomas Curtis' company will be filled up full now.[23]

---

23. Historians have found that seventy thousand Black men in the Mississippi Valley emancipated themselves by enlisting in the Union army. Berlin et al., *Freedom*, 265–266.

I want you to arrange matters so you can enjoy yourself in the very best way possible. If you think you *can not stand it* in Mascoutah much longer, why, I would advise you to accept Polly Ann's offer. It seems as if there is some hidden lurking devil in Mascoutah, who is constantly persecuting or aggravating you, and causing you every now and then, to write the gloomiest kind of letters to me. There seems, from the tenor of your letter received this morning, to be a source of trouble in your mind, which you have forborne to reveal to me, from a fear that if revealed to me, it would cause a state of unpleasant and unhappy feelings. I can assure you, if there is anything of the kind, that your *telling it outright* to me, would cause me less reflections upon you, than to have you *insinuating* in the manner in which you have done. But perhaps I am too severe in my remark. I know your disposition has always been to gather trouble from flying rumors and idle tales; and I have always advised you to put no confidence in them. You know that. And I do hope you will endeavor to content yourself, amidst your troubles, as much as possible. I can assure you, that you have now and always have had, since we have been married, my very warmest and most devoted love, and attachment. And there is scarcely an hour that passes over my head, but what witnesses my longing desires and prayers in behalf of you, and our dear and sweet little Ellie. And I do hope this 'cruel war' will soon come to an end, and we will be permitted to live together *at home*. If I have said anything in the above that would wound your feelings, I ask your pardon: for I did not so intend it.

Your affectionate husband,
Henry.

September 3, 1863

Fort Pickering, Memphis, Tennessee

Dear Cimbaline,
I have not heard any thing about your Ladies Union League, for some time. What has become of it? Do you all intend to let the thing go by the board? Perhaps you think now, that Vicksburg has fallen into our hands, and the rebels are caving in, all around, that there is not any further need of your organization. If so, I think you are mistaken. You should keep the thing alive.

Your affectionate husband,
Henry.

September 6, 1863
Fort Pickering, Memphis, Tennessee

Dear Cimbaline,
Yesterday afternoon I went to market, to lay in a supply of 'rations' for to-day. Saturday is the only day of the week, in which market is open in the afternoon. On this day, there is always an immense crowd in attendance at the 'fair,' which, I think, it might rightly be called; for hundreds go there, it is evident, just merely to see and be seen. The uppertendom of the city is pretty well represented, especially the female portion. It is a crowd and jam in the market house, around it and through it. One has occasionly, in passing through a 'squeeze,' to elevate his basket above his head to prevent it being squeezed' from his grasp. Here you can hear the English, French, and German languages—and can see representatives of those nations, with a large sprinkling of niggers, mulattoes, quarter-oons and octeroons.—all stirring, mixing, winding, twisting, buying and selling, talking and laughing and seeming to enjoy themselves extremely well. The scene is nearly as good as our County Fair, at home. When you come down, we will go up some time, and throw ourselves in among the mess, and, after wending our way round, as long as we desire to, among the *motly* crowd, stop at one of the numerous ice cream stands, which abound there, and refresh our weary selves with a plate of that cooling luxury. I tell you Saturday afternoon market in Memphis, is a pretty good 'institution' after all.
  Your affectionate husband,
  Henry

September 6, 1863
Mascoutah, Illinois

Dear Henry,
In one of your letters, you wrote after you received one of mine I think you spoke out very plain, about some lurkin devel in Mascoutah, allways trying to make a fuss or heard feelinges. I can planley tell you, tha is more than one in this plase which it is the pride of thear life to creat heard feelinges among friendes. That is one great reson why I never loved to live hear so I have often told you, I allso told you when you wos about to enlist in the armey that wos the greatest reson I did not want you to

leave me hear. For I belive all the eanimes I have in the wolrd, lives in Mascoutah. All the fuses and heard wordes I ever had with any one, I have had rite hear, and mite say in your connection with the exception of one person. That is Mrs Nelson.[24] I will not sa any more upon this subject untell I see you.

From your respectfull wife
Cimbaline

Every time I go to write you a letter, Ellie will say, Ma are you agoing to write a letter to Papa, say Ma, are you going to write to Pa Me want to write a letter to pa, give me some paper, and a pensel. Me write some Every time I go downg towen when she misses me, she will run and say to Martha—Polly is Mama gon to the office to git a letter. Every one comes in while I am gon, she will meet tham at the door, and tell tham when I am gon then she will say Pa is gon to Memphis to shoot debles. Gone way off to dixee, Say, do you want to see my pa. Then go to to Memphis and shoot debles tow Every good man goes. My pa is good. he gives me candy. Then she will git up in thear lap, and begin to feel in ther pockets, Say have you got candy. She is the greatest romp you every saw.

September 9, 1863

Fort Pickering, Memphis, Tennessee

Dear Cimbaline,
This forenoon, about ten o'clock, I 'picked up' myself and started for Arkansas. I went up to the city, and took a skiff at the boat landing, and crossed over. I found our boys all in the best of spirits and glee. They are living finely, and are well pleased with their board. I helped them eat some Arkansas fresh pork and sweet potatoes, which the boys had picked up somewhere, lying around loose. When I approached their encampment about the first thing that attracted my attention, was the amount of *feathers* I saw lying and flying around. When I came up close, I saw any amount of chickens tied here, or boxed up there. The boys 'go in' on that line. While I was there, a couple of the boys brought in in a fat hog, just 'captured' which, they said, would not 'take the oath.' They say they *arrest* every thing that *will not take the oath of allegiance.* I found a good

---

24. Many married women with this last name lived in St. Clair County in 1860, and it is unclear which of them Lucy meant.

many persons in, from the interior of Arkansas, who have brought in cotton to sell, with the expectation of laying in a supply of family necessities. There are some restrictions yet resting upon the buying of cotton which has come from Arkansas, & the consequence is that a good quantity of cotton has accumulated upon the west bank of the river, awaiting the removal of these trade restrictions. There are some twenty or thirty wagons over there all the time. I had several hours conversation with a good many of the 'natives,' who are in from the interior. They all seem exceedingly anxious to have the war end and peace restored again. It is impossible for me, in a letter, to describe to you how these people look, what they say, and how they say they have to live. . . . The people down in these back regions see *hard times*, that you all at home have no idea of.

Your affectionate husband,
Henry.

September 10, 1863

Mascoutah, Illinois

Dear Henry,
I will tell you in the commencement of this leter I cannot write very much, I am in so much pain. . . . Dont be fritened when I tell you, some one tried to git in our hous, last Monday night I heard a nois [illegible] in the night and got up and looked out at my window, but I did not see any one. I felt that some one were about the hous, I could rest well. Next morning, Marey Hokenes told us, she saw some one in the night at our front door trying to unlock it, but tha did not succeed in doing so.[25] The person left the door and went to the south window blines, and tryed to git tham open, but tha could not unless bursten tham open. Then he left went aroung the hous. She could not see him any more She were seting up awaiting for her husban to come home That were the way she came to see tham

Donot be unsea about us at home, I have got a six shuter, I lay it by my side every night. If I every see any person aroung our hous after dark, That can not tell his buisness, he will smell poder

---

25. This is perhaps Mary Josephina Hawkins. Ancestry.com, Illinois, U.S., Compiled Marriages, 1851–1900, Provo, Utah, https://www.ancestry.com/search/collections/7857/, accessed December 9, 2023.

So no more at present I will write you a long letter sunday If nothing hapenes yours, Cimbaline

September 13, 1863
Mascoutah, Illinois

Dear Henry

This time, I have commence in the morning, so I mite take my time to write a letter, and not be hurred. We are all well. Except my self. I am still afflicted with biles. Or Dr Land call tham carbunkers [carbuncles]. I have had seven in differant places on my body. During the last week, I have had five to truble me One on each sholder, one on my breast and one on my side and arm. The ones on my side and one sholder, were open yesterday. The others is not redy to open yet. Tha were so large, and the core were so deap. I had Dr Land to cut tham. I tell you it was like cuting my heart strings. Tha were so heard and tuff.

I will tell you all about whot I said to White when I see you. It will take up to much paper to write it all.[26] He did not say more than a dozen wordes to in I tell you I tocked very plane to him. I tolde him no gentle man would act as he did. Tock about a woman in the manor as he had. When her husban were gon, and she left at home alone, and how, if you had been at home, he would not dared to spoken or acted as he had. . . . I did not cear for these little thinges that some people tocked about but when any one spoke of my charker [character] I were thare, and entended to take my one part. Let it be man or woman I told him alls. That he were the first man that I ever knew to speak of me publicley or privetly. If tha had ever been one. I never heard of it. When he spoke of me again I wanted it to be at my face

Last Wendesday night, in the night I heard a noise I got up, and went to the window, and liset I heard some one at the window blines trying to git tham open. I lssent [listened] untell i were sadisfide some one were thare. Then i open the window blines in my beed room, and fired a way. When I fired, Martha said, Thare I heard tham jump over the fence, so I went to the south window, and fired out thare. Next morning, I found I had made a holde in the fence. That were more than I expected I could

---

26. The 1860 census reveals more than a dozen households inhabited by an adult male with the surname "White," but only one of them—James M. White, a twenty-year-old tailor—was found in Mascoutah. USFC, 1860.

do not but, I would hit tham if I could Every sence our hous has been very quite at night. Next time I heare any one a roung, I will take aim and see if I can hit tham, or shoot of some fethers I must close. For I am in so much pain. I can not think of much. It has taken me all day to write this letter. From Cimbaline

Saturday, September 19, 1863
Fort Pickering, Memphis, Tennessee

Dear Cimbaline,
When yours was handed to me, I allowed, from its size, that it contained two or three photographs. But when I opened it, and found that it was only a letter *fourteen pages in length,* I 'understood the joke.' You may rest assured that a broad grin ran over my face, at the discovery of this fact. If, being afflicted like Job, as you were when you wrote it, caused you to think of so much to write, I could almost wish that you would be troubled a little in the same way, once in awhile.[27] However, I am sorry to hear that such a state of feelings was prevalent among some of the neighbors, as there seemed to be, from what you stated in your letter. I always dislike the wrangling strifes and contentions, that frequently occur. But from what you say, I am not disposed to censure you in the least, for the action you took in the matter. If mother and uncle Tommy Rainforth were your advisers, I am sure you acted perfectly right in what you did in the case. If there have been any improper strictures or insinuations cast upon your character, as sure as the Lord permits me to land safely in Mascoutah, I shall cause the perpetrators to retract what they have said. You may rest assured of that. Until then, I think it prudent to say nothing more on the subject.
    Your affectionate husband,
    Henry.

---

27. Job was the Old Testament figure upon whom God cast a series of hardships, including the deaths of his children, the theft and destruction of his property, and painful sores over his entire body.

September 19, 1863

Fort Pickering, Memphis, Tennessee

Dear Cimbaline,
I have something now to write that will surprise you, I expect, & perhaps somewhat disappoint you too. To-day we received orders to inspect and report upon the condition of all our tents and transportation, and get every thing in readiness for marching orders. This would look somewhat like, we were going to leave here soon. We have not yet received orders to go. There is only a strong probability of it. If we have to leave, it will break somewhat into our family plans and arrangements, we had been calculating upon. We do not know how it will yet terminate, and will have to wait.
    Your affectionate husband,
    Henry.

September 20, 1863

Mascoutah, Illinois

Dear Henry
John Curtis has sold out his intrust in the mill. I have heard, he entendes to moove a way from Mascoutah. I do not blame him for wanting to leave such a plase as this. I hope you will be redy to sell out after this wor is over, and leave thes digines, and go some plase wher we can enjoy our selvels. Not live al our life time a mong debles. I feel now, if you ever live with me, you will half to leave this plase. The longer i live hear, the more I dislike it. I have got so now that I hait it
    One month from to day I expect to leave Mascoutah for Memphis. If nothing hapinges. The 20 of Oct. comes on Tusday. I do not know wich will be the best plain to take. For me to git Amos Day to take me and my goods in a waggen to St Louis, rite to the boait, Or go to Belleville, and git on the cares. Or go to Lebanon, Whot do you think is best . . . I want you to write, when you git a hous. How large the room is, and how many windows tha is, so I can bring some window curtings. And carpet. I want tow roomes enyhow. One for a siting room, one to eat and cook. I entend to bring a beed and carpet, and some window curtings. Enufe for one room
    I want you to send me a card with my name writen on it for me to use in traveling. It is more fashenable to use cardes in traveling than it is to

tell you name, and where you are going. I could git one hear, but I can not write as well as you.

From Cimbaline

September 22, 1863
Fort Pickering, Memphis, Tennessee

Dear Cimbaline,
Col. Moore's nigger 'Jim,' who used to cook for our mess when you was here, went up to Columbus about two weeks ago to see his wife and child, who lived with their master back in the country about eleven miles from Columbus. He had the proper passes, and went up on the same boat that Jesse Dupuy went home on. He did one pretty smart trick while he was up there. He landed at Columbus just after dark, one evening, and went out immediately to his wife's, eleven miles, on foot, took two mules and a wagon, and put his wife and child in, and her things, and put back to Columbus, where he arrived about an hour by sun, the following morning. He took the first boat going up to Cairo, where he took his family, and rented a house till Christmas, and paid the money down in advance; gave the mules and wagon to his wife, and started for our regiment and arrived here this evening. He has done all this in eleven days. Don't you think that is pretty good for a 'nigger? What a man will do for the sake of his family, when he loves them! Jim has declared to me, several times, that he intended to take his family to Illinois sometime. He now wants to go with us. He is one of the best fellows, for a darkey, I ever saw.

Your affectionate husband,
Henry.

September 27, 1863
Lebanon, Illinois

Dear Henry
You will see from the commencement of this letter, that I am not at home. I came hear last Friday, for the purpis of haven my teeth repared. I have been truble so much with tham, I though I would have tham out if it cilled me. Yesterday Sarah and I went up to Dr Paynes office. I had all my uper teeth taken out, at one seting. I knew but little a bout it, It were done by the enfluence of Cloaforme [chloroform]. I am glad tha are out.

I entended to gon home to day. But the Do. [doctor] had to make a trip to St Louis yesterday for the purpis of giting some sutible teeth for me. I expect to go home monday evenning. If the Docter gites my teeth finish. It will cost you forty do. [dollars] for me haven my teeth repared I do not know whot you will say about it these heard times. I hope some day or nother to make all the momey for you. So you will not luse it.

Yours with respect.
Cimbaline

October 1, 1863

Mascoutah, Illinois

Dear Henry
I came home last Monday evening from Lebanon with my new teeth in my mouth Some of the nabors thinkes I will pass for sixteen now, and thinkes it is a little dainsours for you to be gon, and leave me at home. For fear some gentleman mite come a long and persuard me to leave this country. Whot do you think of thear opinions. Do you think tha is any daingour of it at present . . . If I git disopinted in my visit to see you, I have got a nother one in my head. I think I shall do. I do not entend to stay in Mascoutah this winter. That is the word with the bark on.

I reamain as ever, your affectionate wife

October 4, 1863

Mascoutah, Illinois

Dear Henry
I take my seat on a nother Sabath day, for the purpis of pening you a few lines, to inform you, that we are in reasonble health. Ellie is better of her breaken out. The Do thinkes it is some thing like the singhles I have sent, and purcured a nother box of Dr Fithes meddisons. Sence I have comenence taken it, I find my health has comencd enproven. I were waid last evening. I waid 1.13 bls [lbs]. Tow pondes more than usel. I am glad to hear your health is good. Nothing I drother hear from you than to hear you enjoy good health. I know when you are well, you can git a long. But when you are sick, I know it must bee very heard for any one to be sick in the Armey, way from home and friendes. I often think of the poor sick solders, that are a way from home In camp, or in Hospitles, I wish it were

my privlige to visit tham, and do tham some good, I have allways had a desire. Every sence this wore commenced to do good to the solders. Those that are willen to give thare lives for our blesed country. I know I am snearld at, At home for talken so, And by some, I thought were our friendes. But I do not cear. I will stick up for the Union, and death to the copperheads. If I lose all my friendes. . . . The lodge of copper heades are a bot to be exposed hear Tha are about eighty in nomber. I hope tha may be exposed and beaten out of socity

   Yours as ever Cimbaline

October 6, 1863
Fort Pickering, Memphis, Tennessee

Dear Cimbaline,
'Nothing new' in camp that I know of. I believe that it has become a settled conclusion that we will remain here, and we have all begun to act accordingly. I find, upon inquiry, that it is the most difficult thing to get houses. I have looked all around outside the fort, and can find none vacant, that are anyways near the fort. And still further I find that it will be impossible, just now, for us to get a house or set of rooms entirely to ourselves.

   Your affectionate husband,
   Henry.

October 9, 1863
Fort Pickering, Memphis, Tennessee

Dear Cimbaline,
There was a nigger man to see us to-day, to offer the services of his wife as a cook and washer-woman for us. He praises her up to be an experienced and skillful hand at the business—having done such work considerably in hotels. We told him to bring her along and we would immediately put her on trial at cleaning up. We will endeavor to make our rooms *clean*, if they are not *nice* and *pretty*. I do not know yet, which I will do, whitewash or paper our room. I will determine by to-morrow. If you can conveniently bring some carpet you had better do it. Our room is about 14 x 16 feet—about as large as our largest room up stairs, at home. The room has no fireplace, but I will get a coal stove with open front, which

will be about as good as a grate. To-day I drew from the Quarter Master some lime, window glass, and nails for whitewashing and repairing up generally.

Your affectionate husband.

Henry.

CHAPTER 4
"A Hard Trip Indeed"

From Vicksburg, Mississippi, to the Red River Valley, Louisiana
and
Memphis, Tennessee
January 1864 to May 1864

Having long grumbled that Mascoutah, Illinois, was the "most miserable plase" she had ever known, Cimbaline Fike made good on her intention to escape the town in the final weeks of 1863. She relocated to the house in Memphis that Henry had secured during his continuing deployment at Fort Pickering. What transpired during the three months that the couple stayed there together remains a mystery. The Fikes' correspondence resumed in January 1864, when Henry and the 117th Illinois embarked on a series of campaigns that took Union armies ever deeper into the South. Confederate defeats at Vicksburg and Gettysburg in July 1863 shifted momentum in the war toward the United States, but Union victory was not imminent, leading new General-in-Chief Ulysses S. Grant to attack rebel armies in as many places as possible.

In the West, these simultaneous offensives included the February 1864 expedition that William Tecumseh Sherman launched into central Mississippi, first against the capital of Jackson and then toward the railroad hub of Meridian. A year spent occupying Memphis had ensconced the regiment in relative safety and comfort, but now Henry and his comrades faced their first real opportunity to go "hunting the elephant."[1] Henry's dispatches in the coming weeks tracked the many challenges endured by an army on the move: daylong marches over rough terrain, a diet of middling coffee and hard tack, sleeping on the cold ground, and skirmishes with rebel troops that resulted in more casualties than his regiment had ever suffered.[2] Their invasion of Mississippi wrought tremendous devas-

---

1. H. Fike to C. Fike, January 30, 1864, Henry C. and Lucy C. Fike Papers (hereafter FP).
2. One local history later stated that the skirmish of February 5 killed two and wounded five members of the 117th Illinois, but Henry's letter of March 8 noted that one of these men died of disease. *History of St. Clair County*, 145; H. Fike to C. Fike, March 8, 1864, FP.

tation, presaging Sherman's future marches into Georgia and the Carolinas, but the campaign was short-lived. The 117th Illinois returned to Vicksburg barely a month after they left and soon sailed southward for what Henry thought would be another brief trip.

That spring expedition up the Red River into northwestern Louisiana proved a galling disappointment on nearly every count.[3] The campaign began well enough, with A. J. Smith's 16th Corps, which included the 117th Illinois, seizing the Confederate earthworks at Fort DeRussy on March 14. Borrowed from Sherman's army, these ten thousand troops made up one of four Union forces that planned to converge on the rebels in northern Louisiana, but many problems bedeviled the other three, threatening to doom the entire enterprise.[4] On April 8 a smaller Confederate force led by Richard Taylor routed the Federals near Mansfield and the Sabine Crossroads. The retreating Union troops rallied at Pleasant Hill and repulsed Taylor's attack the next day, but Union commander Nathaniel Banks chose to withdraw yet again and abandoned his plan

---

3. The capture of Shreveport, headquarters of the Confederate Trans-Mississippi Department and the state's capital since mid-1863, promised to break up rebel forces in the West and establish a base of operations from which Federals could attack Texas and deter further expansion by the French, who had installed a puppet emperor to rule Mexico. The campaign would also extend Unionist control beyond New Orleans at a time when loyal voters eyed the state's readmission to the United States. Major General Nathaniel P. Banks, the commander of the Department of the Gulf and leader of this offensive, quietly believed that success in this effort would burnish his chances of supplanting Lincoln as the presidential nominee of the Republican Party in 1864. What's more, textile interests hoped that this expedition would yield a windfall of cotton, which could break the severe shortages that gripped New England mills. Critics, including Banks's contemporaries and scholars alike, maintain that the general's personal interest in cotton speculation loomed over the Red River campaign, but historian Michael Thomas Smith concludes that such allegations of corruption are "grossly unfair." Hollandsworth, *Pretense of Glory*, 172–189. N. Banks to E. Stanton, April 6, 1865, United States War Department, *War of the Rebellion* (hereafter OR), ser. 1, vol. 34, pt. 1, 194; Johnson, *Red River Campaign*, 49–78; Winters, *Civil War in Louisiana*, 317–399; Smith, "'For Love of Cotton.'"

4. Frederick Steele moved south across Arkansas with some seven thousand Union troops, but harassment from rebel guerrillas and several bitter losses to Confederate regulars forced the Federals to withdraw back to Little Rock. Banks, meanwhile, was slow to arrive from New Orleans with another twenty thousand men, and Admiral David Porter's naval flotilla faced perhaps the most daunting challenge of all, a river whose unusually low level made advancing above the falls near Alexandria exceedingly difficult. Transports heavily loaded with men and materiel, which usually required a channel at least seven feet deep, could not sail through the rapids where the water level was barely three feet, and Union forces thus decided to unload these ships below the falls and move their freight by wagon to a point barely two miles upstream where it could then be reloaded onto smaller vessels. Gosnell, *Guns on the Western Waters*; Whittington, "Rapides Parish, Louisiana," 12–14.

to take Shreveport, rendering this tactical tie a strategic victory for the Confederates.[5]

Henry's letters from this period, less frequent than a year before, captured the frustration of many Union volunteers. Confusion and disappointment tempered his evident pride over the victory at Pleasant Hill, and like many comrades he struggled to comprehend why Banks chose to fall back rather than fight. "We do not fully understand—why we should retreat, after we had whipped our foe," Henry wrote. "Our army is not at all satisfied with the management of the whole affair."[6] Their halting withdrawal, slowed for weeks by the fickle river that nearly stranded the army above Alexandria, left many ragged Federals eager to be rid of the country.

The five letters that Cimbaline wrote during her husband's absence in early 1864 echoed the war weariness she had begun to express a year earlier. The move to Memphis had brought her greater independence and new social connections, including a friendship with a family of "good union folkes" in whose home she boarded.[7] Housing insecurity nevertheless proved to be a challenge in a city turned upside down by the Union occupation, and the prospect of having to move yet again always loomed. Now two years old, their daughter, Ellie, remained a source of delight, charming soldiers and anyone who might buy her treats from the fort's sutler, but also frustration, testing the patience of a mother left alone to discipline a headstrong child. The rambunctious toddler's longing for her father, whose candy she craved most of all, offered a poignant reminder of the emotional burdens that the war cast on children. For Cimbaline, such yearning sharpened her own sense of separation. "She cries so much to see you," she wrote to Henry, "she makes me feel worse than I would."[8] No one in the family, it was clear, was immune to such pangs of loneliness.

---

5. Bergeron, "General Richard Taylor," 35–47; Joiner, "Private Julius L. Knapp, U.S.A," in *Little to Eat*, 119n46.

6. H. Fike to C. Fike, April 12, 1864, FP; For the pronounced frustration toward Banks among soldiers, see Cuccia, "'Gorillas' and White Glove Gents"; Winters, *Civil War in Louisiana*, 340–379; Johnson, *Red River Campaign*, 170–276; Anonymous, "A Vermont Soldier's Experience at the Battle of Mansfield," in Joiner, *Little to Eat*, 51.

7. C. Fike to H. Fike, May 10, 1864, FP.

8. C. Fike to H. Fike, May 31, 1864, FP.

January 30, 1864
Vicksburg, Mississippi

Dear Cimbaline and Ellie,
I dropped you a few lines at Helena, night before last. I wrote the letter and gave it to a little boy who came on board, with a dime for his kindness, who said that he would mail it. I presume he did so. We lay that night at Helena until the moon arose, when the fleet proceeded on its downward course.[9] The day was passed quite pleasantly. The only gloomy aspect attending our trip, arose from the fact, that every revolution of the driving wheel was carrying me further from my dear ones. But, I hope, in due time, to again return to you all. . . . Here our boys are on the ground below the city about a half mile, without tents and no shelter but little roofs they have made out of their rubber blankets, and it raining in the bargain. This, the boys say, will do for their first experience, in this way of hunting up the elephant. . . . Of course we are, as yet, entirely ignorant of our real destination.
  Affectionate husband and 'papa'
  Lieut. H. C. Fike

February 1, 1864
On the Battlefield two miles East of Vicksburg, Mississippi

Dear Cimbaline & Ellie,
Last night I slept in a tent on the ground—it rained very hard for a while, but we kept perfectly dry. This morning we loaded up and moved out here a mile or two east of Vicksburg, on the ground our troops occupied so long last summer, in the siege of Vicksburg. Yesterday Shepherd and I took a little ride around here, and took a peep at things generally. I had heard and read a great deal about the situation and appearance of the country around here.—but never had formed a correct idea of it. It is the most broken spot *I ever saw*. It beats that country we saw, during our trip into Missouri, a few years ago. There are no ends to fortifications, breastworks, rifle pits &c., around here. I have seen dozens of the caves

---

9. Helena, Arkansas, sat some sixty miles downstream from Memphis, or about one-fourth of the journey down the Mississippi River toward Vicksburg.

the citizens dug to live in during the siege last year. The trees and houses bear many marks of the fight.

Yours affectionate husband & 'papa'
Henry.

February 6, 1864
In the field five miles west of Jackson, Mississippi

Dear Cimbaline & Ellie,
The army left [Vicksburg] in three columns, and proceeded eastward towards this section of country. Our division of the army, including the supply train, is about four miles long. The first day we neither saw nor heard anything very interesting, except the roughest country I nearly ever saw. We marched that day about 18 miles, and camped a mile or two west of Big Black river, in an open corn-field, where we burned rails by the thousand.[10] That night we all slept on the ground & did first rate. Next morning we started early and crossed the river. The authorities notified the command that after we crossed this river, we would have to forage for all the feed for our horses and mules. So I instructed 'my boys' accordingly. We had not proceeded more than two miles before we had our wagons as full as we wanted, and have had all that we needed since. The army has foraged a good deal on the route so far. Our boys have 'hauled in' the bacon, chickens, pigs &c. During the afternoon of that day we met and fought the secesh artillery and cavalry, and drove them along before us. As we would drive them from one hill, they would run to the top of the next and so on. That night we camped about twelve miles from where we are now, in another cornfield. Here another large conflagration of rails took place. Next morning (yesterday) we started and met the enemy soon in the morning, and drove them steadily all day. Our regiment skirmished all the forenoon. During this time we had seven men wounded, only one very badly. . . .[11] We are now in an enemy's country and expect to have a lively time of it, from this on.

---

10. From Vicksburg, William T. Sherman aimed to march east across Mississippi and capture the railroad hub of Meridian, from which Union forces might then continue into Alabama. As Henry's letter reveals, the destruction of railroads became a key objective of this expedition into the Confederate interior. Hess, *Civil War in the West*, 233–234.

11. Samuel B. Whiteside, a member of Company K, survived, but the wound, a gunshot through his bowels, left him disabled. Private Samuel B. Whiteside, 117th Illinois Volunteer Infantry, National Archives, Organization Index to Pension Files of Veterans Who Served

I will write to you as often as I can. I am now sitting on a box out in an open field with nothing over me. I hope you will not blame me, if I don't write to you, as often as I would like to do.

Your affectionate husband,
Henry.

February 14, 1864
Memphis, Tennessee

Dear Henry

I take my pen this evening, for the purpis of writing you a few lines to let you hear from us. We are all tolarble well at present I would have writing to you befor now, But I have not been well. I did not know where to drect my letters, as you did not tell me. . . . I am giting a long hear, as well as could be expected. I feel very lonly without you espesly of evening. That is the time I miss you the most. I supose I must learn to do, as I have had to do. . . . I have not heard from home sence you left. I have writing tow letters to Mother, sence you left, but have not received any ansor I think you surly have got out of the world I have not heard from you since you left Vicksburg. . . . The gentalman that onds [owns] this hous came the other day, and said he wanted persesion [possession] by the first of March, so you see, that we half to moove. I donot know where we can git a hous at presant. . . . Ellie is well, except a cold she has been truble with for severl days past. She is not to sick to play with the negroes Every day she wants me to give her money to go to the sutlars to buy candy. If I donot give it to her, she will go over to the shop, and tell any one in the shop that she wants some candy. By this, she has becom quite a pet among the offercers and solders. They ask her who her papa is, and where he is. She tells tham that he has gon to dixia to shoot the rubers. Pa will give tham thunder. She is giting so bad, that I do not know what I shall do with her, unless I whip her. You said, I must not do that. Last night I were seting by the fire, after she had gon to beed, and I thought asleep. I got to studying about things that has past, and at presant. All at once she got up and came to me, and said to me, Take me up Ma She looked up in my fase, and said, what is the matter Ma. Dont cry Mama, pa will come back and

---

between 1861 and 1900, T289, Record Group 15, https://www.fold3.com/image/88010/whiteside-samuel-p-us-civil-war-pensions-index-1861-1900, accessed December 9, 2023.

see you yes pa will come and see you, dont cry. She put her little armes aroung my nake, and kiss me. Than she said Ma rock me to sleep. She oftens speakes of you, and ses pa stays so long. His feet will git cool. pa is a long time coming with his candy, I must stopt for to night. It is late.

Sunday Night, March 6, 1864

Near Vicksburg, Mississippi

Dear Cimbaline,
Although this is the Sabbath day, and should have been observed as a day or rest, yet I never was more busy in my life. . . . We are all as busy as we can be in preparing for another move. I think we will make a brief visit up Red River. We hear all sorts of rumors as to our real destination. But I understood, to-day, that part of the 16th. Army Corps. (to which we belong) will go to Memphis and the other part make a very short campaign up Red River, and then also go to Memphis. I think our brigade will be among the troops that go up the Red River. . . .[12] *I have not received a scratch of a pen from you since I saw you last. What does that all mean?* I can not tell, I am sure. Something must be the matter.
    Your affectionate husband,
    Henry.

March 8, 1864

On the bank of the Mississippi River, Vicksburg, Mississippi

Dear Cimbaline,
    The city of Vicksburg is not a nice place by a great deal. Of all the rough, hilly country, this place exceeds all,—it is indescribable,—and must be seen to be realized by any one. You can actually get lost among the hills and hollows. The health of our boys is *very* good, considering the circumstances. They have marched about three hundred and fifty

---

12. One Louisiana newspaper reported that five federal gunboats moved up the Red River as early as March 1. Within the 16th Army Corps, the 117th Illinois was part of the 3rd Brigade, which the regiment's original commander, Risdon Moore, now led. Joiner, *Little to Eat*, 273.

miles, and our regiment has lost only two men by death—one shot and one died from sickness.

Since I have been detailed from the regiment as Brigade Quarter Master, I have secured, as my servant, a real *white* nigger,—he is as white as I am—and I am not very white now, by a good deal.[13] I obtained him one day, when we went out foraging for corn and mean, about nine miles from camp. His name is *Jerry Davis'*,—he is a good and faithful fellow. He is about thirty years old.

I did not go to bed last night till a few minutes before midnight, and was up this morning at four, so you must excuse me, if I stop, and 'tumble in' for a good snooze to-night.

Your affectionate husband,
Henry.

March 9, 1864

Memphis, Tennessee

Dear Henry
To day I received tow letters from you I was much pleased to heare from you, and to heare you were well. Those tow letters is the first I have received from you, sence the one that were writen neare Jackson Miss. I thought it a long time to be without hearing from you. Some times I git so anixous to heare from you, that I cannot eat nor sleep We are all well at presant, and have been sence you left, except myself. I have been very unwell tow or three times. During the last week I have been truble with a boil oer my left eye. Wich cased me much pain. It is much better now.

We have mooved from Mr Smiths to a hous on Shelbay street, where the ordance office were last summer. The lower part is used now for a poss office. It is a yallow tow story fraim hous, north west of that pretty yard you shoed me last winter We mooved heare the 4. day of March. I am much pleased with our mooveed. We are more in the city. Can see more and enjoy our selveles better. I donot know how long we will remain heare. The Capt thinkes of returning to the Reg as soon as he heares it

---

13. This detail as quartermaster for the brigade, which consisted of several regiments, entailed greater responsibilities for Henry. Boatner, *Civil War Dictionary*, 610–613; National Park Service, "From Regiment to President," https://www.nps.gov/articles/from-regiment-to-president-the-structure-and-command-of-civil-war-armies.htm, accessed December 9, 2023.

has returned to Vicksburg. When he goes I supose Mrs Land and myself will go home. If he does not go in this month my set time to go home, is the first of April. If I find they is not any hopes of the Reg returning to this plase, I have heard tow a three time, that they were some hopes of the Reg returning to Memphis. If this be true I would like to remain heare untell it comes I feare they is not much prospects of it coming to pass....
Yesterday I went to a grand revew of all the negro Reg round Memphis. I never saw so many negres to gether before in my life. They were about six thousand It was a pretty black seen. It all went of well

Write often to me——Cimbaline

March 11, 1864

On board *Thos. E. Tutt*, Near Mouth of Red River

Dear Cimbaline,
We left the city of Vicksburg, last evening just at dusk.... Just a little while before sunset, a cannon sent forth one of its booming reports, which was a signal for us to leave in an hour. Steam was immediately raised on all the boats, prepatory to leaving, and at the appointed time, they dropped out into the stream in the proper order.

The boats generally were from three to four hundred yards apart, and as we passed around a long regular curve in the river, every boat could be seen at once, which presented a very beautiful sight. It is not necessary for me to undertake to further describe the appearance of the fleet, since you have seen similar sights at Memphis.... I have not yet learned the full strength of our army that is expected to work up the Red River.[14] We brought with us, from Vicksburg about ten thousand. To-night, all the boats are tied up to the western shore, just above the mouth of Red River. I have not yet learned when we will start up that stream—perhaps to-morrow morning. I have heard that probably the first place we shall find any rebels, will be at Alexandria on Red River, where they have some fortifications.[15] If this expedition is successful, I think we will about wind up the rebel cause in this part of the Confederacy. We understand the

---

14. The Red River generally runs eastward from its origins in the southern Great Plains, flowing from the panhandle of Texas toward Arkansas, where it then veers southward into Louisiana and finally empties into the Mississippi River.
15. The seat of Rapides Parish, Alexandria, was the largest town on the Red River between its mouth and Shreveport, the wartime capital in the northwestern part of Louisiana.

rebels have one or two gunboats and some transports up this river, which will undoubtedly fall into our hands, if the rebs do not destroy them too soon. The only thing we have to fear, in my opinion, will be the low water in Red River, but I heard this afternoon, that the stream was rising.
Your affectionate husband,
Henry.

March 13, 1864
Memphis, Tennessee

Dear Henry
We had to moove again yesterday. The hous we occoped were signed to some of Gen Shurmen staff, so we had to give persesion in one day. I am very tired, and unwell to day. I received a letter from you friday, and one this morning. I wos glad to hear you were well—and enjoyed your trip. No doubt but you did I am sorry to hear of Don being taken a prisnor It will be sad nuse to his parents I expected you would have been heare by this time, from the rumers I have heard, untell I saw one of Gern Shurmen staff. He informed me that Smiths Div had gon up Red river. He thought it would bee heare in 15 or 20 days. I shall remain heare untell you come. If you do not stay tow long, just a few minuts ago Mr Whitesides came heare to see if I could give him any information about his son. He heard throu Mother that he wos wounded. His wife is with him. Thay hae gon downd to the boat to have her com up. Thay are on there way to Vicksburg I shall hury and send this letter that for by tham. . . . No doubt but I will bee very proud of thouse wise presants you have got for me Pick up all you can git. Hury up and let me see tham. I am becoming very anixous to git a peep at tham. . . . I must stopt writing, for I donot feel like writing to day. I hope you will git this letter This is the third one I hae writing. I would have writing oftener, If I thought you would git tham
No more at presant time Cimbaline

March 18, 1864
Steamer *Thos. E. Tutt*, Alexandria, Louisiana

Dear Cimbaline,
At noon on Saturday, our fleet moved up Red River, and we proceeded up to the Atchafalaya River, and turned down it to the left, a few miles,

and tied up for the night. Next day, in the afternoon, most of our troops disembarked on the north side of the Atchafalaya River, and west side of Red River. Late in the evening they started on the march northwest to attack a fort on the west side of Red River, called Fort DeRussy. By four o'clock in the afternoon, on Monday the 14", they reached the place and engaged the rebels in the fortifications and 'flaxed them out' The fighting last a little over two hours, and was very vigorously prosecuted on both sides. We captured two forts, ten cannons, 300 small arms and about 300 prisoners. The boats arrived in a few hours after the fight, all safe. Our brigade was not immediately engaged, (being held as a reserve) but, was under the fire from the first to the last. There was not a man in our regiment hurt. We had but a few men killed in the fight.—three or four on each side. We remained at the fort until the next day, when the troops, on the boats again, proceeded further up the river, about seventy-five miles, to Alexandria, on Red River, where we are now lying. We reached here, day before yesterday. This is a very nice place of about two thousand inhabitants. I think it is about the prettiest town I have ever seen since I left Memphis. The rebels left the town the evening before we arrived. We have captured here several thousands of bushels of corn, and one or two hundred hogsheads of splendid sugar, and molasses. The sugar is very nice. The soldiers just 'went in on their muscle' on the sugar. You could see them carrying it away, in buckets, cups, pans, sacks, on boards, and every other way. Such sugar as you can get six pounds for a dollar at home, you can get here, for carrying away by the load.[16] I believe the secesh here, are about the bitterest I have anywhere met with; still there are some here who profess loyalty to the old flag, a few of the people are desirous of leaving here when we move.[17]

We have been lying here, now, two days, doing nothing. I understand the Gen. Banks is expected here, with his army, across the country from New Orleans. Rumor says he will be here to-morrow, when we will, (if he arrives) no doubt, move still further up the river, towards Shrevesport. This is a delightful country, and I think you would be much pleased with it.

Your affectionate husband,
Henry.

---

16. Rapides Parish, where Alexandria sits, produced more than twelve million pounds of cane sugar in 1860, which ranked ninth among Louisiana's forty-eight parishes. Joseph C. G. Kennedy, *Agriculture of the United States*, 69.

17. For the complexities of civilian loyalties in the Red River valley, see Ballantyne, "'Whenever the Yankees Were Gone.'"

March 20, 1864
On Steamer *Thos. E. Tutt*, Red River Expedition, Alexandria, Louisiana

Dear Cimbaline,
Yesterday morning a foraging party of our brigade with eight wagons went out into the country on a foraging excursion. They went to the plantation of Governor Moore of this state. He is the secesh governor, and is very wealthy, and has a very nice plantation. The party obtained at his place, about eight thousand pounds of sides, shoulders, and hams; four large hogsheads of splendid sugar, making about five thousand pounds of sugar; and seven barrels of very fine syrup molasses. At another place they got two large loads of sweet potatoes—the largest I ever saw in my life.[18] Besides these articles, they brought in some krout, and about four hundred chickens, ducks and geese. The boys now say, that while they are stationed in a country like this, they are willing to work for Uncle Sam, at 13 dollars per month, and board themselves, in the bargain. The foraging train did not get in until dark last night; and this morning I superintended the dividing of it to the different regiments of our brigade. That kept me busy all the forenoon.
Your affectionate husband,
Henry.

March 23, 1864
Steamer *Thos. E. Tutt*, Alexandria, Louisiana

Dear Cimbaline,
Everything down here in the line of vegetation is quite green;—the trees are covered with leaves and the gardens and dooryards are full of flowers;—and the weather is exactly like real May weather at home. This is one of the finest parts of the country I have yet seen in my wandering down here. There are many large plantations, containing several hundred acres, of nice land. Upon these are frequently some twenty negro

---

18. Thomas O. Moore, governor of Louisiana from 1860 to 1864, lamented to a friend that Union troops singled out his Rapides Parish plantation for despoliation, burning its sugar mills, corn mills, and engines and stripping it of all livestock and blankets. Sacher, "'Our Interest and Destiny,'" 285. See also Cowan and McGuire, *Louisiana Governors*, 84–87.

houses, all nicely whitewashed and, arranged in such order as to resemble a neat little village. These old rich planters, from all appearances, had every comfort at their hand, and lived in almost unbounded ease and luxury. But this war has brought many of these old rebellious 'chaps' to grief, and reduced their splendid plantations to a waste. I think, by this time, many of them have repented, the steps they have taken in this war.

To-day the prisoners, horses and guns, captured a day or two ago, some twenty miles south of here, were brought in,-and the men were confined in the court house. There are about 300 men, 300 horses and four cannons. Late this evening some one hundred refugees came in, from the interior, a good distance; and brought with them about a dozen prisoners, which they had captured themselves. These hundred men, are union men, who raised up, armed themselves, kept hid in the swamps, and when they heard of us, fought their way out to us. They, of course, deserve great credit for this.[19] I am getting very anxious to move away from here. I want to move up the river, and accomplish that which we came to do, and then return up the Mississippi river. From the size of the army we now have, we have no doubts of being able to march any where we want to.

Your affectionate husband,
Henry.

March 31, 1864
Steamer *Thos. E. Tutt*, Cotile Landing, Louisiana, on Red River

Dear Cimbaline,
It has been one week to-night since I wrote to you; and I expect you will begin to think from this, that I am forgetting you. But you know better than to entertain any such ideas as that. The fact is, I receive such poor encouragement in the way of letters that I have no very great desire to write many. . . . I expect, some of these days, that I will receive a bucket full of letters.

On Friday, 25th, we all remained still at the town of Alexandria. During

---

19. Ballantyne, "'Whenever the Yankees Were Gone,'" 36–67. For Unionism in the Deep South, see also Mathisen, *Loyal Republic*; Ruminski, *Limits of Loyalty*, and Bynum, *Free State of Jones*.

the day, all the boats went down the river a few miles and procured wood. That same day, the Infantry of Maj. Gen. Banks' army arrived at Alexandria, which is reported some twenty thousand strong—All this, with his cavalry, and our entire army makes a force that the rebels are not pleased to see in their territory.

On Saturday, 26th Our army, and Bank's cavalry took up the march on land, towards the place we are now occupying. We marched that day 18 miles, and passed through some very delightful country, abounding in large plantations, already plowed and planted in corn; the corn up and growing. But the 'white folks' had all run off towards Texas, with all their able bodied negroes, horses and mules.[20] Sunday 27th. marched on some 8 miles and came to the Red River where we are now stopping. Our trip was somewhat in the shape of a half circle. We left the river and came to it again, some 20 miles above.

March 28th. This day our boats came up—I forgot to mention that the reason why we marched around, by land, from Alexandria to this place, was to lighten up the boats so they could pass safely over a shallow, rapid place in the river called the 'rapids.'[21] But they did not get over without a serious accident. A large hospital boat, the *Woodford*, in crossing the rapids, struck some part of an old sunken boat, and also sunk, but not so deep as to drown any one on board. There were some 200 or 300 sick on board. The boat can be raised, and will not be lost.[22]

Thursday 31. That is to-day. I have been working some on my Monthly Reports for March. Still no news of our leaving. We are all getting *very* tired of remaining so long idle. Some now begin to think that we will not go any further up the river; but will proceed down, when we move, and

---

20. In early 1864 Major-General Richard Taylor, anticipating Federal advances westward from the Mississippi River, redoubled his efforts to impress enslaved laborers and draft animals into the service of the Confederate army. By the time that Henry reached Cotile Landing, slavers and rebel agents had moved much of this property deeper into Louisiana and Texas. Winters, *Civil War in Louisiana*, 325.

21. Rapides Parish drew its name from these rapids in the Red River. Near Alexandria, Banks reported, "There was but 6 feet of water in the channel, while 7½ was necessary for the second-class and 10 feet for the first-class gun-boats. The river is narrow, the channel tortuous, changing with every rise, making its navigation more difficult and dangerous probably than any of the Western rivers." Banks to Stanton, April 6, 1864, OR, ser. 1, vol. 34, pt. 1, 197.

22. Despite such confidence, Union troops could not raise the *Woodford*. After the failure of efforts to move the ship with force-pumps and a diving apparatus sent up from New Orleans, Banks ordered that the boat and its remaining contents be destroyed, lest they fall into the hands of nearby rebels. OR, ser. 1, vol. 34, pt. 1, 240.

go up the Mississippi. But, of course, we do not know anything ahead for certain. The weather, here, is very warm and nice, and the woods are all green, and sweat peas are 'stuck' as we say, and nearly ready to bloom. I shall be glad when we have finished what we came to do, and turn our faces northward. And, also, will I rejoice, when this 'cruel war is over' and we are all home again.

Your affectionate husband,
Henry.

April 5, 1864

Grand Ecore, Louisiana

Dear Cimbaline,
I believe I wrote to you last from Cotile (not Cottie) Landing. That was on the last day of March. The next day, April the 1st, we continued to stay at the same place, and I can assure you, that we all became heartily tired of such a long 'stand still.' 'April fooling' was about the only amusement we had on that day, and many a fellow was 'sold' on the occasion.

On Saturday, the 2nd, the troops all went on board the transports again, and, in the afternoon, we all turned our prows up stream again.[23] The country, for some distance, was very beautiful, and many large plantations lined the river banks. It was Saturday afternoon, and all the niggers seemed to be idle. I suppose they had the afternoon 'to themselves,'—and they flocked to the river banks in hundreds, to see the boats and troops pass; and they greeted us with many cheers and songs. In one crowd, three little nigger boys rode up on a jackass, and one of them cried out, at the top of his voice, 'Hurrah, for Lincoln's side.' As we passed close to the shore, the soldiers would throw 'hard tack' into the crowd, which would cause a mighty scrabbling among the colored population for the morsel. At one plantation, belonging to a Mr. Calhoun, some two hundred niggers flocked to the shore, to witness our passage. On Sunday, the 3d inst, we continued our course up the river, which is the most crooked stream I ever saw, and, at night, arrived at this place. Here, our troops, yesterday morning, went on shore. We will probably remain here all of to-day. The reason we move so slowly up stream, is to

---

23. It took nearly five days for the Union army to move the thirty transports and twelve light-draft tinclads that would accompany its advance on Shreveport past the falls where the *Woodford* ran aground. Winters, *Civil War in Louisiana*, 333–334.

enable Gen. Banks' Army, which is going by land, to keep up with us. I understand they were passing this place all day yesterday. This town contains only some dozen houses.

The rumors here are that the rebels are going to show us fight in the upper country. If they do, we are prepared for them.[24]

Your affectionate husband,
Henry.

April 12, 1864

Grand Ecore, Louisiana

Dear Cimbaline,
No doubt you will hear, before you receive this letter, that our army has had a hard fight with the enemy, and you will, also, no doubt hear all kinds of stories concerning the results of the same. I will now endeavor to give you a brief account of our five days' campaign from this place and back again.

On the morning of the 7th. inst we left here, taking a westward direction into the country, no doubt, intending to come up to Shreveport in the rear. All our sick and those unable for duty were left with all our extra baggage on board the boats. And these boats properly guarded were to proceed up the river, and join us above. During the first day of our march, during which we went about sixteen miles, nothing very strange occurred, more than a very heavy rain;—but that did not hinder our movements to any very great extent. I suppose our column, while marching upon the road, occupied some twenty miles. The 13th and 19th Army Corps were in the advance, and the 16th (ours) was in the rear, with some eight or ten miles between us. The 13th Corps, which was in the extreme front, skirmished with the enemy all day, until in the afternoon, when a general engagement was brought on, which was very severe indeed. The

---

24. Banks, confident that Taylor's rebels would not seriously menace his army until it reached Shreveport, undertook few precautions as his outfit moved northwest from Alexandria. Now separated from the gunboats sailing upriver, the Federal column stretched out for some twenty miles and moved slowly along a narrow inland road, its advance impeded by intermittent rains that reduced much of the sunken road to mud. Taylor, however, worried about the arrival of Steele's Union forces from Arkansas and the difficulty of overcoming this combined Federal force; he therefore decided to attack Banks just south of Mansfield, near the Sabine Cross Roads. Johnson, *Red River Campaign*, 101–145; Meiners, "Hamilton P. Bee," 24.

conflict was exceedingly bloody, and we lost severely. During that fight it is supposed that our loss, in killed, wounded and missing will foot up two thousand men. The 130th. Ills. (Col. Miles' old regiment) lost very severely, going into the fight with nearly four hundred men and came out with only sixty men.[25] Our army that night fell back to within a few miles of a small town in Desoto County, called Pleasant Hill.[26] Our corps came up that night and camped within a half mile of the same town. Next morning we were up at 2 o'clock, and ready for the fight. A part of our division was sent forward early, as skirmishers, and engaged the enemy, in conjunction with 19th. Corps, all day. Our brigade went forward at nine o'clock in the forenoon, and took position in an open field just on the west side of town, among other brigades. Our batteries were stationed around in proper order. The 117th. Reg. Ills. was stationed on the extreme left of the line, to prevent the rebels from flanking us on that side, and were not brought into the action at all. At a quarter before five o'clock in the afternoon the regular hard fighting commenced, and for the first time in my life, I witnessed a hard open field battle. It is entirely useless for me to undertake to give you a description of it. I had read, and read and heard descriptions of battles, but I confess I had never formed any thing like a correct idea of it. For two hours (until dark) the incessant roars of artillery and musketry deafened our ears. During most of the engagement I was in the rear, with our train, but went up once or twice to the open field. One time I took up two loads of ammunition to our men. Our men acted with the greatest of bravery and coolness. The rebels charged across the open field, on to our men, about ten thousand strong. Our men rallied and met their onset, checked them, and finally turned them back, and chased them into the woods some two miles, killing hundreds of them. The firing ceased at dark, and our men returned to the open field, and collected together in their respective regiments, for a good many of them had become scattered during the pursuit we made after the rebels. After the men had assembled, such shouting and cheering I never heard.[27] The hum and buzz of twenty thousand voices

---

25. Most of the 130th Illinois was captured at Sabine Cross Roads and imprisoned at Tyler, Texas, for the next thirteen months. Civil War Soldiers and Sailors System database, National Park Service, https://www.nps.gov/civilwar/soldiers-and-sailors-database.htm, accessed December 9, 2023 (hereafter CWSS).

26. DeSoto Parish sits just south of Shreveport, tucked between the Red River on the east and the Texas border, including the Sabine River, on the west.

27. Only hours after defeat at Sabine Crossroads, the retreating Federals won a tactical victory at Pleasant Hill, where they suffered 1,369 casualties compared to the rebels' 1,626.

is indescribable. After the fight, I rode over the field, and got down and talked with and assisted many of the wounded that lay scattered over the field. Our troops all lay during the night upon the battle field.

Next morning at two o'clock we commenced our retreat back to this place. And here is the part of the whole thing that we do not fully understand—why we should retreat, after we had whipped our foe. We, as I presume you know, are now temporarily under command of Maj. Gen. Banks, who commands this department. Our army is not at all satisfied with the management of the whole affair. As for the various particulars concerning the dissatisfaction of our Army Corps. I will here, refrain from mentioning any. We are now here again at the same place on Red River we left six days ago, and all our boats are up the river above us, perhaps fifty miles. We have heard heavy cannonading up in that direction all morning. We are somewhat fearful that the enemy will plant batteries on the river bank, and possibly destroy our transports. Our only hopes rest in the few gunboats that went up with them—for there were only some twenty-five hundred men with the boats as guards to the same. Still we are constantly looking for our boats every hour, and they may come at any time. If they do get down, you may rest assured that we will be exceedingly rejoiced;—for all our extra baggage and such like are on them. We are here lying on the bank of the river, awaiting the issue of affairs. There is some talk that our forces here will intrench themselves. But it is hard for any one, in my position, to tell what will be done.

You can inform all our Mascoutah friends that Co. 'K' is all right and no one hurt or scared.

Tell all the folks that we are now soldiering it in earnest, and that we shall long remember the battle of Pleasant Hill, on the 9th day of April 1864.

Your affectionate husband,
Henry.

April 16, 1864
Grand Ecore, Louisiana

Dear Cimbaline,
The rebels tried very hard to capture our fleet which was above here, when we returned from Pleasant Hill. They planted a battery on the bank

---

Despite this success, Banks's subsequent decision to withdraw to Grand Ecore rendered the drive to capture Shreveport a strategic failure. Johnson, *Red River Campaign*, 146–169.

of the river below the boats, and thus tried to prevent their return, and capture them. The river is very crooked and narrow, and the banks so high, that the rebels seemed to have every possible advantage on their side. They would hide behind trees and hills and pour into the boats volleys of musketry; still they did not kill but very few.[28] Our gunboats were of vast service to the fleet, where the river was straight enough to give them a chance to see ahead. One of the transports ran aground close to the bank one place, and several hundred of the rebels ran down to the water's edge with the evident intention of boarding and capturing her. But a gun boat near at hand, poured into the crowd, *two* shots of cannister, and left about *one hundred and fifty* dead on the spot. This with some musketry from our boys on the boats, caused them to scamper off on the double-quick. We did not lose a boat; and they all arrived here, yesterday and day-before, though some of them are pretty badly marked.

To-day we received orders to put our surplus baggage on board our boats, which we did; but we have not yet learned what this is for. I take it to mean that we are to march somewhere. And I can assure you that our boys want to turn their faces down Red River, and then up the Mississippi river;—not that they are afraid of the rebels, by any means, but because they are not satisfied with the Department and the way affairs are managed in it. I have not the room, in this letter, to give you the causes, that brought about this dissatisfaction among our men of the 16th and 17th Corps. who came from Vicksburg. They are exceedingly well pleased with our own gallant, brave, and venerable leader, Brig. Gen. A. J. Smith. All the Army here likes him. He will do to 'tie to.'

I have your little pony yet. She is the admiration of every one. Her name is 'Dolly.' Tell Ellie I will bring her a little pony mare.

Your affectionate husband,
Henry.

April 28, 1864

Alexandria, Louisiana

Dear Cimbaline,
We arrived here safely on the afternoon of the 26th inst., after some very warm and dusty marching. A rebel force followed us all the way, and every

---

28. One Union soldier described the rough condition of the ships that eventually reached Grand Ecore: "The sides of some of the transports are half shot away, and their smokestacks look like huge pepper boxes." Quote from Pellet, *History of the 114th Regiment,* 222, in Johnson, *Red River Campaign,* 224.

morning, about the time we would start, they would fire into our rear. But we were always prepared for them, and so 'peppered' the chaps, that they were glad to fall back. The rebels thus followed us up, from day to day, merely to say that they *drove* us from their country.[29] It was a sorry drive to many a poor fellow of their number whom our boys caused to 'bite the dust.' These engagements we had with the rebels, on our retreat, once or twice, assumed the size of a small battle. In one of these the 13th Corps lost some 200 men in killed, wounded and missing; but the rebel loss was still greater, and we took some 50 prisoners in the fight. Our march from Grand Ecore, where I last wrote to you, to this place, is called 85 miles by land. The first afternoon we marched only some four miles, to a town called Natchitoches (*pronounced* Nack-i-tosh) This was on the 20th. inst. We lay there that night and all next day and marched again that night some few miles.

Your affectionate husband,
Henry.

May 1, 1864
Alexandria, Louisiana

Dear Cimbaline,
O, how tired we are all getting of this place and country. The country is nice and pleasant, and the town is quite passable, but then, our time down here is out, and we feel that we should be 'out of here.' A mile or two above town there is a shallow place in the river, called 'the Falls,' where the water is so shallow, that several of our gunboats which went up with us a few weeks ago, can not get down. And the word is now that, that is all that is detaining us here, and we will go as soon as these gunboats can be got down over the Falls. I understood to-day, that our authorities are building a kind of dam for the purpose of throwing the water on one side, and thus raising it so the boats can pass. I think we have enough

---

29. Taylor's rebel force of six thousand men harried the Union army, more than thirty thousand strong, back to Alexandria, which the Federals then set to fortifying with two lines of breastworks, redoubts, gun emplacements, and abatis. As Union ships then began to sail downstream toward the Mississippi, Confederates lined the banks of the Red River beneath Alexandria and inflicted even more losses on the Federals, whose casualties in the first week of May alone included three transports, two gunboats, and nearly six hundred sailors and soldiers. Bergeron, "General Richard Taylor," 45–46; Johnson, *Red River Campaign*, 256–257.

'Yankee' ingenuity in our army to carry any such project through. Red River is quite a small stream, and easy enough to manage, in a matter like this.[30]

We have no special 'war news' in this locality worth mentioning. Several boats which lately have come up here, from New Orleans, started down stream this afternoon, bound for the same place. They met a gunboat of ours a few miles below here, which informed them that the rebels had a battery planted on the bank of the river some eighteen miles below the town; so just a few minutes ago, since I commenced this letter, they all came back. This announcement may give the boys something to do. I can assure you the battery will not remain there many days;—for if it attempts to do so, some morning it will wake up and find itself 'taken out of the wet.'

This morning the church-bells rang in town, calling the people to the house of God. The sound of these bells reminded me more of home, than anything I have seen or heard in this region. O, how I longed to be at home, with my dear family and friends, and with them have the privilege of attending the Sabbath School and Church. I hope to have the opportunity of enjoying this blessing again with you. Although the surroundings and fortunes of war prevent me from having the opportunity of enjoying many Christian privileges, still I thank my heavenly Father, I still have a desire to be found in his service. I can say, with a truly clear conscience, that *none of the public vices and immoralities have ever yet touched me*, and *shall not* while I remain in the army. I hope you are still endeavoring to put your trust in One who never fails in his promises to the faithful. My daily prayer ascends to the throne of our God, that you, Ellie and myself may be preserved, kept and spared to meet again on earth,—and finally all be housed in heaven, where no wars shall cause loving hearts to be separated.

Your affectionate husband,
Henry.

---

30. Banks later credited the ingenuity of Lieutenant Colonel Joseph Bailey, an officer of the 4th Wisconsin Volunteers who served on the staff of General John Franklin. A former lumberman with experience running logs to downstream mills, Bailey suggested the creation of a wing dam along the banks of the Red River, which would force its waters into a narrow stream, allowing heavy ships to float along the rising channel and to sail past the rapids. Banks to Stanton, April 6, 1864, OR, 209; Johnson, *Red River Campaign*, 249–250.

May 3, 1864
Alexandria, Louisiana

Dear Cimbaline,
Yesterday our Division was ordered out a few miles to the front,—the command taking one day's rations along. At night the Col. sent me an order, and I sent him out sixty boxes of ammunition. They were encamped four miles from town, and had been skirmishing pretty heavily with the enemy. I might say that all of our headquarter mess was gone, but myself, and a few of the boys.... This afternoon an order came in, and I had two days' additional rations sent out to our men. Our troops have moved out some nine or ten miles from town. I do not know how strong the rebel force is, in that region, nor do I know exactly what is the object of the expedition out in that direction. Our army is hard at work, building a dam across the river above town a piece, to raise the water, so as to enable the gunboats to get over the 'falls'—I think they will succeed, and have the thing completed in a very few days.[31]
Your affectionate husband,
Henry.

May 10, 1864
Memphis, Tennessee

Dear Henry
To day too weekes a go, I received a letter from you. That one is the last I have had untell to day. I received too to day I was glad to heare from you. I have been looking for you for the last month, But I have not see you yet, only in my dreames. I often dream of seeing you and passing plasant hours of confersation with you I all ways find it out to be a dream. I am bording, at the same plase we have had roomes for the last too months on

---

31. African American troops, said one Louisiana historian, "did the greater part of the rough work" needed to build the wing dam. Banks noted, "The construction of the dam was exclusively the work of the army," which "labored sedulously and zealously night and day, in and out of the water." He added, "But little aid or encouragement was rendered by officers of the navy." Soldiers gathered materials for the dam from the Alexandria buildings they demolished, including the military academy that William T. Sherman once led, and the nearby pine forests and the stone hauled from local quarries. Bailey's ambitious effort ultimately spanned a river that was 758 feet wide. Quotes from Whittington, "Rapides Parish," 16, and Banks to Stanton, April 6, 1864, OR, 210; Johnson, *Red River Campaign*, 260–261.

Union street, at Mr Densons. I like the famly very much. They are poor pepole, but good union folkes. Mrs Denson is a no one woman, next to Mother. Ellie calls her, gran ma, all the time. I thought I would borde with tham a week or too, and wait and see if you did come or I could git a letter stating whot you entended to do, as soon as I know that you do not expect to returne to the plase, I intend to go home The wether is giting very worm heare, and I have not been well for the last tow weeks. I am very fearful that I will have poor health when hot wether comes. I am using meddison now, that Mrs Denson has recomended, for my diseasus. I hope it will have the affect she ses it will I would give all I am worth, if I could enjoy good health. i would have writing oftener latly if I had not been looking for you heare I hope you will come. I want to see you, before I go home. If you donot come before I leave I do not expect to see you soon. (*Mabe.* never.) This wore is a very croul and weaked one. Making some very unhappy famlys. For my parte I am very tired of it, and wish it wos over with. . . . Ellie has not been very well She is as bad a girl as you ever saw She tockes of her pa so much. Tell me whot her pa will by her when he comes she thinkes her pa is the greatest man that ever lived.

From Cimbaline

May 23, 1864
On board Steamer *Hannibal*

Dear Cimbaline,
We all reached the mouth of Red River, by land, day before yesterday. In our march from Alexandria down, we had to fight the rebels every day. Our boats kept along the river, opposite our train, and thus they were protected from the rebels. We did not lose any boats in coming down from Alexandria. As soon as we reached the mouth of Red River, all the troops got upon their respective boats. . . . The boat I am on, came up from Red River ahead of the balance of the fleet. We arrived here last night, and the others will come to-day, I think. We came ahead to procure clothing for the troops. I guess we will remain here a few days—I hear some little talk that we will be sent up into Arkansas to assist Gen. Steele who is reported to be in a tight place.[32] A great many think we will not go

---

32. Major-General Frederick Steele ultimately abandoned his plan to invade northwest Louisiana from Arkansas. Bedeviled by rebel guerrillas, his Union forces suffered bitter

on that expedition, but will proceed further up the river. I suppose we will know in a few days. If we do go on that trip we will be nearer Memphis than this place is. If we go up there I shall try to come to Memphis a few days anyhow and see you.
Your affectionate husband,
Henry.

May 23, 1864
On board Steamer *Hannibal*

Dear Cimbaline,
The Red River Expedition has been a hard trip indeed, and one that tried the pluck and endurance of our boys. The troops are real bad off for clothing. When we left here on the 10th of March last they did not have what they wanted, and now, you may rest assured they present a *ragged* appearance. A great many of them, from necessity, have procured citizens clothing, and straw hats, and such like articles as they could 'press into' the service.'

I have enjoyed the trip well,—and saw many things entirely new to me. We passed through some of the nicest of country, and I saw some dooryards and flower gardens, that exceeded anything of the kind I ever saw before. As for evergreens and flowers, there is no end to them. About all the growing crops I saw, were plenty of corn, some little cotton and sugar cane. On our last day's march, I saw corn about as high as my shoulders. Corn grows well in the state of Louisiana, and they raise a great deal of it.
Your affectionate husband,
Henry.

May 25, 1864
On board Steamer *Hannibal*, Vicksburg, Mississippi

Dear Cimbaline,
We are still lying here at Vicksburg, not knowing exactly what we will do. The boats have been taking on coal last night and to-day, and appearances indicate that we will move somewhere before many days. A boat

---

losses to Confederate regulars at Poison Spring, Marks' Mill, and finally Jenkins' Ferry, after which the Federals retreated back to Little Rock. Johnson, *Red River Campaign*, 170–205.

arrived here to-day, from above, which was fired into by a rebel battery between here and Helena, at a place called Columbia. She was struck several times. I should not be surprised if the rebels, would take courage of their recent success in Louisiana and Arkansas, and give us some trouble, by harassing our boats on the river, for a while. But I think the gun-boats will be able to attend to them.

Brig. Gen. A. J. Smith, who commanded our troops on the Red River Expedition, has received his commission as Major General, since our return. We all think he well deserves the promotion.

Your affectionate husband,
Henry.

May 27, 1864

On board Steamer *Hannibal*

Dear Cimbaline,
I hardly know what to say; for I have the same old story to repeat, about our being here, and when we will move, and where we probably will go, when we do move. . . . We can hear all kinds of rumors here in camp. It would almost run any one crazy, that was not used to these camp stories. I guess you have been 'soldiering' long enough to know something of these things, and to know that we fellows never know what we are *going to do*, till we are ordered to do it. The soldiers' life is one of *waiting, waiting, expecting, expecting, hoping and hoping*. Sometimes when *I wait*, and *expect* and *hope* so long without realizing anything, I almost become discouraged. But, experience has taught me, to exercise patience, do my duty, and always hope for the better. This course I have always found to be the best.

Your affectionate husband,
Henry.

May 31, 1864

Memphis, Tennessee

Dear Henry
I am glad to say to day, we are all well as usul. Ellie and I have not been very well untell the wether become cooler. We have emproved ery much in the too last weeks. I receied 9 letters with in the last three days from

you. It has been three weekes sence I have heard from you befor I had given up all hopes of hearing from you again soon. I had made up my mind to go home. I had sold every thing, and packed my box, and set the time to start home. The time I set to go was yesterday May the 30. Sunday I received too letters from you staiting you wos at Vicksburg. I just received tham in time, not to go. I entend to stop a while longer hear and see if you are coming. . . . Ellie received her mony long ago and has spent it. She has plenty all the time. She meets with great many firends, and thay ceep her in plenty of mony. She wos delited with her little letter. She lafght all the time I wos reading it. When I got through, she said my papa is a good man, he send me mony, and a little letter, and he is going to bring me a little pony horse I want my pa pa to come and see me and ma She cries so much to see you, she makes me feel worse than I would, for I feel it is heard enuf for us to bee seperated at the very best. I have enjoyed myself very much, sence you left, much better than I thought I would. But still I often think how much happyer I would bee if I could enjoy the company of one who I love better than all the company I ever meet with. When we are at home your company is all I cear to enjoy. I know you have thought me selfash for it, But I never could help it. You never appresiated my love for you, as I thought you out to I feel very thankful to hear you say, that you are still praying and endevering to live a riglious life, and you have not taken up with any weaked habits. I know thare is many ways to lead any one from the right way in the armey. I know if they ever wos a wife that ever offerd up sincear prayers in behalf of her husban. It has been me. They is never a day passes, but I ask gods blesings and protection to rest up on you, that he may deliver you frome all temtions that is roung We at home often hear of good morel men in the armey pertaken of weaked habits. My prayer is god for bid that you should ever rebell a gainst his holey law. Nothing neve would greave me more then to heare of you action so

Yours in love, Cimbaline

CHAPTER 5

"The Terrors and Trials of War"

St. Louis, Missouri, to Harrisonville, Missouri
and
Mascoutah, Illinois
September 1864 to November 1864

Henry was justifiably relieved when the 117th Illinois docked at St. Louis on September 18, 1864. Three days earlier the *Stephen Decatur,* the steamboat that carried him and hundreds of comrades north from Memphis, became snagged in the shallows of the Mississippi River and almost sank. Quick work by the passengers and crew salvaged the ship and allowed them to complete the journey safely. To have both his life and good health after two years of military service was a blessing to be savored. What's more, the regiment's arrival at Jefferson Barracks meant that Lieutenant Colonel Fike and his neighbors-in-arms were now physically closer to family members on the east bank of the great river than at any point in their long deployment. They had endured hard marching and bitter disappointments during their first campaigns in the Deep South, but a trip to St. Louis brought them familiar sights and a welcome reprieve from the oppressive summer heat. After sultry months near Vicksburg, an "exceedingly cool" Sunday morning offered bracing comfort but also portended a hard fall to come. "It pinches us 'mightily," Henry noted in his diary, as he again set about procuring blankets for the men of his regiment.[1]

Confederate armies had not seriously menaced St. Louis since the Union victory at Pea Ridge, Arkansas, in March 1862 had effectively driven organized rebel forces from Missouri. Two summers later, Confederate General Edmund Kirby Smith, eager to divert Union troops from Atlanta and the eastern theater, authorized an expedition from Arkansas into the Missouri Ozarks under the command of General (and former

---

1. Henry C. Fike Diaries, September 18, 1864.

Missouri governor) Sterling Price. Like many secessionists, Price saw this campaign as an opportunity to liberate his state from the clutches of a hostile Federal occupation.[2] He was confident that Missourians would rally to his army of liberation and strengthen its ranks of twelve thousand men, many shoeless or lacking guns, with additional recruits and supplies. By September 20, when the three divisions of Price's army crossed into Missouri, some eighteen thousand Union troops were scattered across the state, many of them serving in the Missouri State Militia or the Enrolled Missouri Militia (EMM).[3] Thinly defended Ozarks garrisons were vulnerable to rebel capture, and even the fate of St. Louis, the largest city and most prized strategic point in the West, seemed in doubt.[4] Even after the timely arrival of Henry Fike and forty-five hundred additional Federal soldiers, General William Rosecrans, Union commander in Missouri, appealed to Illinois governor Richard Yates to provide any men that he could spare for the city's defense.[5]

Thirty miles to the east of St. Louis, Cimbaline shared her neighbors' fears that the Confederates might yet strike across the river. Aside from Robert E. Lee's failed Pennsylvania incursion that led to his defeat at Gettysburg, civilians in the North had largely been spared the threat or reality of invasion. Now, however, in the Civil War's fourth interminable year, even Mascoutah seemed vulnerable. The potential attack sharpened anxieties over the ongoing draft, but Cimbaline insisted that the local men who avoided or complained about military service were shirking their civic obligation. "It does my sould [soul] good to see some of tham feel so bad about it It will do me more good when they will half to do," she wrote. Of the men who were wealthy enough to hire substitutes to take their place, she added, "I think that dont show much love for there country."

By the first week of October, just as rumors of Price's invasion into

---

2. Mark E. Neely, *Civil War and the Limits*, 41–71.

3. The Unionist provisional government in Jefferson City established the loyal Missouri State Militia after much of the Missouri State Guard, the antebellum state militia, withdrew under the leadership of exiled secessionist governor Claiborne Fox Jackson. The EMM, created in the summer of 1862, was called out on September 24 to confront the Price invasion. Filled with the able-bodied men who had not already volunteered for or been exempted from military service, the EMM augmented the existing federal and state forces in Missouri but faced sharp criticism for the dubious loyalty of some members. See Lause, *Price's Lost Campaign*, 161, and Hamilton, "Enrolled Missouri Militia."

4. Blevins, *History of the Ozarks*, vol. 2, 114–122.

5. United States War Department, *War of the Rebellion* (hereafter OR), ser. 1, vol. 41, pt. 3, 532.

Illinois reached their fevered peak, it became clear that the rebels were not likely to strike St. Louis. The Confederates instead headed northwest toward the Missouri capital of Jefferson City, with the rear-guard actions of Joseph Shelby's cavalry holding at bay the Federal troops who now pursued them from the east. Among the Union soldiers who followed the rebels was Henry Fike, who after two uncertain weeks of waiting now marched west on the Manchester turnpike. Henry's once-daily letters home became less frequent as the Federal pursuit intensified, but the 117th Illinois, always a day or two late, never caught up with Price's rebels, nor did it participate in major battles that fall.

Henry's writings nonetheless captured the cheering reception of loyal Missourians as well as the destruction that the war, especially the recent Confederate invasion, wrought upon the countryside. He was smitten with the rolling prairies of western Missouri, even as that once-bucolic landscape bore the scars of a guerrilla war too brutal for outsiders to comprehend. His fall dispatches provided a rare glimpse into the desolation that followed the Union army's General Order Number 11, which had depopulated parts of four Missouri counties a year earlier.

Price's resounding defeat at the Battle of Westport spelled an end to Confederate hopes of retaking Missouri. Meanwhile, news of that fall's presidential campaign engrossed Henry and many of his comrades, particularly those eager to secure furloughs to return home and cast ballots. Many in the 117th Illinois failed to obtain such furloughs, but days later they took great satisfaction from the news that Abraham Lincoln had nonetheless won reelection, a triumph that meant that the United States would prosecute the war until the Confederacy finally surrendered. Cimbaline, too, celebrated Lincoln's victory as a signal moment for the Union cause and one that could soon bring her husband home.

Until then, chronic fears continued to haunt her. Troubled as ever about Henry's safety and the churning feuds in Mascoutah, Cimbaline also despaired about the family's financial situation. Assuming responsibility for the management of the family's farm and accounts had revealed outstanding debts that were far greater than what her husband had admitted. The family's vulnerability, she confided, "trubles me more then eny thing elce on earth." Letters thus became the medium through which she confronted their precarious finances and expressed her own sharp disappointment. Henry's response, likely hindered by the long, snowy trek back to St. Louis, remains a mystery. Holding onto hope that he might yet visit her by the coming holiday, Cimbaline took comfort in the company of nearby relatives and perhaps in her dawning sense, nurtured by an exodus of Mascoutah residents, that the couple might soon be able to relocate and start anew. Until then, however, they would still rely on the letters that kept them fastened to each other as they stepped uncertainly into a third autumn apart.

༄

September 18, 1864
Jefferson Barracks, Missouri

Dear Cimbaline and Ellie,
We don't exactly know what we are going to do up here. There are various opinions as to the object of our coming. The most prevalent one just now, seems to be, that we are here to attend to Gen Price, should he attempt to invade Missouri, as rumor says he intends doing. Others have the story that we are here, to be handy in case of any disturbance when the draft is being enforced. I expect if we remain here many days, that lots of the boys' friends and relatives will be flocking in to see them; and a good many of the boys, no doubt, who live near by, will get permission to go home for two or three days.

I expect to go up to St. Louis, in the morning with the Division Q.M. to see about getting supplies for our troops. I hope I shall get letters from you often, while we are so handy. I think a good many of the Mascoutah folks might come down and see us, while we are so near at hand. It would be nothing more than a pleasure trip. Come to St. Louis, take the Iron Mountain RailRoad, and go ten miles to Jefferson Barracks, and you are within a few hundred yards of my tent, where I am writing this letter.

Your affectionate husband and 'papa'
Henry.

September 18, 1864
Mascoutah, Illinois

Dear Henry
I am still at Mothers. So lonsom I do not know whot to do with myself. I do not think I can live heare any more contented. I do not know whot to do. You did not give me any advise whot I should do. I have not made any visits yet I have not felt well sence I came home Ellie is not well. She has taken a very seveare cool, and cauft very much I have not received

but tow letters from you sence you left. I suppose you have seen some of the Mascoutah folkes by this time. We heare all sorts of rumer heare we have heard that Smiths Division has been ordered to St Louis to do duty If that be so, you may look for me soon, and all Mascoutah, I think they is not any such good luck as that

from Cimbaline

September 22, 1864
Jefferson Barracks, Missouri

Dear Cimbaline and Ellie,
It is very windy to-day and the dust blows so, one can hardly breathe. It comes in my tent and settles upon everything. There are a great many citizens here on visits to see their friends in the army. Every train that arrives brings them by the dozens. They come, men, women, and children—fathers, mothers, sisters, brothers, wives and swarms of little ones, all anxious again to see their soldier friends, husbands, sons, and fathers in the army. You can see many officers and private soldiers going around and showing their wives the 'sights,' and carrying their babies upon their arms. Every train that arrives at the depot, finds a vast crowd there, most every one looking for *his* friends or relatives. And many are the happy greetings between those who have been so long absent from one another. The encampment, in consequence of the presence of so many females and children, has quite an appearance of a camp meeting or county fair. . . .

We have, as yet, received no orders in reference to moving from here. The papers state that Gen. Price is pretty active down in Arkansas; and it may be, that we will be called on, some of these days, to go out in that direction to attend to the 'old gentleman.'[6] The boys are beginning to manifest some considerable interest in political matters, and feel a little concerned in election affairs. We have no fears, as to the final result of

---

6. The rebel troops that a scouting party from the Missouri State Militia confronted at Doniphan on September 18 were the advance elements of the Confederate army that was still mostly in Arkansas. Known to many as "Old Pap," Sterling Price was a Mexican War veteran and commander of the pro-Confederate Missouri State Guard. He also served as Missouri governor from 1853 to 1857 and presided over the February 1861 convention where Missouri delegates voted overwhelmingly to remain within the Union. Castel, *General Sterling Price*, 3–24.

the whole matter. The glorious news of Gen. Sheridan's splendid victory, in the Shenandoah valley in Virginia, is quite encouraging.[7]

I will close. Tell Ellie not to forget her
'Papa'

September 24, 1864
Jefferson Barracks, Missouri

Dear Cimbaline and Ellie,
About four o'clock this afternoon our brigade received orders to be ready to move by Monday morning. I think the same order was given to all three brigades. I do not know that we will certainly move from here on that day; but I presume we shall go shortly. The impression seems to prevail that we are to go to Pilot Knob on the Iron Mountain R.R. or to Rolla on the Pacific R.R. from present prospects my little visit I contemplated taking home next week is about 'played out;'—that's too bad—isn't it? Well, I don't intend to despair over it. There will some way turn up for me yet. I feel perfectly confident that I can get home this fall sometime. So you may depend upon that much. . . . The women who are in camp seem to be disposed to make themselves useful, and help along the 'soldier boys' all they can, while they are with them. As I was passing along through the 117th. this evening, I saw one soldier's wife sitting on a stick of wood, mending a shirt for her husband;—a little farther along, I saw one take a poker, and lift the lid from a skillet, and take a peep inside to see how things were going on, in a manner that none but a woman can do. I passed on a little further, and I saw a middle aged woman, sitting by the side of man, smoking her pipe. Just as I passed, she turned her face toward him, and said, 'You didn't write, for such a long time.' I expect she was giving him a kind of reproving lecture for his neglect. Well, *you* can't play that tune to me.[8]

To-day I received a copy of the last issue of the *Belleville Advocate*, in

---

7. On September 19, U.S. troops under Philip Sheridan defeated Jubal Early's Confederates at the third battle of Winchester, part of the Union's aggressive fall campaign to exhaust rebel forces in the Shenandoah Valley of Virginia. See "General Sheridan's Victory," *Daily Missouri Republican*, September 21, 1864, 2, and Gallagher, *Shenandoah Valley Campaign*.

8. Despite the remarkable steadiness of their correspondence, the teasing from Henry or Cimbaline about the infrequency of the other's letters remained one of the most consistent features of their exchanges.

which are published the names of the 'drafted' in St. Clair Co.[9] Among the number, I find a host of my *friends* from Mascoutah and vicinity. I wonder how the prizes drawn in Uncle Sam's lottery pleases them. 'How are you, conscript?' Tell them all to come along, for there is plenty of room. What is the price for substitutes about Mascoutah? The market, in that business, is lively in St. Louis.[10]

Your affectionate husband and
'Papa.'

[post-script] Sunday September, 1864

Jefferson Barracks, Missouri

The rebel Gen. Shelby is reported to be at Fredericktown Missouri with a pretty strong force. Fredericktown is about 25 miles south-east of Pilot Knob. Rumor says he is advancing on towards Pilot Knob, or some point near by. The 2d Brig. of our Division went down the R.R. during the latter part of last night, and early this morning. There is considerable stir and bustle in camp, in consequence of the move on hand.[11]

Your affectionate husband,
Henry

---

9. Historian Arthur Cole noted that the draft finally went into effect in some parts of Illinois in October 1864, but elsewhere it took until March 1865. Cole, *Centennial History of Illinois*, 278–279.

10. News related to the Union draft filled many of the September newspapers in St. Louis. On September 23, for example, the names of the 913 men conscripted from the Fifth Ward took up nearly an entire column of the *Daily Missouri Republican*. Adjacent entries in the local news illuminated unusual stories under titles like "Oddities of the Draft" or "Freaks of the Draft." One such report described how a prosperous merchant in the Fourth Ward arranged to pay substitutes $800 each for his two stepsons, only to discover that he himself had been conscripted, adding, "Instances of peculiar ill fortune are so numerous in connection with the present draft, that some new and remarkable one comes to our knowledge every half hour." See *Daily Missouri Republican*, September 22, 1864, 3.

11. Henry likely gained this intelligence about the movements of General Jo Shelby, who commanded one of Price's three invading columns, from that Sunday morning's issue of the *Daily Missouri Republican*. See "Important Military News—Shelby Captures Fredericktown," September 25, 1864, 3.

September 25, 1864
Mascoutah, Illinois

Dear Henry,
This is Sunday morning. The town is full of people. To day is the time for the Girmans to have there new church Dedicated Mother has gon to see the sight.[12] I would have gon, if I had felt well enufe. I have taken the worst cold I most ever had. I have ben beed sick with it. Ellie has got a cold to She fell downg the other day and brok tow of her upper teeth lose. I do not know where she will luse tham or not. She has ben cring with the teeth achoke [crying with the tooth ache] for tow or three days past. She is so cross that we can not do much with her. She is for ever more crying to see you They are conciderble excitement heare about the Draff. They are a good many about Mascoutah Drafted. It does my sould good to see some of tham feel so bad about it It will do me more good when they will half to do. I suppose you have seen the list of those who are Drafted be fore this time. Anderson Fike and Jim Padfeild has gon to Olten [Alton] to see if they can hire substituts to go in there plases.[13] I think that dont show much love for there country.[14] I am thankful that all that wont go, will half to pay a good price for there substituts. I wish they would *not* alow any one to pay monney to git out. I think they are no better to go, then those that has gon.

I have been at home more than tow weekes. Only four letters to show from you That is the poorest you ever have don in your life to me, or sence you have been in the servis. I expect you feel so much releaved from your burden, that you had through the summer, that you have forgot to write I have paid for a box at the office for my letters If I do not

---

12. One local history suggests this might have been the dedication of a German Methodist Episcopal church in nearby Summerfield, which was erected in 1864. That same volume lacks detail about the founding of the German Methodist church in Mascoutah, but it notes that 1864 was also the year when German Methodists in Belleville purchased the sanctuary, parsonage, and schoolhouse from the town's Lutheran church. See *History of St. Clair County*, 176.

13. Here, Cimbaline probably meant Alton, the Mississippi River town that sat just upstream from St. Louis and more than thirty-five miles northwest of Mascoutah.

14. James R. Padfield was a thirty-seven-year-old constable in Mascoutah who was married with two children. The full version of Henry's September 20 letter to Cimbaline reveals that Anderson Fike and Padfield were among the many well-wishers from Mascoutah who visited Jefferson Barracks. United States Federal Census (hereafter USFC), 1860.

receive only four more in the tow weeks. I will not pay for it a nother quarter

No more at presant, From Cimbaline

September 26, 1864

Jefferson Barracks, Missouri

Dear Cimbaline and Ellie,
I am still here in camp. All the troops of our brigade left last night. . . . None of the regiments have yet taken their transportation (teams); and each regimental Q. M. is left in charge of the same. . . . All the troops which have gone from here, have taken three days rations with them, and have gone down along the R. R. somewhere. The St. Louis papers of this morning give accounts of a good deal of excitement over the rebel movement of troops up into this state, under Gens. Price and Shelby. General Rosencranz [Rosecrans], commanding this Department, has called upon the State Militia to come out promptly to the rescue. I presume you all get the daily St. Louis papers, and keep posted—*if you don't you should.*[15]

Your affectionate husband and
Papa.

September 29, 1864

Jefferson Barracks, Missouri

Dear Cimbaline and Ellie,
No doubt you have learned long before this of the state of excitement and feeling in the city of St. Louis, relative to the advance of the rebel forces up into this part of the state. There is no doubt of the matter, that Gen. Price is now in this state with quite a strong force, that he has his force, under the command of Shelby and Marmaduke, advancing side by side, for some object.[16] It is rumored, that his ultimate object, is the capture of Jefferson City, the capital of the state. The city of St. Louis is awake to the

---

15. One day after reporting that some six thousand men moved north with Price, the *Daily Missouri Republican* wrote that a Confederate force as "no less than 15,000 cavalry, with three batteries of artillery" was sixty miles south of St. Louis. "The Rebel Raid," *Daily Missouri Republican*, September 26, 1864, 2.

16. The rebels found scouting near Jefferson Barracks were likely Shelby's cavalry.

state of affairs now existing—all the business houses are closed—the militia is all called out—volunteer companies of 'exempts' are formed, and preparations generally are making for the defence of the city, should the rebels turn their attention in that direction. All the troops at the disposal of the Department commander (Gen. Rosencranz,) have been properly posted or sent out. Troops have also been ordered from Springfield, Illinois, and other places. So I think that everything is safe in this region.

Your affectionate husband and

Papa.

P.S. Since closing my letter, I have learned that all our troops are returning from the direction of Pilot Knob—the rebels having made demonstrations of coming around to the westward.[17]

September 30, 1864

Mascoutah, Illinois

Dear Henry,
They wos quite a excitement in town last night. The nuse wos that Price had crossed the River with his men in to Illinois. they call the men together by ringing the Bell. Had a meeting. This morning at 10 oclock They rang the Bell again, that was for drill All the buisness houses wos shut up untell a bout 12 oclock. I had to lafe to see some of our nuse careres [news carriers] when they come along. They look like there eyes would pop out of there heads, when they would tell the nuse they had heard

I all most wish some of Prices men would come heare just to see some of tham, take a fit I am sorry you wos disopinted about coming home this week I hope you will come soon. I am afraid you will not enjoy you self very much if you do come.

Write often as you can

From Cimbaline

---

17. Price turned toward the central Missouri valley with hopes that southern sympathizers would provide his army with fresh recruits and supplies, but historian Kyle Sinisi argues that the rebel commander also believed that capturing the capital, thought to be poorly defended, would confer political legitimacy on the effort to liberate Missouri from Union control. See Sinisi, *Last Hurrah*, 91–94, and Brownlee, "Battle of Pilot Knob," 271–296.

October 3, 1864
Kirkwood, Missouri

Dear Cimbaline and Ellie,
We are now about due west from St. Louis, perhaps a little southwest. The town of Kirkwood is on the Pacific R. R. and contains about twenty houses. The people along the road which we traveled, yesterday, seemed to be, generally, quite loyal; and manifested great satisfaction at seeing us coming out in this direction. At a great many of the houses the people stand at the roadside, with buckets, and pitchers, and hand water to the boys as they passed along.

We are encamped in a large meadow, at the edge of a wood, with good water handy.

We heard yesterday that our brigade has had a little brush with the enemy, some ten miles west of here. Our boys are out at Franklin, now, on the R. R. west of here, where they had the skirmish. It was not much of a fight. No particulars yet received—except the rebels skedaddled.

Yours affectionately,
Henry.

October 4, 1864
Gray's Summit, Missouri

Dear Cimbaline and Ellie,
We proceeded some half mile north of town, and struck a turnpike road leading westward from St. Louis. We took this road, and marched some eighteen miles, before we went into camp. The day was quite drizzly and wet, and in consequence of this, somewhat unpleasant. The road was splendid for teams, but a little *too solid* for men to march upon with ease to their feet. All along the country we saw every indication, on the part of the citizens, to do their share towards driving the invader from their soil. They have organized themselves into militia companies, and have drawn arms, and prepared to defend themselves. The great difficulty, however, seems to consist in their being scattered over the country in such small bodies—too small to withstand the assault of a large attacking force. There are a good many Germans living in this part of the state, and they are, generally, loyal. . . .[18] On last Saturday, the rebels came into

---

18. For the German American settlement of Missouri, see Gerlach, *Settlement Patterns in Missouri*.

this place, about three hundred strong, burned the depot and robbed a store of all its clothing, boots and shoes. The rebels' chief aim, seems to be, to procure clothing, and supplies. Their main force is reported to be some fifteen miles to the westward of here. . . . Good night to you. Give Ellie a kiss for her 'papa'—and tell her I think of her whenever I see little children along the road.
Yours affectionately,
Henry.

October 4, 1864
Mascoutah, Illinois

Dear Henry,
James Johnson is moving to day. Dr Land[19] mooved yesterday. Mr Huff will move next week to Clay County[20] you can see our nabors are leaving fast. Not meny left. Old Jetter is at home. His time is out. Yes Uncle Tommy is moving to, yesterday and to day[21]

I received a letter from you last evening, stating that you expected to leave the barecks. I am sorry to heare that. I am affraid you will see hearder times than you ever did. I wish you could have come home before you left. I am affraid you cannot come home soon.
Yours with love and respect
Cimbaline

October 6, 1864
Gray's Summitt,[22] Missouri

Dear Cimbaline and Ellie,
This looks very much like we are to have some marching to do. I think this quite probable. If there is any late news from Price's army, within two

---

19. Perryman Land, an Alabama-born physician, who appeared just two households away from the Fikes in the most recent federal census enumeration. USFC, 1860.

20. Cimbaline likely meant Clay County in Illinois, some eighty miles east of Mascoutah.

21. The wartime departure of so many neighbors was a stark contrast to the population spike in St. Clair County after the war. According to the federal census enumeration, Mascoutah had 2,076 residents in 1860, but a decade later its population jumped to 2,790, an increase of 34 percent. Kennedy, *Population of the United States,* 99; Walker, *Compendium of the Ninth Census,* 119.

22. Gray Summit sits in Franklin County, some thirty miles west of Jefferson Barracks.

or three days, I have not got hold of it. I have not seen a St. Louis paper, of a later date than the 3d inst. Yesterday some thirty or forty paroled soldiers and citizens came in here, from the west. They stated they had been taken by Price's army—some of them at Pilot Knob—and had finally been paroled, some thirty miles west of here. They state that Price's army was making its way towards Jefferson City. I think their principal object is to plunder the country, and procure horses and clothing; as they take all the good horses they find, and rob all the stores of all their clothing, boots and shoes. . . . I expect that you would think that I look a little odd, if you were to see me now, as I have got my *scattering* beard all shaved off. I thought I would try a smooth face awhile. As I do not know of any more to write, I will close.

Your affectionate husband and
Papa

October 7, 1864
Gray's Summit, Missouri

Dear Cimbaline and Ellie,

I am well pleased with your arrangement of renting our house.[23] I hope the place will work well. Tell all the people to not get 'scared out of their boots'; for Price will never put his foot upon Illinois soil.

I will write to you as often as I can. If you do not receive two or three letters a week from me, you may take it for granted, that there are no facilities for sending mail matter. I want you to write as often as you can, and the letters will get to me some time. I love to read them, if they are old. Tell me, who all of the drafted men are going to the army—and who are getting substitutes. I will close.

Your affectionate husband and
Papa.

---

23. During the first two years of the war, Cimbaline sought direction from Henry about how to handle the collection of rent, payments on outstanding notes, and other financial questions. By the fall of 1864, he apparently deferred to her judgment about rent collection more often, but her next letter revealed a partnership that was less collaborative than she imagined.

October 9, 1864
Mascoutah, Illinois

Dear Henry

We are all well, but very tired. . . . I have not perticular nuse to write at presant. Old Mascoutah is about the same old The lonsomest plase I ever lived in. I donot know how I will stand it this winter. I expect I will die with the blues. If you heare of my death, you will know the case of it.

I have paid Charles tow houndred dollars on his note. He ses they are a bout eighty more coming. he ses the note at first called for tow houndred and seventy dollars. I do not know as you never tell me any of your buisness. Mother thinkes it is a mistake, I supose you know, I wish you would let me know in your next letter

You never told me what rent to ask for the Michel farme, or where I should rent it or not. Narcisia Mc Clure[24] is downg on a visit, I do not know how long she entends to stay. I have not seen her yet

I must stopt writing and git redy to go out in the country.

From your wife., Cimbaline

October 12, 1864
"Out in the Country" in St. Clair County, Illinois

Dear Henry

I am out at Mr Rayhills on a visit. I come out last Sunday evening. The famly are all well. We are all well allso. Mr Flanry[25] commenced teaching at the Rayhill school house last monday. The children all go to school, except Betty and Hellen, that is at home.

I have not any thing very interresting to write, I thought if I did not write while I wos out heare you would think I was neglecting my deuty tourdes you

---

24. Narcissa McClure and her husband, Edward, had lived in St. Clair County in 1850. The 1860 Census lists a couple with corresponding birth years in Sangamon County, but the different places of birth listed in each enumeration suggests they may not have been the same couple. USFC, 1850, 1860.

25. Thomas A. Flannery, a twenty-six-year-old Irish immigrant who rented the home next to the Rayhills, was apparently the schoolteacher referenced here. As recently as August 20, 1864, applicants who sought certification to teach had to swear an oath of loyalty. See *History of St. Clair County*, 113, 278.

James is out heare halling wood for Charles this week Helen was in town yesterday, she saw Mother, she is well. Every man that was drafted about Mascoutah has hired substiuts that is able, and a good meny that is not able. Charity ses if you will come home about Chrismas, she will kill a turkey and make a dinner for you on our ninth aneversary day. I think that will be very nice. Do not you think so

If you come home this year, try and come about that time, if you can. Then if you can not come any more while you are in the servis, it will not be so long untell your time is out

From, Cimbaline

October 13, 1864

California, Missouri

Dear Cimbaline and Ellie,

I expect you have been looking for some time, for a letter from me. But, when I tell you that I write to you, as soon as I have an opportunity, I know you will pardon my delay in the matter. On Friday the 7th inst. I wrote you my last letter previous to this, from Gray's Summit. I will now give you a brief sketch of our march, from that time, up to the present.

On that afternoon, we were joined by two brigades of Enrolled Militia from St. Louis, under command of Brig. Gen. E. C. Pike. That afternoon we marched ten miles & encamped at a water mill on a creek, where, we got some corn meal. Next day we marched about twenty-eight miles, over a very rough country—up steep and rugged hills,—almost young mountains. The country reminded me, very much of that, along which we passed south of Pilot Knob. That night we encamped a Buff Creek. Next day we did not march. The militia could not keep up, and we had to wait. . . . All along the country, through which we passed, we saw, on every side, evidences of the march of Price's Army. All the farmers told the same story—Price had taken all their good horses—killed and eaten many of their cattle—fed up a great deal of their corn, without paying for it, and plundered their houses and stores of all clothing and any goods.[26] On Monday, 10" inst. we marched to, and camped upon the west side of the Gasconade river. This is a splendid stream, which we forded—the

---

26. One of Price's generals, M. Jeff Thompson, recalled that the rebel army "left in its track a line of robbery, almost as bad as that of Sherman's bummers." See Sinisi, *Last Hurrah*, 98–102, for depredations committed by Price's men south and east of Jefferson City.

men pulling off their pants, and wading right through. Tuesday 11"—we marched some twenty miles, through the same kind of country—still on the track of Price. Next day, the 12th we marched to the Osage river, which is quite a stream. This we crossed, and proceeded to Jefferson City immediately, where we arrived at dark. We got on the cars forthwith (our brigade only) and came out to this town this morning, which is 25 miles west of Jefferson City, on the Pacific R.R. Our other two brigades will be here to-morrow, I think. Price went through this town, and pillaged it on last Sunday.[27] The towns we passed through, from St. Louis, here are: Kirkwood, Franklin, Gray's Summit, Union, Mt. Sterling, Lynn, Jefferson City, Lookout and this town, California. . . . This town contains about one thousand inhabitants—located in a nice country. The country around here has some prairie land, and is very nice.[28] They have a good school house, and an apparently good school. I paid the school a short visit this afternoon. It looked somewhat natural to witness the exercises of a school room again. . . . Price army was at Booneville,[29] on the Missouri River, yesterday. Scouts from there to-day report him as having evacuated that place and gone westward. We will have to 'keep on the jump' to catch him—for he is mounted, and can travel so fast. But we have now got several thousand cavalry after him, giving him a good deal of trouble and anxiety. My sheet is full—so I will close, I am quite well.—feel sleepy tonight—only slept about two hours last night. Good night. sweet dreams to you both.[30]

Your affectionate husband and
Papa.

October 15, 1864

California, Missouri

Dear Cimbaline and Ellie,
The 1st & 2d Brigades of our Division arrived here yesterday, from Jefferson City, over-land. They call our brigade the 'pet brigade' of Gen.

---

27. Sinisi, *Last Hurrah*, 113–116.
28. Geographer Walter A. Schroeder's research into the native prairie of Missouri suggests that Henry wrote this letter near the point at which the wooded hills and valleys that dominated his march from St. Louis opened up to the native tallgrass prairies that dominated the Osage plains of western Missouri. Schroeder, *Presettlement Prairie of Missouri*, 33.
29. Boonville, roughly thirty miles north of California, sits upstream from Jefferson City.
30. General Alfred Pleasanton led the Federal cavalry who pursued the rebels into western Missouri.

Smith—because we have got to ride on the cars, two or three times, while they had to 'foot it' over the country. . . . The glorious news of the Union triumphs at the state elections in Indiana, Ohio and Pennsylvania, a few days ago, gladdens every patriot's heart in our command, and, we think, most surely indicates the reelection of Lincoln, and the consequent vigorous prosecution of the war, and the ushering in of an early peace. . . .[31]
I am highly pleased with the looks of this town and surrounding country. The town is situated in the edge of a rolling prairie, with timber on the east, north and west, within a mile—while on the south you can see ten or fifteen miles over hills and valleys of timber, which present a most magnificent appearance. I understand that land is, just now, very cheap in this region, and if I wanted to buy a location, I think I should look around some here. This is the county-seat of this county, and necessarily creates an amount of business here. Tell Ausby or any of our friends, who have an idea, of looking out for a new home, to give this part of the country a call.—as I think they will be well pleased with it.

Your affectionate husband and
Papa.

October 17, 1864

Lamine Creek, 1 mile east of Otterville, Cooper Co., Missouri

Dear Cimbaline and Ellie,
We left California yesterday morning at 7 o'clock, coming westward to this place, marching during the day some twenty-five or twenty-eight miles. This morning I hear a good deal of complaint from officers and men on account of sore feet. During our march, yesterday, we passed through some as nice country as I wish to see any where—nice rolling prairie land, with strips of timber crossing it, and giving the whole, a most romantic appearance. The country very much resembles the country between Lebanon, Trenton and Highland, except that it is somewhat rocky or grav-

---

31. The National Union ticket of Abraham Lincoln and Andrew Johnson won 53.5, 56.4, and 51.6 percent of the votes in Indiana, Ohio, and Pennsylvania, respectively, in the presidential election held on November 8, 1864. Here, Henry referred to the mid-October elections for statewide and congressional offices, in which the Republicans' strong showings augured well for Lincoln's chances of reelection. See Waugh, *Reelecting Lincoln*, 332–346. For election interest within Henry's regiment, see James Krafft Diary, November 10–11, 1864.

elly. Our march yesterday was along close to the R.R., first on one side, and then on the other, never more than probably one mile from it. We followed the State road. We are now encamped on Lamine creek, within two or three hundred yards of the railroad. The rebels have burned the R.R. bridge over the creek. Yesterday we passed through Scott's Station, Tipton, and Syracuse—three places on the railroad.[32] Tipton and Syracuse are two nice thriving towns, or were before the war stopped their growth. On last Saturday week, the 8th of this month, the rebels came into Syracuse, about one hundred strong, under the noted bush-whacker Todd, and burned the R.R. depot, and murdered some six or seven men in cold blood.[33] Four of the men, they called out into the street, and drew them up in line, and shot them down, like dogs, without even giving them any more reason for doing so, than saying, 'You Union sons of bitches, we have heard of you before.'[34] I talked to several citizens about it, and saw the wife of one of the men who was shot. His name was Yard, and a shoemaker by trade. He has a son in the 33d Reg. Missouri Vols, which will be here in a day or two.[35] The people all through here, who are loyal, can't express their joy at our coming. They wave flags, which, no doubt, many times they have had to conceal from the enemy—and even shout, and many times weep for joy, as they see our boys pass by. Yesterday afternoon, as we passed through Syracuse, one woman stood with a national flag, by the road-side, which she waved for nearly an hour; and our boys kept up a loud shout and cheer, all the time they were passing. It was a good sight to see. Our people and friends at home, cann't begin to imagine, much less realize, the terrors and trials of war. It has to be seen and felt, to be fully understood.

Your affectionate husband and

Papa.

---

32. For two years Pacific City (later renamed Syracuse) served as the western terminus of the Missouri Pacific railroad. *History of Cole*, 433–434.

33. Here Henry likely referred to guerrilla George Todd. See Hulbert, *Ghosts of Guerrilla Memory*, 37.

34. *History of Cole*, 418–420.

35. Milton Yard served in the 33rd Regiment Missouri Volunteer Infantry. USFC 1860; Civil War Soldiers and Sailors System database, National Park Service, https://www.nps.gov/civilwar/soldiers-and-sailors-database.htm, accessed December 9, 2023 (hereafter CWSS).

October 17, 1864
Mascoutah, Illinois

Dear Henry,
We have returned frome our visit, and feel quite well. I had a very plesant time with your people. Beter than I expected. Nothing new to write about Mascoutah, as I know of. Amos Day[36] has gon to serve his year in the armey, and John Hilworth allso that is about all I know has gon from heare All the rest has haired substitutes, I think I will go to Summerfield on a visit, and other places, the last of this week, or the first of next week, if nothing prevents From all reportes, I need not write this letter to you It is all a float, that all of you are taken prisnors by Price. I do not entend to belive it, untell I know it. Then I suppose I will half to believe it
 No more at presant
 From Cimbaline

October 19, 1864
Mascoutah, Illinois

Dear Henry,
I received a letter from you last evening. The first one i have had for more than a week. Not meny lettrs received from our Reg. for some time. I tell you they has been some anixous hearts to heare the nuse
 Mother has not come home yet, I hope she will soon. It is rother lonsom liven with out her Espesly at her house We are all well, the only compalint is, I hae got a very sore toe, I can not ware my shoe with any ease, If it donot git better soon, I cannot take my visit as soon as I expected
 Another big fuss among the womens, One in town, and one in the country, and one among the Town women and some of the country womens, they to have great times, they think, I have nothing to do with it and

---

36. Amos Day, thirty-five, mustered into the 43rd Illinois Infantry regiment at Alton, Illinois, on September 21, 1864. A private in Company C, he and his company served garrison duty at Little Rock, Arkansas, through November 1865. Fred Delap, Illinois Civil War Muster and Descriptive Rolls Database, Illinois State Archives, Office of the Illinois Secretary of State, https://www.ilsos.gov/isaveterans/civilMusterSearch.do (hereafter Delap, ICWMDR). A search of Illinois muster rolls and the St. Clair census manuscripts from 1860 does not reveal John Hilworth or a name similar to it. Its absence might be explained by desertion or perhaps Cimbaline's erratic spelling.

do not entend to, I think they are haing a bolly time about there old men, I am glad you are not home, for fear they would have you in It semes all the marred men are brout in to their conversasion at their big fusses. Some of them have been fighting, Both men and women.

I told some of tham I thought it was enought to have wore aroung us, let a lone having it among us. The worst is the women fight Don't you think they are giting along in the world.

From, Cimbaline

October 22, 1864

Lexington, Missouri

Dear Cimbaline,

I snatch a moment or two to drop you a few lines. Our troops are leaving this place, and I am seated by a camp fire, on an old broken bucket, writing on my knee. My desk is loaded up in the wagon, and gone, and I had to get this paper from a soldier. I am very well. . . . I believe, I wrote to you last from Lamine Creek. Since then, we have marched some seventy-five miles. By looking on the map you will see that Lexington is on the Missouri River.[37] We are now getting near the Kansas line. We have come through some very fine looking country. I am quite well pleased with its appearance. Good land and well improved farms can be bought out here at from five to twenty-five dollars per acre. I have heard of some real good bargains. A great many people have become so annoyed with the war, that they are willing and desirous of selling out at any price.

We followed Gen. Price's army pretty close, getting in here a few hours after he left.[38] We are off this morning in hot pursuit of him. I have some doubts of our catching him—his forces all being mounted. We have considerable cavalry, however, which may annoy him, so as to detain him, till we can get up with him. If we can only get a chance at him, we are perfectly willing to risk the consequences.

---

37. Three years earlier, Price's Missouri State Guard overwhelmed the Union garrison at the Missouri River town of Lexington, an engagement perhaps most famous for the advancing rebels' use of hemp bales as a rolling breastwork. See "Letters from the Battle," 53–58; McCausland, "Battle of Lexington as Seen," 127–135.

38. Price's army clashed with a smaller Union force at Lexington on October 19. After slowing the rebels' advance during six hours of skirmishing, James G. Blunt's outnumbered Unionists retreated westward toward the Blue River, with the Confederates in pursuit. Sinisi, *Last Hurrah*, 71–80.

Your affectionate husband,
Henry.

October 23, 1864
Mascoutah, Illinois

Deare Henry

I have not received but one letter from you during the past week. I think you must have got all most out of the world, From the way your letters come. . . . After I finished my letter, Ellie thought she must write one to you, after she wrote it, or while she wos writing Mother came up to look at her write, She said Gran Ma go and sit downg, after I write my letter, I will come and read it to you. This was what she read

My Ma brout my Ponney over to Gran Ma My Pa must come home and see me, and play with me, and I will kiss him

I kiss my Grand ma every night, and my ma tow weeks a go to day. I want my Ma to bring the cow over heare

and let me milker I want my pa to come home and bring me some aples, and lotes of candy. If he will. I will love him and kiss him all night

Must I make those shirts for you, by the time you come home.[39] Or have you got some. Whot do you think the prospect is, a bout coming home. Is they any or not. Write and let me know what you think about it, and about whot time you can come. Yours, from Cimbaline

October 26, 1864
Mascoutah, Illinois

Dear Henry

To day I paid Polly Fike for our cow. I have sold all of our funiture that I can do with out while it is a good prise, we had to much for our famley. I thought I better sell it and pay some of our debts, Then have it laying aroung in the dust I sole it tusday, and paid polly to day. She tole me she had a note on you for 4.00 Do I told her you could pay that your self, that I did not know anything about it: that was the first I ever heard of

---

39. Cimbaline repeatedly supplied Henry with homemade shirts. See C. Fike to H. Fike, September 2, 1863, and C. Fike to H. Fike, January 3, 1865, Henry C. and Lucy C. Fike Papers.

it. I never heard you say anything about it. Henry I donot know how you ever got your self in dept [debt] so much. I have found out, that you owe about $5000. How it ever hapen I can not tell. I have about $100. on hand I thought I would ceep part of it, and git me some thinges I have wanted for a long time. Sence I have found out how much you ow, I will not git tham If I should, I would be ashame to ware tham heare. It has been all ready said, that I better stay at home, and take care of our property, and save money, and pay our depts, No one can say that that I am waistful, and say the trouth. I do not care who it is, *white or black*, I have tryed to live as saven as I could. In every respect. Many times I would like to have things, and would have got tham. But I would think how much you wos in dept [debt]. I would try to git along without tham. That has been the way I have lived for five or six years, I can not see that it is giting any better. If anything worse, I am giting out of heart. I can not see our way out. It trubles me more then eny thing elce on earth I hope you will come home soon, and arange your buisness better then whot it is. Osbay never will see, or attend to eny thing for you All he cares for, is to make money out of sider and apples I can not git him to count intrust for me while they are a apple on the ground[40]

From Cimbaline

October 27, 1864

Harrisonville, Missouri

Dear Cimbaline,

One week ago this morning I wrote to you from Lexington. Since then we have marched a good deal and seen much, which I shall be unable to speak of fully in this letter. I will, however, give you a brief account of our last week's doings:

On Saturday 22d, we marched some 22 miles south west of Lexington. Our army consisted of about ten thousand infantry and twenty-six pieces of artillery, with enough cavalry for scouting ahead, and serving as an escort for the General. I might here say, that the balance of our force, some

---

40. Like many fortune seekers, Ausby ventured to California in 1849, but he returned to Mascoutah three years later and settled into a comfortable livelihood as a merchant and member of the county court. His property holdings, according to the 1860 census, were more than four times greater than Henry and Cimbaline's, which perhaps explains her resentment here. USFC, 1860; *History of St. Clair County*, 278.

ten or twelve thousand cavalry under Gen. Pleasanton were on ahead in Price's rear, while Gen. Curtis was on his front with some two thousand cavalry and eight thousand infantry. Gen. Curtis brought his army from Kansas, and operated in Price's front, and contested his advance.

On Sunday 23d, we marched about 25 miles westward and a little northwest towards Independence. We went into camp about 8 o'clock p.m. and received orders to eat and feed our teams and be ready to march in three hours. This order arose from the report that our army in front had got Price hemmed in, and we were needed on the following morning to go into a general fight to capture his entire army. So, about midnight our boys shoved out, shouting and cheering at the top of their voices. We reached Independence and passed through the town about three o'clock in the morning; and then took a southwesterly direction. By eight o'clock a.m. we reached the expected battle ground; but 'the bird had flown' the day before. On this last stretch our men marched forty miles in eighteen hours. Most of them stood the tramp well, though they were quite tired. We here camped for the day on Big Blue creek. This was the 24". Where we encamped, and also three miles west of us on the prairie, there had been a fight the day before, and there were two hospitals here, one ours and one containing about forty rebel wounded. I visited both hospitals and the place where the fighting occurred. I saw and conversed with the rebel wounded and the two surgeons left by Price in charge. There were 13 dead rebels left on the battle ground which our men buried. The loss on each side something near seventy-five in killed & wounded. Our wounded were all sent to Kansas City or Independence.[41]

On Tuesday, 25 we marched a little south west and passed through New Santa Fee [Fe], right on the line between Missouri and Kansas. I took a ride out about a half mile into Kansas; so I can say I have been in 'bleeding Kansas.'[42] From this town we marched a couple of miles east of south, and camped for the night. Rumors and despatches here stated that Price's army, having been checked in the front by Curtis' Army had turned south, and now were some thirty miles to the south of us.

Next morning 26", which was yesterday, we marched about twenty-five miles, southeasterly and came through Harrisonville to this place. We marched yesterday, through a prairie some twenty-miles wide and passed

---

41. "Fight on the Little Blue!" *Western Journal of Commerce*, October 29, 1864, 1.

42. Although the partisan violence that inspired this phrase had largely subsided by 1858 in many parts of Kansas, the counties along the Missouri remained plenty bloody through 1864. See Etcheson, *Bleeding Kansas*, 190–206.

only two or three deserted houses. This neighborhood has been pretty well settled once. This county and Jackson county north of this, have both been depopulated by an order from military authority—causing all citizens of the counties to move within four miles of some military post, thus affording themselves better chances for protection, and removing harbors for bushwhackers.[43] This is a magnificent looking country. Many of the prairies I have seen, far exceed Looking-Glass prairie in grandeur and beauty—Our cavalry are still in pursuit of Price's retreating army.[44] Word came to us to-day which is quite creditable, that our forces engaged the enemy yesterday, capturing Gen. Marmaduke, five hundred prisoners and seven pieces of artillery. This is quite encouraging news; and we hope it may be confirmed. I forgot to state that we had already previously captured six pieces of artillery.

We are lying here in camp to-day, and the boys are enjoying the resting spell very much. I think our infantry troops will not, probably follow Price any further. We are now on our last days' rations, but expect a large supply train here, to-night, from Warrensburg, on the railroad. There is not much news in camp;—only one rebel spy was hung to-day, and one bushwhacker shot and another hung. This is, no doubt, right, as they deserved the fate.[45]

We are all getting along well, and I think we will, probably, start towards St. Louis, in a day or two.

I will close by saying good-bye to you, Ellie and mother, until I write again.

Your affectionate husband,

Henry.

---

43. Frustrated by the long-simmering guerrilla war along Missouri's western border, Union general Thomas Ewing announced General Order Number 11 on August 25, 1863, four days after pro-Confederate raiders under William Quantrill sacked Lawrence, Kansas, and killed more than 170 men and boys. Order No. 11 expelled the disloyal inhabitants from Cass County, where Henry wrote this letter, and three neighboring counties. The fires that swept across the native tallgrass prairies of this depopulated area led observers to describe it as the "Burnt District." Niepman, "General Orders No. 11," 185–210.

44. Henry's adoration of Looking-Glass prairie, which stretched across St. Clair and neighboring counties in western Illinois, contrasted sharply with the deflated impressions that Charles Dickens documented in his 1842 visit. Said the Englishman, "Great as the picture was, its very flatness and extent, which left nothing to the imagination, tamed it down and cramped its interest. I felt little of that sense of freedom and exhilaration which a Scottish heath inspires, or even our English downs awaken. It was lonely and wild, but oppressive in its barren monotony." Dickens, *American Notes*, vol. 2, 135–136.

45. See also James A. Black Diary, October 27, 1864.

7 1/2 o'clock P.M.

I send this letter to Warrensburg by one of our men who is going there with Major McWilliams.[46] The officers of Indiana and Illinois regiments are making an effort to get Gen. Rosencranz to allow them to go home to vote; and Major McWilliams starts with a dispatch to him, at Warrensburg, to night, on that subject. Warrensburg is thirty-five miles from here; and the party expects to be back here to-morrow night. Gen. Smith is willing to do the thing, and I think it somewhat probably that we will be home to vote, and give 'Old Abe' a lift.[47]

October 28, 1864

Harrisonville, Missouri

Dear Cimbaline,
The latest news from Price is that he is skedaddling in hot haste for Dixie, with Gen. Pleasanton after him 'with a sharp stick' or something else as unpleasant. Tell Ausby and Polly that their son Capt. John Fike, is hearty and well; and the whole company is getting on very well.

There is a very current rumor in camp, that an order has been issued by the war authorities that after this campaign is over, and we return, our Division and the First Division which is with us, will be sent down the Mississippi river, to do garrison duty again along the river. We are all very willing to serve the remaining months of our time, in some good garrison post, where we will not have to tramp around so much.

I hope we may soon be able to come home, and spend a few days with our friends again. Tell Ellie to not forget her papa, and to take good care of her pony, for when she gets a little larger, I will buy her a little saddle, and then she can ride whenever she wants to.

I hope mother will not think hard of me, for not writing to her oftener. I know she gets to hear all the letters I send to you, which keeps her well posted. My compliments and love to all the friends and connexions.

---

46. Major Robert McWilliams, 117th Illinois Volunteer Infantry. Fold3.com, "National Archives, Organization Index to Pension Files of Veterans Who Served between 1861 and 1900," T289, Record Group 15, February 4, 1911, https://www.fold3.com/image/293149643, accessed December 9, 2023.

47. The presidential election of 1864 marked the first time in American electoral history that states allowed men in active military service to cast votes while in the field. Soldiers from states that had not yet embraced that innovation needed to secure permission to return home to cast a ballot. Waugh, *Reelecting Lincoln*, 332–354.

From
Your affectionate husband,
Henry.

October 30, 1864

Dear Cimbaline,
I am sorry to say that Gen. Rosencrans would not grant our request. He said the exigency of military affairs, is such as will not admit of so many of our troops going home at once. You may rest assured that his refusal has not made him many friends in our Division; for all our boys think that they deserve an opportunity of going home to vote, since they have been campaigning it with all their might, for nearly the entire past year, marching during that period over one thousand miles, through heat and cold, dust and rain. This evening, since arriving here, we have heard it intimated that our command will probably be divided in a day or so, and some of them, be sent north across the Missouri river, I suppose to go 'whacking' with bushwhackers; for there is no other rebel force on that side of the river. If this is so, it will not please our boys very well; but I only give this as a talk in camp. There are many strange things occurring in this world every day, of which we never dreamed; and in military affairs it is peculiarly so. One never knows what the next day may bring.
Your affectionate husband,
Henry.

November 5, 1864

Lookout Station, Cole County, Missouri

Dear Cimbaline,
When we arrived at Sedalia I there had thirteen more put in my charge, which now makes one hundred and twenty eight. Twenty four of these wagons are loaded with various kinds of ammunition, and in the remainder I haul forage gathered in the country, and about one hundred and thirty men from our Division, who had sore feet and could not march. These are coming back with me. However, to-day, as we passed through the town of California, I left the most of these there, to be sent down on the train to Jefferson City. I did this to lighten the wagons, which are now so heavy since the recent snow. Having the responsibility of so many teams on my hands—and having to attend to settling with every man,

for the corn, hay and oats we have had to take, and then the care of my lame, halt and sore footed, has given rise to enough business to employ my time very well.

We have had excellent roads and weather, until the recent snow storm, which I presume was experienced in Illinois. On the 3d inst. it commenced snowing before daylight, and snowed all day. It was the most disagreeable day, by all odds, that I was ever exposed in.

Your affectionate husband,
Henry.

November 7, 1864

Jefferson City, Missouri

Dear Cimbaline,
This afternoon I had a leisure hour or two, which I spent in walking around town, looking at the 'sights.' I was up to the Capitol building, which I found full of soldiers, who were stopping in there, out of the weather. The building is a very common one for a State Capitol.[48] It has no fence around it, and the ground is muddy, and has no trees or any kind of shrubbery to ornament the place. In fact, this whole town is a poor looking, dirty muddy place. It looks very much as all towns generally look, that are surrounded by and contaminated with seceshdom. It looks like war was in the land. There appeared to be no public improvements going on, and things, generally, seem to be on the stand still. However, when this war is over, and Missouri becomes a free state, as she is bound to do, matters and things generally, will appear in another light. Tomorrow, I suppose, is election day—the great day of our nation. I should like very much to be home to-morrow, to give 'Old Abe' the benefit of my one feeble vote. I think that would elect him, and thus save our country.

Your affectionate husband,
Henry.

---

48. Henry refers here to the second building that served as the seat of Missouri government. Completed in 1840, this second capitol—like the first, destroyed in 1837—burned down after a lightning strike on February 5, 1917. Shoemaker, "Dedication of Missouri's Capitol," 300–303.

November 9, 1864
Trenton, Illinois

Dear Henry,

Health is genrly good. The Election came of yesterday in this town. Old Abe got the margarety, no doubt.[49] We have not heard yet, but we are satesfide. Last night we had a very heard rain. This morning the hold town wos nearly coverd with watter. . . . I will not attempt to write a long letter this time. When I returne home, I will write you a long letter and give you all the puticulers of my visit

I hope when you come to St Louis you will come home and see us
Yours in love, Cimbaline

---

49. The Union ticket won a one-thousand-vote majority across St. Clair County. "The General Result," *Chicago Tribune*, November 11, 1864, 1.

CHAPTER 6
"What We Enlisted For"

Nashville, Tennessee, to New Orleans, Louisiana
and
Mascoutah, Illinois
November 1864 to March 1865

After a difficult march across Missouri and back, Henry relished his November reunion with Cimbaline. His regiment had traveled more than four thousand miles since January 1, nearly half of them on foot, but a pleasant fortnight spent in the family's Mascoutah home eased the ache of long months spent on the march. His brief homecoming came to an incongruous end on Thanksgiving Day, when new orders put the 117th Illinois aboard a steamboat once more, again bound for points unknown. Henry and his comrades nonetheless faced the upcoming leg of their sojourn with good cheer and gratitude. Most of the men had less than a third of their three-year enlistment left to serve, and hopeful signs suggested that the war might end before these terms expired. President Lincoln had been decisively reelected, a victory owed in large part to the ardent support of Federal troops. What's more, the Union army's capture of Atlanta and the Shenandoah Valley of Virginia suggested that the fall of other Confederate strongholds, including the capital of Richmond, was now within reach.

After steaming up the Cumberland River into central Tennessee, the 117th Illinois joined the Union army that George Thomas had assembled at Nashville.[1] In mid-December these Federals routed John Bell Hood's

---

1. Union forces had occupied Nashville since February 1862, shortly after the capture of Forts Donelson and Henry, and it held a depot that became crucial in the supply of Federal troops west of the Appalachians. Confederate troops led by John Bell Hood now aimed to liberate the Tennessee capital and perhaps Kentucky to its north. The rebel advance was an unsuccessful effort to divert Sherman's Federals after the Confederates' loss of Atlanta, with each misstep proving to be worse than the one before. On November 29, Hood's Army of Tennessee clashed with Union forces near Spring Hill, some thirty miles southwest of Nashville, but failed to outflank the Federals, sever their supply line, or pre-

Army of Tennessee, a defeat that one local newspaper said "will convince the rebels not only of [the] hopelessness of regaining Tennessee, but of the cause at large."[2] The Union victory was a heady counterpoint to the failed Red River expedition of the preceding spring, and it left Henry and his comrades in the highest of spirits.

Their jubilation soon yielded to the grinding hardships of soldiering in winter. Assistant Quartermaster Monroe J. Miller likened the cold, wet conditions at the battle of Nashville to a "living death," and the weeks that followed were little better.[3] Following a fruitless pursuit of the retreating Confederates, the 117th Illinois established winter quarters at Eastport, Mississippi. Within weeks the regiment's supplies ran dangerously low, and gnawing hunger gripped the camp. Flour and even hard tack vanished from the soldiers' daily rations, which now consisted of corn and little else, leading one man to ask when the commissary sergeant would draw the men hay as well. "This is only soldiering," Henry mused. "And that is what we enlisted for."[4]

The army's adaptations to such challenges came at the expense of southern civilians, whose farms and woodlots surrendered the livestock, grain, and timber that barely sated the demands of plundering Union troops. "An army traveling through a country is a terrible & awful affair, to the inhabitants thereof," wrote Henry.[5] An insoluble contempt for Confederates, however, tempered whatever pity he felt for families who suffered the desolation of war. Victory lay just beyond the Union's reach,

---

vent their retreat northward. A day later the Confederates attacked John Schofield's Army of the Ohio once more, but their repeated assaults on the Union line at Franklin met with disastrous results; among the six thousand rebel casualties were six generals and dozens of other regimental commanders. Hood's army of thirty thousand rebels possessed few good options as they eyed their strongly fortified enemy. Schofield's men withdrew from Franklin to join Thomas at Nashville, bringing the size of their combined force to fifty-five thousand men. The Union forces held a strong position, as the Cumberland sliced north of the city and protected both of the army's flanks, and a wide ring of earthworks defended them from the south. Henry and his comrades, on arrival, threw themselves into the expansion of these breastworks, which eventually stretched for ten miles. John R. Lundberg, "Errant Moves on the Chessboard of War: The Battle of Spring Hill, November 29, 1864," in Woodworth and Grear, *Tennessee Campaign of 1864*, 46–65; Cooling, *To the Battles of Franklin and Nashville*, 265–298.

2. "Another Great Battle Yesterday," *Nashville Daily Union*, December 17, 1864, 2. See also "The Great Battle Yesterday!" *Nashville Daily Union*, December 16, 1864, 2; Cooling, *To the Battles of Franklin and Nashville*, 299–340.

3. Monroe Joshua Miller Papers (hereafter MJMP), December 12, 1864.

4. H. Fike to C. Fike, December 21, 1864, Henry C. and Lucy C. Fike Papers (hereafter FP).

5. H. Fike to C. Fike, December 26, 1864, FP.

and until it came, those he blamed for the rebellion deserved whatever hardship they might suffer.

Cimbaline continued to write Henry after his November departure, but unfortunately only five of her letters from the next several months have survived. They reveal a woman who looked to the end of the war, or at least the completion of Henry's service, with acute anticipation. Too often alone in the family's home, she battled sharp headaches and painful lesions, but managed to elude the deadly smallpox outbreak that afflicted many neighbors, including her brother- and sister-in-law. Ever frustrated with life in Mascoutah, Cimbaline exclaimed, "How glad I will be to git out of this dirty hole and git some pure are [air]."[6]

An extended visit to the nearby farm of Charles Rayfield, the Fikes' brother-in-law, was a relief, especially to Ellie, but subsequent letters reaffirmed Cimbaline's desire to leave St. Clair County for good. When Henry asked what line of work he ought to pursue after the war, she replied that her greatest hope would be that he pledge to never settle in Mascoutah again. "That would have just pleased me to a tea," she wrote.[7] The final paragraph of Cimbaline's last extant letter urged her husband to consider relocating to California. Moved by his wife's pleas, he likewise fixed his eyes toward the future and began to seek buyers for their Illinois property. "A good many Americans are selling off their farms, and leaving this vicinity," he noted in his diary. "Good land is bringing a good price—some $75 per acre. I think some of selling mine."[8] Where they might go was a yet-unsettled question.

❧

November 30, 1864

Steamer *Mollie McPike*, Cumberland River, Tennessee

Dear Cimbaline,
We have not yet learned our destination—whether we will disembark and remain near Nashville, or push out into the interior south. I suppose our

---

6. C. Fike to H. Fike, January 3, 1865, FP.
7. C. Fike to H. Fike, January 22, 1865, FP.
8. Henry C. Fike Diaries (hereafter HFD), February 11, 1865.

movements will depend upon the maneuvres of the enemy. As soon as I can learn what we are going to do, I will immediately apprise you.

Our boys are all well, and in good spirits. Nothing new. I will close for this evening, and probably add a few words in the morning.

Your affectionate husband,
Henry.

December 4, 1864
In Line of Battle, Two Miles South West of Nashville, Tennessee

Dear Cimbaline,
I expect you will think that I am a long time writing to you. From the circumstances surrounding us, it has been impossible for me to have an opportunity to write at all.

The day before we arrived here, our forces, two corps strong, had a hard engagement with the enemy, under Gen. Hood, at the town of Franklin, only 18 miles from this city. Our loss, in this engagement, was about one thousand men, while that of the enemy was some eight or ten thousand. The heavy loss on the part of the enemy, compared with ours, was owing to the fact that our men fought behind fortifications. After this engagement, the enemy being in very large force, our men fell back to this city. That was on the night of the 1st of this month. On the next day, all the forces of ours were placed in line of battle, around the city, about a mile from the suburbs of town. Our line must be some twelve miles long. Our troops have all thrown up breastworks in front of their line. Since we have landed here, we have been placed in four different positions. Night before last our men worked all night on their breastworks, and yesterday afternoon we were changed to another locality, and the men worked again most of the night throwing up works.[9] The enemy came up yesterday, and engaged our pickets. It is very hilly where we are, and from some of the hills, one can see a good distance. Our men could discover the enemy moving from place to place. Several of our batteries have shelled the woods where they are, but brought from them no response. During last night, the gunboats carried on a most vigorous shelling on the river

---

9. Miller noted that government employees, including clerks, mechanics, and other laborers, constructed some of the inner lines of fortifications. MJMP, December 2–3, 1864.

a few miles below the city. Since I have been sitting here writing, some of our batteries close by have been shelling the enemy. A good many think we will have a fight here, before the thing is done. If the enemy does come, they may expect to get a good thrashing, for we are fully prepared for them. If we should have a fight, I will write immediately and give you the full result, so far as we are concerned.

Your affectionate husband,
Henry.

December 6, 1864

Camp at the Breastworks, Nashville, Tennessee

Dear Cimbaline,
Yesterday, I went outside our breastworks, down to the picket lines, and watched our boys skirmishing with the enemy. I could very plainly see the 'Johnnies' come out and fire at our men, some of them mounted. Later in the day Col. Merriam and I took a ride for a couple of miles round the breastworks to our left. We could see the rebels' line of fortifications very plainly, a half or three quarters of a mile from ours. Our batteries shelled the enemy more or less all day, but it did not seem to scare them much. In fact, they don't seem to be of the 'scary kind.' It is yet difficult to form an opinion as to what they design doing here—whether they intend fighting here, or merely aim to engage our attention here, while they attempt something elsewhere.[10] But you may rest assured that we are prepared for them at any point.

Your affectionate husband,
Henry.

December 7, 1864

Camp at the Breastworks, Nashville, Tennessee

Dear Cimbaline,
The line of breastworks our men have thrown up, when viewed from some one of the numerous high hills around here, presents one of the

---

10. Hood's options, had he liberated Nashville from Union occupation, included moving from middle Tennessee into the Union state of Kentucky and, if successful, reinforcing Lee in Virginia or attacking the rear of Grant's army at Petersburg, while Sherman's army remained further South. Daniel, *Conquered*, 319.

grandest spectacles ever beheld. We have here in the line of battle, most of whom are visible, some forty thousand troops, whose camps dot every hill and speckle every valley. The enemy, too, is near at hand in strong force, to all appearances. Although our boys feel well prepared, yet, every day, they are adding something to their works—making a slight change here, or adding on something there. Our batteries have been at work an hour this morning, shelling the woods. I can hear a dozen shots a minute while I am writing. . . . Nashville is not as nice a town as Memphis, in my opinion. The State Capitol building is a fine structure, and there is one mansion near our camp, which exceeds anything I have yet seen in Dixie.[11]

Your affectionate husband,
Henry.

December 11, 1864

At the Breastworks, Nashville, Tennessee

Dear Cimbaline,
This is a cold morning. We are all as closely housed up as you please. Last night every thing froze up hard. The rumor, yesterday, was, that the rebels had withdrawn a few miles from our immediate front. There are some in our front, anyhow, whether the enemy has gone or not. I suppose, this cold snap, the 'Johnnies' don't feel much like fighting.[12]

I feel quite well and hearty, and am standing the cold weather very well.
Your affectionate husband,
Henry.

December 19, 1864

Near Franklin, Tennessee

Dear Cimbaline,
I suppose you will want to hear from me. You, no doubt, will be surprised at my short letter. We had two hard days' fight at Nashville, on the 15" and

---

11. The Tennessee state capitol had been completed in 1859, after fourteen years of construction.

12. The Nashville press, affirming Henry's diary, wrote, "Friday night five rebel soldiers came in on one part of our line, and gave themselves up. They stated that their sufferings from cold and hunger were too great; so they concluded to change their mode of life." *Nashville Daily Union*, December 11, 1864, 3.

16th of this month. . . . The fighting was terrific and grand. I never saw it equaled. You, will no doubt, get all the particulars in the newspapers. . . . Our boys are in the highest of spirits, and we are after Hood. I have not slept any hardly for the two past nights. It has rained for the last three days, & we are all wet. . . . I hope you are well by this time. I wish I had more time to write. I could tell a great deal about the fight, &c. &c. . . . I must quit. We are on the move. I hear cannonading in the front. We must be off. We captured 300 prisoners out here yesterday morning, or rather the night before.

Your affectionate husband,
Henry.

December 21, 1864
Near Spring Hill, 33 Miles South of Nashville, Tennessee

Dear Cimbaline,
Since we left Nashville, we have suffered more from inclement weather and irregular marching, than we have any where else experienced, during the same length of time, since we have been soldiering. This is the fifth day out; and we have marched only thirty odd miles in that time;—but it has been done by little odds and ends—sometimes going into camp in the forenoon, then breaking up camp, perhaps near sundown, and then be on the road, till eight or nine o'clock at night;—and all this through mud and continuous rain,—for it has rained nearly all the time we have been out. Two of these nights I could not get up to the regiment with my teams, on account of other wagons being mired down or upset in the road ahead of ours. We had to camp our teams right by the roadside, and wait until daylight, before we could proceed. All the sleep I got one night, was under the shed of an old corn-crib where I lay on three rails, without any thing to cover myself more than the clothes I had on. Another night, we camped our teams in the road; after we fed our animals and ate a cracker or two, and supped a little coffee, I made my bed on top of the fence by the roadside. You may think it pretty strange for a person to sleep on top of a fence, but I did so. It was a stone fence, and I pushed off the top stones to make my bed something near level, though not by any means, smooth and soft, and stretched myself out upon it, with the same allowance of covering I had on the other occasioned referred to.

You may imagine this kind of comfort, when thus situated, and the wind blowing, and the rain falling by spells. But this is only soldiering. And that is what we enlisted for. I am, however, somewhat glad our time is now only something over eight months more. Notwithstanding all thus, our men stand it very well.

I have lost so much sleep lately that I must quit and go to bed. We have a good place to sleep to-night, and I want to make up some of my lost time.

Your affectionate husband,
Henry.

December 23, 1864
On Duck River, 40 Miles South of Nashville, Tennessee

Dear Cimbaline,
I hardly know what the real news is relative to Hood's position and movements in our front. All I do know certainly is, that he was badly whipped at Nashville, and is now retreating as fast as he can, while we are rather hurrying him up a little; though he has managed to retard our movements very much by destroying the bridges after he passes over them;— and the streams are so high from recent rains, that we have to bridge all of them before we can pass.[13] Still rumor places Hood not so very far in our advance after all; as his rearguard were seen at this river, when our front arrived here. Hood's teams must be giving out, as we find abandoned wagons all along the roadside, and various 'traps and trumpery' scattered everywhere. We found some twelve or fifteen wagons and two pieces of artillery, which he had been compelled to leave at this river, no doubt, for the want of transportation, or rather teams.

We all feel that we have done our duty. And the greatest wonder of all, and for which we should be ever grateful to our Heavenly Father, is that while we gained our victory by one charge after another upon the rebels

---

13. L. H. Eicholtz explained the predicament faced by his fellow Federal engineers: "We are making but slow progress, on account of the high water and the mass of wreck and iron in the stream, which it is next to impossible to remove. Our ropes freeze and stiffen, and the men are scarcely able to hold themselves on the scaffolding on account of the ice.... We are doing all that can be done under the circumstances." L. H. Eicholtz to Wm. D. Whipple, United States War Department, *War of the Rebellion* (hereafter OR), ser. 1, vol. 45, pt. 2, 299.

works, causing them to fly in consternation, this done, with so little loss on our part.—only about one thousand in killed and wounded.

Your affectionate husband,

Henry.

December 26, 1864

Near Lynn,[14] Giles County, Tennessee, 65 Miles South of Nashville

Dear Cimbaline,

You will discover from the heading of my letter that we are getting down pretty well into the land of Dixie in our pursuit of Hood's retreating army. . . . We are traveling upon a turnpike road, otherwise our march would be impossible; and even this road is so badly cut up, that it is nearly impassable, in some places. But if Hood can go it, we will be found trying. My understanding is that Gen. Thomas has ordered troops from Chattanooga, Murfreesboro and other places, to move across the country, and head off Hood's army. I am afraid bad roads will prevent the full accomplishment of this. But, should they succeed, we will have Genl. Hood in an extremely tight position; and he could hardly, then, get across the Tennessee river.[15]

Many of the citizens of this country have been entirely stripped of ever bit of moveable property they possessed, in the shape of stock, grain and eatables. This after now I stopped to warm my feet at a man's house, on the roadside, where one of our wounded cavalry men had been left. The man was quite along in years, I should think fifty-five or sixty years old. He told me he raised 26 acres of nice corn, & had a good stock of horses, cattle, hogs &c., but now, he has nothing—yes, nothing—everything gone—corn and all, and even all his fences torn down and burned up. An army traveling through a country is a terrible & awful affair, to the inhabitants thereof. When we camp, we always look out for a good fence, from which to get dry wood. Even while I am writing these lines to you,

---

14. Here, Henry likely meant Lynnville, a Giles County village situated between Columbia and Pulaski.

15. A Unionist paper in Nashville was equally skeptical of the rebels' chances of eluding Federal pursuit, observing, "Our forces are still pressing Hood, who appears to have lost most of his intelligent qualities. The Tennessee is very high, its banks being overflowed at several points." "Latest from the Front," *Nashville Daily Union*, December 28, 1864, 2.

I am warming my feet by a fire made from rails. I pity these people, for humanity's sake alone—most of them are rebels at heart, and deserve no mercy at our hands. What ought a rebel and traitor to expect from his country;—or those fighting in its defense? . . . I should have like to have been home yesterday, and taken a Christmas dinner with you. Thank fortune! I think my last Christmas has passed in the army. Capt. Whitaker and I had a talk about our last Christmas dinner in Memphis. I presume you well remember it.

Your affectionate husband,
Henry.

January 2, 1865

Cliffton,[16] on the Tennessee River, Tennessee

Dear Cimbaline,
We arrived at this place this afternoon about 4 o'clock, after marching some sixteen miles to-day. Yesterday we marched about fifteen miles. For the last two days, the roads have been very good, and traveling was consequently much better. During the night of the 30th inst., the weather turned extremely cold, and snowed a little, and the day following was very cold. Many of our soldiers suffered from cold feet. We have been marching over such rocky and gravelly country, that their shoes have become badly worn; but this difficulty will now be done away with, as we expect to draw all the shoes and stockings we desire to-morrow.

This town is situated on the east bank of the Tennessee river, about 35 miles below Pittsburg Landing. The place, to all appearances, has, once, contained some seventy-five houses; but nearly all that is now left, is the naked chimneys, which seem to stand as monuments of the desolating effects of war. There are now but four or five houses here.

Since we left Nashville we have marched about 130 miles. We went about 65 miles a little west of south, to Pulaski, where we turned to the west, or rather a little to the north of west, and 65 more miles of hard and muddy marching brought us to this place. We found several boats here with supplies. Our destination now seems to be, still further up the Tennessee river,—rumor says, to Eastport, which is some 80 miles from here. There is also a vague rumor in camp, that we are going there, and

---

16. Clifton sits in Wayne County, just north of the Alabama border.

will go into camp and rest awhile. We hope so; for I can assure you that it would be relished. Since our regiment left Memphis, last January, it has marched 2000 miles by land, 300 miles by railroad, and 2500 by steamboat, making in all 4800 miles it has moved in a little over eleven months. I think that ought to do for one year.

Our boys are in very good health, and fine spirits. The war news, as it comes up from every corner, giving such flattering information, inspires us all with the belief, that our term of service will see this war terminating.

Your affectionate husband,
Henry.

January 3, 1865
Mascoutah, Illinois

Dear Henry,
My health is not emproving very fast. I seam to linger along and feal bad all the time, yet I am able to be up and aroung in my room, I have been truble for the last four weekes with geathers and ulcers in my head and lounges. I think I have cought and raised more than a galen of corruption within the last tow weekes I am not better within a few day, I entend to see Dr Welch,[17] and know his opinon Polly Fike is very sick. She was taken last Saterday with the winter fever. Dr Welch is attenden her case. Osbay is still improven conciderble of a small pox in town. The famly south of us had severl cases, allso west of us, Mr Cranes[18] famly. Nothen new agoing on in town to my knoweledge, The 27. of Dec the Masons gave a Masonick supper, had a dance in the flower house, neare the drug [sic?] tree. Evry body was thare of course, but me

Mother went out to Charles yesterday to spend the week. Charles started for [?] and to see his daughter at Jackinville[19] Next Saderday. If i am able, thay are going to send aftr me, and takes me out to there house to stay tell I am better. Thay come after me last Saterday and yesterday to git out and stay untell I am better, but I was not able to go. I think by Sa-

---

17. This physician, the Bavaria-born Wolfgang Welsch, was also a resident of Mascoutah. United States Federal Census (hereafter USFC), 1860.

18. Neighbors Isaac and Mary Crane had six children, ranging in age from three to fourteen. USFC, 1860.

19. Jacksonville, Illinois, sits about a hundred miles north of Mascoutah, between Springfield and the Mississippi River.

derday I can go if it is a good day How glad I will be to git out of this dirty hole and it some pure are. I think it will do me more gud than meddison
No more at presant
from, Cimbaline

January 4, 1865

Clifton, Wayne County, Tennessee

Dear Cimbaline,
I have spent a good part of this day in reading. After marching through mud and rain and cold for nearly three weeks, as we have had to do, since leaving the city of Nashville, one is well prepared to fully enjoy a little rest and comfort in good quarters. . . . I believe, in my last letter, I stated that Eastport is in northern Alabama. Since then, I have found I was mistaken; it being in the extreme northeast corner of Mississippi, about 20 or 25 miles east of Corinth, on the Tennessee river. . . . It is very monotonous and tedious waiting day after day, this way, for an opportunity to move, and I shall be exceedingly glad when orders come to get away from here.

We have no mail facilities here, and consequently can get no letters or papers. I hear, that probably a mail boat will come up in a few days, and bring us some information from our friends at home.

Your affectionate husband,
Henry.

January 6, 1865

Mascoutah, Illinois

Dear Henry,
Polly is very sick yet. She has the winter fever. Anderson little girl is very sick. Osbay has been growing worse every sence Polly has been sick, at times he will rave just like he had no sence

We have very cool wether hear now, snow on the ground about five inches deep, small pox still ragen in town yet

I have plased my self under Dr Welch treatment, I hope he will cure me soon. He gives me a great deal of incourgement Where he told me the truth or not, I am not able to tell yet, I suppose time will prove it I have promist to go out to Charles to morrow. I suppose I will rop up good and try to go. I expect to remain out thare untell I am better, If it is all winter.

Ellie is quit well, and is so bad I do not know what to do with her, while she is with Perry

No more at presant From Cimbaline

January 8, 1865

Clifton, Wayne County, Tennessee

Dear Cimbaline,

Just before daylight, this morning, a boat reached here from above, bringing Genl. A. J. Smith. This also brought an officer and some men from each regiment of our command, who are going back to Nashville, to get the baggage and stored property we all left there, when we started in pursuit of Hood. They will go down the Tennessee river, and then up the Cumberland to Nashville, and return the same way by boat. Capt. Randall[20] is the officer in charge, from our regiment. I presume I should have been sent back myself, were I not in charge of all our transportation, and must see it up safe with the command. The officers from above report that it is the calculation to go into something like winter quarters at Eastport, for about two months. Every thing, just now, looks a good deal that way. I am sure we are entirely willing on that score.

Your affectionate husband,
Henry.

January 11, 1865

Out in the Country, Illinois

Dear Henry,

I am out at Charles Rayhills I came out last Sadordray evening. I had a very pleasant day to come out. It has been very coold every sence I came out [struck out]. Sunday it begain to snow, and Monday night untell last eening. To day is clear and very cold, just right for slaying We have had

---

20. Captain Andrew J. Randall, forty-two, was a farmer from Aviston, just to the northeast of Mascoutah. Fred Delap, Illinois Civil War Muster and Descriptive Rolls Database, Illinois State Archives, Office of the Illinois Secretary of State, https://www.ilsos.gov/isaveterans/civilMusterSearch.do (hereafter Delap, ICWMDR).

so much cool wether this winter it allmost freazes me.[21] I have no nuse to write that will be interresting to you, only Dr Ross came out yesterday, he and Charles went hunten and killed six prara [prairie] chickens We had a chicken dinner. . . . The nuse is that the sick folkes were some better yesterday, That duchman came and tld me. he could not git the money to pay downg for the forme now. He thought perhaps he could withen five or six weekes. He wos not positive. If he could not git the money he wanted to rente it again. I told him he could have it for three do. per achar . He said he would not pay it, he wantes the house repaired and a well dug.

He paid me the rent for last year. he charged me $9.50 cents for repairing and maken railes for the forme he said, you promist that he should take it out of the rent. They are all well and hear and in good spirets, and think they will git some good slay rides. Charles is in a hurry to go to town. I must close. From Cimbaline

January 13, 1865
Eastport, Mississippi

Dear Cimbaline,
I have been busy, to-day, in and around my tent, 'fixing up' and making things as comfortable as I can. John McGowan and I have made for our selves a good 'bunk,' so we can now sleep up off the floor in something like a decent manner. Besides this, we have our tent floored and a good stove for heating purposes. Taking all things around our 'shebang' into consideration, we have a good cozy warm place. It would much amuse you to go around through the regiment, and see the various kinds and sizes of the shanties and huts the boys have built or are now constructing. They are of all imaginable lengths, widths and heights;—some made of round logs, some of split logs, some of slabs, and a few of boards;—some are large enough for eight or ten persons, while others will accommodate not more than two. The usual number living 'together' is generally four or five. The ingenuity displayed in building and fashioning these huts is very various, and sometimes quite amusing. After all, notwithstanding the soldier has a hard life to generally endure, there are many little spots

---

21. One central Illinois paper agreed, reporting, "A considerable fall of snow occurred on Monday and Tuesday, to the depth of six or eight inches. . . . The prospects for sleighing is good." *Champaign County Gazette,* January 13, 1865, 3.

of pleasure and comfort scattered along, through his military history. If so, I am sure that, after campaigning constantly for nearly a year, the privilege of enjoying good 'winter quarters' is one of these 'spots.'[22] . . . Our command very much stands in need of a good supply of almost every thing that the soldier needs in the way of clothing—it has been so long since they have drawn any.

Your affectionate husband,
Henry

January 15, 1865

Out in the Country, Illinois

Dear Henry
Again I take another opportunity of writing you another letter to informe you that we are still out in the country. Last Thursday evening I received five letters from you, all maild at the same time. Sence then I have not received any from you. . . . They have been good slaying all the past week. Of course we have had a great many collers, The girles had had some young men to call on tham John Griffin called hear one evening last week to take them slayriding to Mrs Rentehlar.[23] They went and had a very plesant time. He is a widower, lives foure miles wst of Mascoutah, he told me he knew you very well. Friday after noon Mrs Van Winkle[24] came out, and brout her brother who is hear on a visit, he has served three

---

22. Miller recorded that soldiers scavenged whatever building materials they could find from nearby houses, which they destroyed to construct their own winter quarters. MJMP, January 8–12, 1865.

23. Elizabeth Rentchler, fifty-nine, was a wealthy widow who lived outside of Mascoutah. USFC, 1860; *History of St. Clair County*, 357. The most recent census enumeration in St. Clair County listed a John Griffin, a fifty-seven-year-old farmer, who was married to Melinda Griffin, but she did not die until November 25, 1878. USFC, 1860; "Malinda Jane (Rains) Griffin," Find a Grave Index, https://www.findagrave.com/memorial/70917698/malinda-jane-griffin, accessed December 9, 2023.

24. Lucinda (Padfield) Vanwinkle, who married Jesse Vanwinkle on September 18, 1856. "Illinois Statewide Marriage Index, 1763–1900," Illinois State Archives, https://apps.ilsos.gov//isavital/marriageSearch.do, accessed December 9, 2023. The 1850 census enumeration lists four Padfield brothers who would have been old enough to serve in the military during the Civil War—William, Thomas, James, and Joseph. It appears that only Joseph served, in Company C of the 117th Illinois, but records show that he, like his brothers, was a farmer and not a surgeon. USFC, 1850; ICWMDR; Civil War Soldiers and Sailors System database, National Park Service, https://www.nps.gov/civilwar/soldiers-and-sailors-database.htm, accessed December 9, 2023 (hereafter CWSS).

years in the armmy as a Surgen. He appeared to be quite a gentleman he wos dressed in full unaform. Ellie was very much pleased with seeing sholder straps again She went to him and got up in his lap, and asked him if he was a soldier, and told him her, papa, was downg in Dixiea shouten copper heads and rebles, That what he is a doing, The Do. was quite delited with her

Polly is giten well. She has had a very heard spell of sickness. I hope it will be the meanes of maken a better women of her, It can be plainly seen, that Osbays affliction has made quite a change in him, at least we can see that he appears to be much better man and expreses him self the same I think I am approven sence I come out in the country at enerste. Charles tock Charity and I last Thursday evening slayriding in town. We call on Dr Ross and famly, and Wille Fike and lady.[25]

I will study on the contents of one of your letters, will give you my opinon some other time concerning to whot buisness you will go in to, when you come home. I much rather heard you say, that you did not feel that you could ever come home and settle in Mascoutah again. That would have just pleased me to a tea . . & . . I must close for this time.

Yours from Cimbaline

January 16, 1865
Eastport, Mississippi

Dear Cimbaline,
Our location here, as a military camp, is very nice, though the country is very hilly. We are in the extreme north-east corner of the state of Mississippi. The front of my tent opens to the eastward, and we are situated on a high eminence. As I sit in the door of my tent, I can look just across Bear creek, only about a quarter of a mile distant to the eastward, and see the hills and pines of Alabama; while, just across the Tennessee river, to the north of camp, only some half a mile distant the woods and hills of Tennessee greet the gazing eye. . . . Maj. Genl. Thomas arrived here yesterday morning, and has established his head-quarters upon shore, in our corps. I presume his advent among us signifies something; though, what that 'something' means, I am, as yet, unable to form a definite opin-

---

25. Here, Cimbaline likely means William Fike, twenty-five, and Julian Fike, twenty. USFC, 1860.

ion. I expect his plans and operations will depend considerably upon the movements of the rebels. Rumor says Hood has been superceded by Forrest; and, if so, we may expect to have to run about considerably this spring and summer after the old 'cunning fox,' who is always so hard to catch or pen up. But, we are ready to try him, when the time comes. . . .[26] Give Ellie a kiss for he papa and tell her to write to me how 'Dolly' is getting along—if her 'family' has increased any yet. My love and regard to all.

Your affectionate husband,
Henry.

January 19, 1865
Eastport, Mississippi

Dear Cimbaline,
The winter quarters of our regiment and, the troops generally, continue to improve, as the men, from day to day, continue to bestow more labor upon their huts and shanties. The consequence of the vast amount of cutting and chopping which has taken place, is, that most of the hills and hollows are being almost entirely stripped of their timber and wood; and, should our stay here be prolonged to many weeks, we shall have to commence procuring our firewood from some other place, than just at our doors. A person that never saw the like, can form no conception, whatever, of the vast amount of timber an army of fifteen or twenty thousand troops will consume, in the short space of a few weeks.

Yesterday and to-day, camp has been full of all kinds of expressions and comments upon the probabilities of peace,—commenced by the reports brought here in northern papers of the 13" inst. About the only information these papers give is, that Rebel Commissioners, three in number, had started to Washington City, with propositions for peace from Jeff. Davis' dominions, and were at Genl. Grant's headquarters desiring per-

---

26. A day earlier, General Thomas reported to Washington that Forrest's cavalry remained active amid the Army of Tennessee's harried retreat southward: "Forrest is at and about Okolona with his main force, with small advance parties at Jacinto, Boonville, and Corinth. Forrest's command, as well as Hood's infantry force, is said to be very much broken up and in a disorganized condition." G. H. Thomas to H. W. Halleck, January 15, 1865, OR, ser. 1, vol. 45, pt. 2, 593.

mission to proceed on their mission of mercy.[27] It would be impossible for me to undertake to give you the remarks made, upon the strength of these rumors, by our men. Conversation and an expression of ideas would be carried on for a while, when perhaps, the crowd would commence to introduce their witty remarks upon the probable issue of the affair. One would say he was 'sorry he couldn't get to serve Uncle Sam three years, as he had agreed to'; another one would remark that he 'would write home, and tell them he would be there to assist in sowing spring oats'; and still another, 'that Susan would have to 'hurry up her cakes', as that wedding would have to come off a few months sooner than heretofore calculated.

Your affectionate husband,
Henry

January 22, 1865
Out in the Country, Illinois

Dear Henry,
Ellie enjoyes her self finley out in the country She said last night, Ma, let us live out hear all the time. I like to live in the Country I have not enjoyed myself as well as I expected to. I thought if I would come out hear and stay tow or three weekes, it would entirley cure me. All this past week I have been very unwell with another seveare cold. I have taken in my head. My simptoms was the same as they was when I was sick I am better than I was. I am inhalen some meddison now for my head. I think it helps me some I hope it will cure me entirley any one to have there head diseased, it makes them feel that they are diseased all over, I never was trubled in this way before I think I will go home to morrow if I can Our quartly meeting comes of tow weekes from yesterday and to day in Mascoutah

Osbay thinkes of starten to California as soon as Polly gites well, for his health. He thinkes a trip thare will cure him. I would like to go with him

---

27. Such reports were confirmed on January 29 when the three Confederate commissioners that Jefferson Davis sent north—Vice President Alexander Stephens, Senator Robert M. T. Hunter, and Assistant Secretary of War John Campbell—arrived at Petersburg, Virginia, to inquire about terms of peace. The so-called Hampton Roads conference broke down soon after Lincoln flatly declared his unwillingness to discuss any terms or conditions until the Confederates submitted to the authority of the United States and agreed to reunion. Sanders, "Jefferson Davis," 803–826.

if you are willing. What do you think about it. Write soon and let me know Tell Mr Marcal, I was glad to hear that he is still liven. I allway think of him when I look at fancy soap, and when I see ice cream ask him if Mrs Sirel is still in Memphis I must stopt writing. Charles is going to town to mail some lettrs for himself. I will give him this one. No lettrs sence last Thursday a week
 From Cimbaline

January 28, 1865

Eastport, Mississippi

Dear Cimbaline,
For four entire days, prior to yesterday—our entire command was out of bread and flour. A good many began to think 'hard times' had set in. The Commissaries issued *corn* to the troops instead of 'hard tack' or flour. A great many jokes and quaint remarks have been called forth by this issue of corn. One of our boys asked the commissary sergeant when he was going to draw *hay* for them, Another one said he wanted the Quarter Master to get him *shod* as the ground was hard and rough. Another good joke perpetrated was by some of the 178th N. Y. Vols, a regiment which belongs to our brigade. About half of one company got *halters* and put around the necks of the other half, and led them about a quarter of a mile down to the creek *to water*, passing, in their route, by Maj. Gen. Thomas' Head Quarters. You can conjecture the sport and laugh this proceeding brought forth. But this reign of *parched corn and hominy* is now about over. A lot of good flour arrived here yesterday, and slap-jacks, and biscuits have been the rage for the past twenty-four hours. I presume plenty of breadstuff will be here in a day or two. . . . I hope to be able to come home in the course of —— a few weeks.
 Your affectionate husband,
 Henry.

February 24, 1865, 2 1/2 o'clock p.m

Steamer *Missouri*. About 40 miles above Memphis

Dear Cimbaline,
There are about one hundred white soldiers and two hundred colored ones on board our boat, going down the river, to join various regiments

into which they have enlisted as recruits. . . . Although I am going away from home, perhaps to be absent from you and Ellie longer than I ever have been at any one time, in my life, yet, I am happy to think that this is my *last time* of being so long away from my dear family and mother. As time will probably slip away rapidly with me, while we are moving from point to point, I want you and Ellie and mother to pass off your time in the most pleasant manner you can, by visiting around among the connexion and friends. As soon as the nice spring weather sets in, set out on a long campaign of visiting, and see if you can find any better home for us than our present one. I am perfectly willing now, to sell out completely and leave Mascoutah, and, I am in earnest, when I say I want you to think about where we shall go, and what kind of business you would prefer I should engage in when I return home.[28] I know you will say to yourself, when you read this, that you don't know what kind of business to select for me. Well, you can think about it, and make a suggestion or two, any how.

Your affectionate husband,
Henry.

February 27, 1865

Steamer *Missouri*, Lying at Vicksburg, Mississippi

Dear Cimbaline,
Of course, you can't expect me to have much news to send you, while I am on the river. All we can see are a few old houses, and burnt up towns, and deserted, lonely-looking plantations. I notice that down in this latitude, spring is near at hand. The earliest budding trees, such as the elm, are beginning to swell their buds and look green. I presume I have bid adieu to winter, and will find that spring has fully set in, when I arrive at New Orleans. . . . As I feel considerable interest in the sale of my land, I hope you will keep me thoroughly posted in that matter. Who is selling and buying, and what land is bringing, &c. &c.

Tell Ellie I will write to her before very long. There is a little girl about her size with her mother, on board our boat, going to New Orleans, to see her father, who is a surgeon in our army.

---

28. Henry's diary entry the following day revealed that he had nearly accepted P. H. Postel's offer to buy his property for seventy-five dollars per acre. HFD, February 25, 1865.

Your affectionate husband,
Henry.

March 1, 1865

Steamer *Missouri*, Lying at New Orleans, Louisiana

Dear Cimbaline,
The weather down here is warm and pleasant. The woods and fields are green, and plenty of niggers can be seen in the plantations plowing & hoeing. For about fifty miles above the city of New Orleans, the banks of the river are covered with the most beautiful plantations I have ever seen in the south. The houses are all situated along on the immediate bank of the river, and the sugar mills to the rear a short distance; and these are so close to each other that they present the appearance of one continuous village on shore. Many of the houses are surrounded by nice groves of evergreens and orange trees, which are loaded with bountiful harvests of the golden fruit. You should have heard the remarks of some of the soldiers when they would pass an orange orchard. How they 'would like to forage around that plantation' one fellow said 'Just look at those niggers walking around there and *not eating oranges.*'[29]
Your affectionate husband,
Henry.

March 2, 1865

Camp Chalmette, Near New Orleans, Louisiana

Dear Cimbaline,
I arrived at camp this forenoon and found the boys generally well and in excellent spirits. Our camp is situated about six miles from the city of New Orleans, on the old battle-ground fought upon by the contending armies under Gen A. Jackson on the part of the United States and Gen.

---

29. Oranges were a somewhat expensive novelty to northern soldiers. During a Chicago winter, the price of one barrel of oranges—shipped from Havana, Cuba—sometimes exceeded twenty dollars, in contrast to green apples, more readily grown in a temperate Illinois climate, which could be had for $3.50 per barrel. "Chicago Daily Market," *Chicago Tribune,* January 2, 1865, 3; Chas. Hamilton, "Fruits and Fruit Trees," *Woodstock Sentinel,* March 1, 1865, 4.

Packenhous commanding the British forces, on the 8th day of January 1815. Since our troops arrived here, it has rained an immense amount, and the ground being so exceedingly level, it has been the muddiest military camp I ever saw; though it is now commencing to dry up some. ... Our command is under marching orders to go to Dauphine Island, at the mouth of Mobile river, as soon as proper transportation can be furnished, which may be in a few days, or may be a week or two.

Your affectionate husband,
Henry.

March 6, 1865
Camp Chalmette, Near New Orleans, Louisiana

Dear Cimbaline,
During last night our brigade received orders to be ready to embark upon steamers to-day. It is now 1 o'clock p.m. About an hour ago our regiment left camp and went down to the river. I have not ascertained the name of the vessel that they go aboard. The officer who takes my place in the old brigade has not yet reported; so I am still in camp. He will report some time this afternoon. Our teams do not go on the steamers with the troops, but will move across the country to the lake, and there take shipping, and go out into the gulf through another passage. If you will look at the map of the vicinity of New Orleans, you can plainly see how our troops can move down the river by steamers, and the teams can go a few miles to the lake, and then get out into the Gulf and reach the vicinity of Mobile. I think our teams will start to-morrow.

Your affectionate husband,
Henry.

March 9, 1865
Three Miles Northwest of New Orleans, Louisiana

Dear Cimbaline,
Our regiment bid adieu to New Orleans on the morning of the 7th inst. on board the Empire City. This ocean steamer was large enough to transport the entire brigade, of five regiments, making some 2000 men in all. All our 16th Corps. has not yet succeeded in getting off. This is owing to the difficulty of getting ocean vessels. Ordinary steamboats are not safe to

cross that part of the Gulf we shall have to traverse. The same day our brigade left, (the 7" inst.) our teams, and the supply train, moved from the old camp, six miles east of the city, to a much better encampment some three miles northwest of the city. We are close to the famous 'shell road,' which is considered the 'fashionable drive' of this city. The road is quite a fine thing, though considerably out of repair. Instead of McAdamizing the road with rock broken up, as we do in the north, this road is covered with small ocean shells, such as you frequently see in flower gardens and door yards, and the shells have become broken up and disintegrated, so that they make a road as smoothe as a floor.[30] The street rail-road, which is the finest in this city I have ever seen, runs out on this 'shell road', as far as where we are encamped, where the race grounds are located. I forgot to mention that this famous road continues on to the lake which is some three miles further to the north of us.

It is quite tedious, being separated as we are from our command, and not knowing when we will get with them again. We expect, probably, to move over to the lake in three or four days, where we are to embark upon the water and go across to Dauphine Island. I believe I mentioned in my last letter to you, that I was back with the regiment again. I have about fifteen of our men with me, to assist in getting our transportation along.

It has been wet and rainy most of the time since I arrived here. Night before last it rained and the wind blew almost a tornado. Yesterday it was clear and warm. Last night it rained again, and it is showery and windy to-day.

Your affectionate husband,
Henry

March 13, 1865

Camp Chalmette, Near New Orleans, Louisiana

Dear Cimbaline,
I was glad to learn that you and Ellie and mother were all well. One would think, from the tenor of your letter, that you was in ecstacies over my letter, intimating my willingness to sell off our property and seek another home. It is a serious and important matter to sell home and everything

---

30. Macadam roads drew their name from Scottish civil engineer John Loudon McAdam, who advocated roads made of small, broken stones, which traffic then compacted into a smooth traveling surface. Guldi, *Roads to Power*, 52–53.

belonging to it, and to launch out into the world among strangers, to find new friends and form new acquaintances and associations; and we should study the subject well, and act carefully and wisely. I want you to give the subject all the consideration you can while I am absent, that you may be enabled to give me the benefit of your counsel and advice.

It will be a week, to-morrow, since our brigade left here, and I am here yet; but I think, now, that we shall, very likely get off with our transportation, in two or three days.[31] It is only three miles from where we are now encamped, to the lake, where we are to go on board the boats that are to transport us to our destination. There is a report in the evening papers of this city, that there has been some little fighting near Mobile, between the rebs. and some of our troops who were sent there before we arrived here. But, I think no general advance upon that place will yet be made, until we are a little better organized for moving.

Your affectionate husband,
Henry

---

31. Fike, Miller, and others remained to await ships that were capable of hauling the brigade's horses, wagons, and ambulance trains. See MJMP, March 6, 1865.

CHAPTER 7

"The War Is at an End"

Fort Morgan, Alabama, to Montgomery, Alabama
March 1865 to July 1865

The last months of Henry Fike's enlistment found him farther from Cimbaline than at any point in his Civil War service. Previous campaigns had taken his comrades hundreds of miles from their Illinois homes, from the Louisiana bayous to the Kansas prairies, but the white sands and rolling waves of the Alabama gulf coast, where they arrived in March 1865, were another world away. The quartermaster of the 117th Illinois nevertheless gave thanks for the "the blessed privileges of the pen," which collapsed the physical distance that kept him from family and home. Through the end of the war the Fikes kept alive the correspondence that sustained their relationship across broad stretches of time and space, but of these final exchanges, only the letters from Henry have survived. A compelling testament of the Civil War's final days, these dispatches illuminated a deep yearning for peace and family after long years of sacrifice and separation.

From New Orleans, Henry sailed into the Gulf of Mexico toward Mobile Bay brimming with a confidence that Union victory was assured. Federals had gained control of the inlet that led into the bay a summer before, seizing the forts on the barrier islands that lined its entrance. Admiral David Farragut cautioned against a direct assault on the city, which was strongly fortified and tucked into the northwestern corner of the bay. "I can not believe that Mobile will be anything but a constant trouble and source of anxiety to us," he warned.[1] Seven months later, however, Union brigadier general Edward R. S. Canby prepared to capture Mobile by seizing the land on the east side of the bay and then firing on the city from across the estuary formed by the mouths of the Mobile and Tensaw Rivers.

---

1. McPherson, *War on the Waters*, 212.

Despite the news from Virginia that Grant and the Army of the Potomac threatened to overwhelm Lee's dwindling rebel force, residents of Mobile were ever determined to resist the Federal advance.[2] Two weeks later, just after Henry reached Dauphin Island, the *Mobile Evening News* declared, "This place will be fought to the last extremity. Whenever the Yankees see proper to open the ball, we are ready for the dance."[3] Yet after weeks of heavy shelling by Federal batteries, Confederates finally abandoned the city on Easter Sunday.[4]

The three divisions of A. J. Smith's 16th Army Corps marched northward into central Alabama after the fall of Mobile. Henry passed through the country's piney woods eager to receive war news but heard little more than croaking frogs and the anxious rumors of peace that bounced between comrades. Mail and news of any kind reached the 117th Illinois more slowly and sporadically than ever, thanks to the regiment's isolation and the cumulative destruction of the railroads, bridges, and telegraph wires that once linked the Deep South to the outside world. The Union forces in Montgomery, Alabama, did not receive official word of the surrenders by Generals Lee and Johnston until April 26, more than two weeks after the hostilities in Virginia and North Carolina had finally ceased. Such reports prompted cheers and hopes that Union troops might return home by Independence Day; the belated news that an assassin had murdered President Lincoln arrived days later, puncturing their exultation. One week later, Richard Taylor surrendered his Confederate troops in Alabama and Mississippi, and peace at last reached Henry's corner of the Civil War.[5]

For Union troops who garrisoned Montgomery and nearby towns, their mission now shifted to preserving law and order across the devastated countryside. Henry marveled at the revolutionary transformations evident in the former cradle of the Confederacy. Now empty was

---

2. As Confederate leaders in Richmond debated the enlistment of enslaved men, one local editor condemned the slowness of legislators and argued that desperate circumstances required swift action. He wrote on March 5, "Let the master take down the rifle from its rack, and with the servants who are willing and whom he can trust, volunteer in companies and troops for the defence of the land." "Negro Volunteers—The Duty of Masters," *Weekly Advertiser and Register*, March 4, 1865, 2.

3. "Local Intelligence," *Mobile Evening News*, March 20, 1865, 1; Andrews, *History of the Campaign*, 32–33.

4. Canby, Report No. 1, June 1, 1865, United States War Department, *War of the Rebellion* (hereafter OR), ser. 1, vol. 49, pt. 1, 91–99.

5. Hess, *Civil War in the West*, 291–292.

the statehouse where southern rebels had congregated "to devise those wicked and rebellious schemes for the destruction of our Union."[6] The arrival of a Federal fleet carrying a large number of United States Colored Troops inspired raucous jubilation among the area's formerly enslaved population. Thousands of Black men, women, and children thronged to the bluffs above the river landing, singing "John Brown's Body" and "The Battle Cry of Freedom." This scene of excitement, Henry wrote, "exceeded anything I ever saw of the kind." Local civilians, especially the most impoverished households, welcomed the end of war, as did the paroled rebel troops who returned to the area, but the presence of these Black troops elicited discernable unease among white residents, who looked, in Henry's soldierly slang, "chawed" by the sight.

His brief stay near Montgomery yielded other glimpses of the double-edged meanings of emancipation. Freed people proved eager to aid the advancing Union army, alerting Henry and his comrades to the presence of hidden caches of food and horses. The bodies of Black people who streamed into town, however, bore proof of the brutal fury that whites unleashed on the formerly enslaved.[7] An Alabama newspaper claimed that Union soldiers held people of color in even greater contempt than did southern slavers: "The negro has never found a friend except in his master. Of all persons the Yankees hate him most and treat him worst."[8] Henry's observations from this period, filled with more racist slurs than his early letters, do little to contradict such assertions. After watching an overseer whip a Black woman on April 22, he purchased a strap used for such floggings and justified the acquisition as a southern "curiosity."[9]

Stifling heat and poor health loomed over Henry's impatient final weeks in the South. Once soldiers had arranged their quarters in the camp established just outside of Montgomery, they found diversion wherever they could, often by swimming, singing, or reading; many turned to alcohol.[10] Officers preferred to play games of "town-ball," and Henry,

---

6. H. Fike to C. Fike, April 29, 1865, Henry C. and Lucy C. Fike Papers.
7. "Shocking Brutality," *Montgomery Daily Mail*, May 15, 1865, 2.
8. *The Journal*, April 13, 1865, 2.
9. Henry C. Fike Diaries (hereafter HFD), April 24, 1865.
10. Years earlier, the assistant quartermaster praised Henry as one of the regiment's sober officers, but Henry's June purchase of two bottles of wine, noted in his diary, perhaps suggests an erosion of his temperance beliefs. See Monroe Joshua Miller Papers (hereafter MJMP), August 6, 1863, and HFD, June 30, 1865.

according to his assistant, emerged as the best player in the regiment.[11] When Cimbaline encouraged Henry to consider resigning and return home, he was at first conflicted, but a week's consideration convinced him that he could wait no more. After sporadic complaints of high fever and diarrhea, he obtained a medical certificate of physical disability, which he tendered with his immediate resignation on June 21, months before his scheduled September discharge. He waited three uncomfortable weeks to learn that his superiors finally accepted his resignation, during which time illness swept across even more of the Montgomery encampment.[12] Although shadowed by lingering sickness, his long-anticipated journey home retraced familiar steps, taking him to Mobile, New Orleans, Memphis, Cairo, and then, at last, Mascoutah. The reactions of Cimbaline and Ellie to Henry's return have been lost to history, but the finality of his clipped diary entry on July 26—"Though not well, I came home—'*Home again Home again*' from the war, for the last time"—suggested happiness enough for all.

March 19, 1865
Near Fort Morgan, Mobile Point, Opposite Mobile, Alabama

Dear Cimbaline,
I expect it will be a good many days before you will receive this letter, now that I am so far away from home. The distance from here to Mascoutah, by river &c., must be nearly fifteen hundred miles. I cann't fully realize the great distance between us, and feel that I could not endure the absence, were I not possessed of the power of communicating with you, by the blessed privileges of the pen.

On the morning of the 17" inst. I mailed a letter to you, in the city of New Orleans, as I went to town to get some Commissary stores for my mess. . . . We did not run the first night, and lay up near Fort Pike. Next morning we shoved out early, and had a fine and pleasant run all day. We coasted along some three to six miles from the shore of the main land, and passed, in our route, near Cat, Ship and Dog Islands, passed be-

---

11. MJMP, May 20, 1865.
12. HFD, July 12, 1865.

tween Round and Horn Islands, near Hurricane Island, through 'Grants Pass," on the north side of Dauphin Island, round to Fort Gaines on the east end of this Island; which we reached about 4 o'clock p.m. on the 18" inst.[13] The troops on our boat, here, got off, when the boat crossed over to where we are now, & we took off our teams here, last night. This 'Mobile Point' on which we are now 'stopping' or camping whichever you please to consider it, is connected with the mainland. The regiment is yet on Dauphin Island, and I have not seen them since they left New Orleans, and I may not join them for several days, yet, as I understand that the troops are being sent from the Island to the mainland several miles up Mobile bay.

From all appearances, it is very evident that a large expedition is to start from this coast for the purpose of penetrating the central portion of Alabama. Probably, the first place, and a strong one it seems from all accounts, to be taken is Mobile. After that, no doubt, Selma, Montgomery and other important places will succumb to the victorious march of the Union Army. But, of the plan and operations of these movements we shall have to wait and see.

Mobile Point is a long, narrow point of land, consisting mostly of sand, some mile wide where we are camped. Round the edges, the waves from the Gulf and Bay have thrown the white sand up some fifteen feet high, which make a good breakwater against any incursions from the tempestuous waves. I took a ride with one of the boys, this afternoon, out along the Gulf side of this Point. It was a most beautiful sight to see the huge, majestic waves from the Gulf come rolling, & foaming towards the shore, bringing in with them the nice sea-shells &c. For the first time I 'snuffed' the pure sea-breeze; and I can tell you, that I never inhaled as sweet and exhilarating atmosphere in my life. It is beyond description. I know it would cure you sound and well in a short time. We are camped on a small arm of Mobile Bay, on the inside of Mobile Point,—the side next to the main-land. My tent is within 25 feet of the waters' edge. The weather is nice and warm here, and I had a pleasant bathe in the bay to-day. These waters are full of oysters and crabs, and our boys are in the water after them all day long. The oysters are very nice, and I had a fine mess of them for supper about an hour ago. I have eaten 'lots' of them since I came to New Orleans, and like them, now, very well.

---

13. Confederate forces surrendered Fort Gaines on August 8, 1864, during the battle for Mobile Bay. Andrews, *History of the Campaign*, 17.

Your affectionate husband,
Henry

March 22, 1865
Near Fort Morgan, On Mobile Point, Opposite Mobile, Alabama

Dear Cimbaline,
I am still lying here on Mobile Point, awaiting moving orders to march and rejoin the regiment. Within the last three days our Corps has been moved from Dauphin Island which is at the mouth of Mobile Bay, across and landed on the east side of the Bay, about ten or twelve miles north of where I am. From all appearances our Corps is to march northward on the east side of the Bay, while the 13" Army Corps is to go up on the west side. I presume the two armies will unite somewhere in the vicinity of Mobile. . . . I have heard heavy cannonading yesterday afternoon, and all day to-day, seemingly from ten to twenty miles up the Bay. I think it was the gunboats shelling the coasts, and probably 'peppering' some rebel batteries along the shore. The expedition moving from this region is a grand one, and on a much larger scale than I, at first, supposed; and I think there is that care and management displayed, which will undoubtedly win success. The time has come for Mobile and several other important places to fall, and yield they must. Mark what I say.
Your affectionate husband,
Henry

March 26, 1865
Near Fort Morgan, Alabama

Dear Cimbaline,
Time passes off slow and tedious while we are lying here awaiting orders to move. . . . I heard from our command yesterday morning. They are some twenty miles from here, up on the east side of Mobile Bay. They had not, up to yesterday morning, had any fighting more than merely skirmishing a little with the rebel cavalry scouting around. Some of the rebels made a dash upon our pickets, a few mornings ago, but were easily repulsed, in which we captured seven of their men, which proved to be Forrest's men—which proves that, at least, some of Forrest's command

has been sent to assist in the defense of Mobile. From rumors and information gathered from deserters, it appears that the rebels are determined upon endeavoring to defend Mobile; but I think when our entire army comes to confront them, if we don't get them entirely surrounded, and thus prevent their escape, some pleasant morning will reveal to us an evacuated city.

While lying here doing nothing but eat and sleep, all the past time we have, is gathering and eating oysters, gathering sea-shells upon the Gulf beach, or riding upon the bay in some little sail boats we have rigged up for our pleasure.

Your affectionate husband,
Henry.

March 28, 1865

On board steamer *Tarascon*, Anchored out in Mobile Bay, Alabama

Dear Cimbaline,
The reason for this delay of our boats (there are some two or three others also loaded with teams and waiting as we are) I understand to be this: Our troops have left Fish river, and are pushing their way further up on the east side of the bay, and we are waiting for them to clear the shore of rebels and rebel batteries, so we can land further up. There is no telling how long we may have to wait here; but I hope we shall get orders to leave here to-day.

Your affectionate husband,
Henry

March 31, 1865

Near Sibley's Mills, Baldwin County, Alabama[14]

Dear Cimbaline,
I reached the regiment this afternoon, at this place, and found all generally well. I put my things on the boat last Monday morning, down near

---

14. This flanking movement toward Cyrus Sibley's Mills, which sat near the southern branch of Bayou Minette between Spanish Fort and Blakely, forced Confederates under Brigadier General St. John R. Liddell to withdraw northward. See Canby, Report No. 1, OR, 93.

Fort Morgan, and we remained anchored out there until the evening of Tuesday, when we moved up the Bay about twenty miles, and anchored out again in the bay, opposite 'Stark's Landing' were [where] we remained on board with all our wagons and animals until this forenoon, when we disembarked and came up to our camp, some eight miles from the landing.[15] While we were on the boat lying out in the Bay, we could plainly see the city of Mobile just across the bay about eight miles from us. We could plainly see about twenty transports tied up at the city wharf. Also I could plainly see some rebel gunboats and a sand fort or two of the rebels at the upper end of the bay. Our army is on the land east of this fort and another one on the eastern shore of Mobile Bay. Our gunboats in the Bay are keeping things stirring in their line of duty. The rebels have filled all the waters in the upper part of the Bay with torpedoes, which make it dangerous for our vessels to run around much. One of our gunboats has been sunk and another one disabled temporarily by the explosion of torpedoes. Our army has fixed up machines for fishing out these torpedoes, and have found and got out between 80 and 100 of them. They are dangerous concerns. This morning two men were carrying one along, and dropped it, when it exploded and killed one of the men and badly wounded two others. These men did not belong to our regiment. The rebels here are spunky and seem disposed to show fight. They have some very strong forts and fortifications around Mobile and on this side of the bay. In my opinion our army has got a good big job on its hand in the capture of Mobile, and I think it will require weeks to accomplish the thing. Their works are so strong that we shall have to bombard them, and to do this, we shall have to fortify against their works and plant siege guns, which we are busily doing now, working night and day.[16] Their largest and strongest fort on the east side is 'Spanish Fort.' After we take this, we have to move some further north and take another small fort or two, and then cross around on the north side of the Bay, across two or three rivers that come into the Bay on the north, and then down the Bay again some five miles before we reach Mobile. All this will require much hard work and a great deal of hard fighting, unless the

---

15. The use of Starke's Landing as the logistical base for Smith's troops, rather than Fort Morgan, considerably shortened the Union supply line. Jordan, *Operational Art,* 136.

16. Union troops working day and night placed fifty-three siege guns and thirty-seven field pieces during the assault on Spanish Bay. The battery established on the bluff above Bay Minette, which Henry likely described here, included eight thirty-pound Parrotts and a pair of Whitworth rifles. Canby, Report No. 1, OR, 94.

rebels skedaddle, which I think they will hardly do without some fighting. Our troops have been shelling Spanish Fort for five days, and the rebels are replying warmly. But we are planting several more mortars and siege guns brought up to-day, and we shall make it warmer and warmer for them every day. Our men are working night and day; and now it is past nine o'clock at night and the rebels are shelling our works. Our Division (the 2d) is not in the front line, but is back in the rear held as a reserve, and as a guard against any advance on us from the rear. We have breast-works thrown up all around us on the east. I have got hold of a good map of Mobile and vicinity, and as soon as I can I will draw off a kind of sketch and send you, so you can fully understand our position. . . . To-day, who should come walking up to me, at the landing, but George—my servant who came with me from Red River to Memphis. He is now working on a Government boat. He was the gladdest fellow you ever saw to find me, and says after the boat makes one more trip, he is coming to me again. He says, in New Orleans, he saw some niggers who came from the plantation where I got Ellie's pony,—and they say the pony's name is 'Nancy Black.' . . . There has been a religious revival going on in our regiment for about a month, and a great many have professed religion and joined the church. Much good has been done among our regiment. And right here, let me mention one of the many strange things that sometimes occur in the tented field: To-night about nine o'clock while our chaplain was holding a warm lively prayer meeting in our regiment, and men were singing and shouting aloud the praise of God, only some three miles from our camp, could plainly be heard the loud booming cannon and exploding shells of deadly war, perhaps sending many a poor fellow mortal to the bar of God. War is terrible and dreadful thing and presents many strange features and contranieties.

Your affectionate husband,
Henry

April 4, 1865

Near Blakely, Baldwin County, Alabama

Dear Cimbaline,
Day before yesterday, as our command was marching on the road, going out on a reconnoisance, a torpedo in the road bursted and killed two

horses of officers riding along.[17] Col. Merriam was close by at the time, and was badly shocked. The rebels have filled the roads with these torpedoes all through this country. These torpedoes are shells filled with powder, and have a kind of friction match or percussion cap attached, so that the hoof of a horse, or wagon wheel will strike it, and cause it to explode. I saw, eighteen of these infernal machines yesterday, which our men had found and dug up.

5 1/2 o'clock p.m.

Just at 5 o'clock, one half an hour ago, our siege guns which have been getting into position around Spanish Fort, opened out upon the fort, and the fire is terrible. I can count about *forty or fifty explosions in one minute.* The fort will surely have to surrender to-night or to-morrow.

Your affectionate husband,
Henry

April 7, 1865
Near Blakely, Baldwin Co. Alabama

Dear Cimbaline,
This afternoon I climbed to the top of a tall pine tree, standing on a hill near by our headquarters, from which I had a splendid view of the rebel lines, and the river and bay. I could plainly see two gun boats of the rebels out in the water, which seemed to be watching us like two bull-dogs. The shells from the rebels' guns fall within from three to six hundred yards of our camp at all times during the day and night; And it is strange how accustomed to them a person can become; for I sleep soundly every night, scarcely ever aroused by the explosion of the shells near by. We have not replied with artillery, to any extent, to the rebels in our front; but we commenced planting artillery and siege guns last night, and will be ready soon to go to work in earnest. The bombardment at Fort Spanish on the 4" inst. did not, so far as I can ascertain, result in anything more definite than that a hundred or two cannons, firing at once, can 'kick up a big dust' and make a big smoke. We are bringing to bear, some larger guns, upon, that fort, that will, no doubt, tell in time.

---

17. Soldiers during the Civil War often used the term "torpedo" to describe both land mines and underwater ordnance. Bell, *Civil War Heavy Explosive Ordnance*, 471.

We manage to get hold, somehow, of Mobile papers occasionally, three or four days old. They state that a good deal of anxiety is felt for the security of their city, and call upon all, white, creole, and black to come forward in the defense of their homes, families and firesides. But I think their cry will prove in vain—for the city is doomed to fall, sooner or later. We have all about concluded that we have a job of one or two months on our hands, but we are bound to 'put it through' if it takes all summer.

Your affectionate husband,

Henry

April 10, 1865

Blakely, Alabama

Dear Cimbaline,

Night before last, 8" inst. a general charge was made upon Fort Spanish by the 1st & 3d Divisions of our Corps and one Division of 13" Army Corps, in which we captured the entire fort. The attack was made about 10 o'clock in the evening, but the rebels had been evacuting since dark, and most of them had escaped out to the rear by wading through the marshes in the rear of the fort, and in small boats; so we only got about 550 prisoners and 36 pieces of artillery. The assault and charge probably occupied about an hour. The only pity was that the charge was not made two or three hours earlier, when we should undoubtedly have captured about 2000 prisoners. But, as it was we captured some valuable artillery.[18] Next day (yesterday) I took a ride down to and all over the fortifications of Spanish Fort, and saw the whole thing, including several torpedoes which had been found sticking their noses up out of the sand; but I took good care to not explode any of them. Our loss in this action probably amounted to 300 in killed and wounded.

But a better part of my narrative is yet to come. Our Division, and a part of the 13" A. C. and a command of colored troops made a grand and very successful charge upon the entire rebel line of fortifications surrounding

---

18. Subsequent reports noted that during the Mobile campaign Smith's 16th Corps suffered 537 casualties, including sixty-eight men killed, and that the attacks on Mobile, Spanish Fort, and Blakely resulted in the capture of more than five thousand Confederate prisoners, nearly three hundred artillery pieces, and several thousand guns. Canby, Report No. 1, OR, 99; Christensen, General Orders No. 40, April 23, 1865, OR, ser. 1, vol. 49, pt. 1, 101.

Blakely. It is unnecessary for me to say that our boys 'went in' in the true and full sense of the term. The charge was made about six o'clock in the afternoon, over the roughest ground, made so by the rebels, I ever saw. The rebels had placed all kinds of obstructions to hinder the charge of our men, such as logs, brush, sharp sticks, and wires stretched across and through the brush; but away went our men, with a defening shout, and never stopped until they had scaled the enemy's works, and had full possession of the entire fortifications and contents. Some of the regiments in the extreme advance lost pretty severely. One regiment lost 58 in wounded and killed. I do not know the entire loss of our army in this engagement. But one thing which occurred through nothing else than the providence of God, was, that our regiment which was in the midst of the fight, *did not have a man killed or wounded—not one touched.* We all should feel exceedingly grateful to our Heavenly Father for his shielding care and protection evident on this occasion. We captured here about 2500 prisoners, 64 pieces of artillery, 200 mules, 100 or 200 beef cattle, sheep, & hogs—a lot of commissary stores, corn and tents; also the rebel hospital and wounded. Among the prisoners were three Brig. Generals—Thomas, Liddell & Cockerell.[19] Our regiment chased some of the rebels about a half mile through the woods to the river, where some of them had waded out some distance into the water, I presume, thinking they would try and swim the river; but our boys soon brought them to shore. Our Division captured about 1600 of the 2500. Our regiment took about 150 prisoners. Our Brigade about 800 prisoners.

Your affectionate husband,
Henry.
P.S. Boys all well—and in most excellent spirits. I think that Mobile will have to fall soon. H.

April 11, 1865
Blakely, Alabama

Dear Cimbaline,
I hardly know what to write in consequence of the various rumors afloat in camp, in reference to military matters. Yesterday our Brigade was or-

---

19. Brigadier Generals Bryan Morel Thomas, St. John Richardson Liddell, and Francis Marion Cockrell. Eicher and Eicher, *Civil War High Commands*, 179, 348, 612–613.

dered to come into the fortifications and take possession of every thing in the way of property captured from the enemy, and account for it all by reporting the same. This we have been doing. To-day one rumor reaches us, that Genl. Grant has had an engagement with Johnson [Johnston], or rather Lee, in Virginia, and badly whipped him, compelling Lee to ask for a suspension of hostilities to enable him to prepare for a final and general surrender of the entire army, and yielding up of the Confederacy;—also that Grant had telegraphed to Camby to stop further operations until orders from him.[20] This story, of course, set up a big shout in camp. Another story quite current is, that the city of Mobile is being evacuated. This rumor seems to be currently believed by all who have means of knowing. But amidst all this, this evening we received orders to be ready to march to-morrow, but Genl. Gilbert, commanding our brigade, thinks we shall hardly move so soon.[21] Taking it 'all and all,' I do not profess to know anything definite concerning any of these matters.

Your affectionate husband,
Henry

April 12, 1865
Blakely, Alabama

Dear Cimbaline,
Since I had been absent from home this last time, I had been felicitating myself that you would spend the remaining portion of my term of service pleasantly and agreeably to yourself. But to my disappointment your letter of the 28th contains expressions indicating that all things have not been going on smoothly. It grieves me to learn that any thing of such an unpleasant nature should have occurred. I do sincerely trust that no more such unpleasant occurrences will transpire before I return home. You state that a 'dozen words' from me, when I was at home, would have

---

20. Confederates abandoned Petersburg and Richmond on April 2, and four days later Grant's army caught up to the retreating rebels and won an emphatic victory at Sailor's Creek. On April 9—Palm Sunday—the generals met inside the McLean House at Appomattox Court House, where Lee surrendered his Army of Northern Virginia. Varon, *Appomattox*, 7–78.

21. Brigadier General James Gilbert led the First Brigade, Second Division, of the 16th Army Corps, to which the 117th Illinois belonged. Report No. 2: Organization of the Union Forces, OR, ser. 1, vol. 49, pt. 1, 107.

set things all straight. I honestly confess I do not know what you mean. If there was any misunderstanding between you & any others, that a 'dozen words' from me would have corrected, I here declare my entire ignorance of it. That any cause for words of an unpleasant nature should have arisen between you and mother, greatly surprises as well as deeply mortifies me. I hope that will be passed over immediately and forgotten.
    From your affectionate husband,
    Henry

April 14, 1865

In the Field, on the March, About 20 Miles Northeast of Blakely, Alabama

Dear Cimbaline,
On the night of the 10" inst. the rebels evacuated Mobile, and our troops entered and occupied the place next day. I did not get to hear what they found there. Report says that the citizens heartily welcomed our army when it entered the city. If so, I expect they were the poor class unable to get away, and who had been overrun by the domineering confeds. One thing certain, Mobile has 'gone up,' and the rebel army that has occupied it so long, has moved up the country, and we probably are following up to attend to them. But I think the days of the Confederacy are numbered. We have received northern news as late as the 4th inst., in which we learn of the joyful success of our army in Virginia, and the capture of Richmond, Petersburg, 25,000 prisoners &c. &c. all of which fills our hearts with joy, and makes us feel the war is speedily drawing to a close. If Lee's Army is whipped and captured, which we hear is true, I do not see what more the enemy can do, than to succumb, and give up the struggle. They, now, can surely see that to fight longer, is needlessly prolonging a wicked and rebellious course. As the saying is, the boys 'count big' on coming home soon. May this prove true. I guess you will agree to this—won't you? . . . Tell Ellie I have got the nicest kind of a china cup and saucer for her, which I shall try and bring home for her to drink tea out of. She must be a good girl and learn to read, so she can read for me, when I come, all about the kitty and dog and cow, and all the nice things.
    As ever,
    Your affectionate husband,
    Henry.

April 16, 1865
Don't Know Where We Are, About 45 Miles N.E. Blakely, Alabama

Dear Cimbaline,
Since leaving Blakely, we have marched some forty-five miles in a northeasterly direction; and in that distance I have seen but about five families, and eight or ten houses. The country is covered, so far, nearly exclusively with dense pine forests, and the land is very sandy, and the people can raise a little corn and rice. For the first time I saw rice growing to-day. It was just up out of the ground an inch or two high. The few people I saw seem to be of the poorest and most ignorant class—long slender bodies, pale sallow faces, light hair, sharp noses and raw-boned faces. . . . None of these people seem to know anything more than what just concerns their house and 'tater patch.' All the families seem to be well supplied with a good large stock of children, with fair prospects for their continued increase. I heard a soldier remark to-day that all this country was good for, was to raise sweet potatoes and children. As for the sweet potatoes I cann't say much; but in reference to the other portion of the remark, I can, from observation, bear special testimony. But, let us pass by these poor, ignorant fellow beings and let them remain in their 'glory,' if they enjoy any, for the war will soon come to an end, when, it is to be hoped, their condition may be improved.[22]

I have no news to write, for I see nothing but pine woods, hear nothing but the frogs croaking in the cypress swamps, and learn nothing from the various rumors among our boys.

A citizen told me, to-day, that he saw some Confederate soldiers a day or two ago, who told him that Montgomery had fallen into the hands of the Yankees, some ten days ago.[23] Every thing looks towards a speedy

---

22. Four days later, Henry observed in his diary, "A good many of the citizenry, especially the poorer class, seem glad to see the advent of the 'Yankees' into their midst." HFD, April 20, 1865.

23. Union troops arrived in Montgomery on April 12, and the city, according to the terse Federal report, "surrendered without a fight." Pro-Confederate newspapers in the city offered a strikingly different account and described the Federal army's pitiless destruction of cotton and other property in the city. The scene, one paper noted, "beggars description. Dense columns of smoke piled above the city and almost shut out the light of the sun. Women with affrighted countenances were seen running hither and thither, crying and wringing their hands, and hundreds of excited persons were endeavoring to secure the furniture from the adjacent houses. We have never witnessed a more heart rending specta-

close of the war, which I sincerely hope may prove true, so I can come home and stay with my dear family, which I know I am loving more and more every day. Nothing can induce me ever again to bind myself to remain for three long years from you and Ellie, when once I am with you again.

As ever your affectionate husband,
Henry

April 26, 1865
Near Montgomery, Alabama

Dear Cimbaline,
We are out about five miles from the city on the main public road leading to Mobile. I think we shall move up nearer town this afternoon or to-morrow. As I said before, we are expecting our gunboats and transports up from below with supplies for our army. We have been foraging off the country for the last week, for what subsistence our animals required, and if our boats do not come to-day we shall be compelled to look to the country for subsistence for our men. But this section of the country is well off, and can easily supply all our wants for some time.

The news from all parts of the army is of the most encouraging nature. We have received the official intelligence of the surrender of Genl. Lee and his army of northern Virginia. And through rebel sources, yesterday we learned that Genls. Johnson [Johnston] and Beauregard had subsequently surrendered on the same terms.[24] And we have rumors of the surrender of other portions of the rebel army, in different localities. The city of Montgomery seems desirous of peace. So does all the country through which we have lately marched. The news from the state of Mis-

---

cle." Itinerary of the Cavalry Corps, Military Division of the Mississippi, OR, ser. 1, vol. 49, pt. 1, 391; "Evacuation of Montgomery!" *Montgomery Daily Mail,* April 17, 1865, 1. Union commanders disputed that their troops set the fires that consumed this property. See J. H. Wilson to W. T. Sherman, April 21, 1865, OR, ser. 1, vol. 49, pt. 2, 424–425.

24. Lee, as General-in-Chief of Confederate forces, appointed General Joseph Johnston to lead what remained of the rebel Army of Tennessee against William T. Sherman's Federals in the Carolinas, where Pierre Gustave Toutant Beauregard had previously been in command. Sherman and Johnston struck a tentative armistice on April 18, which followed the lenient terms that Grant had extended to Lee's Army of Northern Virginia, but the new U.S. president, Andrew Johnson, rejected these terms. The final surrender came at Durham Station, North Carolina, on April 26, the same day as this letter to Cimbaline. Jamieson, *Spring 1865,* 175–203.

sissippi expresses a similar sentiment as prevalent in that state. Taking all things into consideration, we are disposed to flatter ourselves that the war is about over, and that peace will be fully restored in a few weeks; and further, that a month or two will find us all at home with our families and friends. The boys say they expect to spend the coming Fourth of July at home. I wish their desire may be granted.

Day before yesterday (the 24" inst.) we received, through rebel sources, rumors to the effect that President Lincoln and Secretary Seward had been assassinated in Washington on the 14 inst. We do not want to believe the story, and hence do not credit the rumor; and will not, unless better evidence is furnished than we have already received.

I do not pretend to know what our army will do here, more than merely occupy the country for a while, in order that the southerners may get accustomed to look upon the blue coats with respect. . . . We are exceedingly anxious to get the news from the north, and learn what is going on there. We are about fourteen days behind the news you have at home. So you may judge of our anxiety to hear from there. . . . Yesterday morning, before we left camp, some niggers told me where some meat was hid in the woods. I took two men and a team with me and went out three miles into the swamp, and found two wagons loaded with good bacon. The owner didn't 'save his bacon' that time. Coming through the country I have managed to get my share of sweet milk, honey and eggs &c. &c. We have not suffered.

Affectionate husband,
Henry

April 29, 1865

Near Montgomery, Alabama

Dear Cimbaline,
We are in a nice shady grove of pine and oak trees. Water is plenty, near at hand, though not of the best quality, and we have sunk wells. In coming to this camp, from our last encampment we had to pass through the entire city. . . . To-day I payed the city a visit & took a peep 'around town,' to look at the 'elephant.' The place, once, has, probably, contained from fifteen to twenty thousand inhabitants. The city, in time of peace, would be a delightful place to live. I am much pleased with it. It contains a good number of fine residences, and what is nicer still, bountifully supplied with shade trees and shrubbery. In this respect, it exceeds Memphis by

far, and you know something of that place. The State Capitol of Alabama is here. This is nothing of an extra building for that purpose. Montgomery was the first capital of the entire Southern Confederacy, before they located it in Richmond, Va. I was in the State house here, to-day, and saw the legislative halls, where southern traitors, first congregated to devise those wicked and rebellious schemes for the destruction of our Union. The place looked deserted and sin-stricken

The people, as far as they have expressed themselves, seem desirous of peace, and greatly rejoice at the prospect of an early cessation of war.[25] Confederate money is flat here, and nobody will take it. Greenbacks are 'all the go.' But there are not many of them to 'go,' for our boys are generally out of money, having received no pay since they left St. Louis, last November. The people here, for a long time would not believe Lee had surrendered his army to Grant. But the arrival of a good many paroled prisoners from Lee's army, who have come in here, within a few days, have fully dispelled from their minds all doubts on that point, and they now acknowledge they are 'gone up.' You can see any amount of rebel soldiers paroled, and some who have come in and given themselves up, and taken the amnesty oath, and our own soldiers, all mixed up, and walking round town, laughing and talking, and enjoying themselves 'hugely.' This look, indeed, strange. But all feel the war is over, and everything will soon be settled and quiet again.

Sunday evening, April 30, 1865

The transports arrived this afternoon bringing about six thousand negro troops and some commissary stores for our army. The arrival of these boats, which I witnessed, exceeded anything I ever saw of the kind, in the effect produced. We are encamped about a mile and a half from the landing. When I heard the whistle of the first boat, I mounted my horse, and put out to the 'scene of action.' The curiosity among the niggers of the city to see the Yankee boats and nigger soldiers was indescribable. They congregated on the bluff at the landing, to the number of about three thousand—men, women and children, of all colors, from black to creoles. As the boats neared the landing, the nigger soldiers began to sing, with a thousand voices "John Brown's body. &c." and "Down with

---

25. A Montgomery paper urged local civilians to reciprocate the generous treatment extended by Smith's troops: "We can assure the sturdy veterans of the 16th army corps that their kindness towards the people of this city are fully appreciated and have excited the liveliest feelings of gratitude. . . . Our people should bear in mind that a kind word, gently spoken, melts the heart and disarms a brave soldier, quicker than the angry flash of steel." "Kindness Reciprocated," *Montgomery Daily Mail,* May 1, 1865, 1.

the traitor, and up with the stars. &c", and at the same time they were greeted with thousands of cheers from their fellow blacks on the shore.[26] The wildest confusion and enthusiasm prevailed. The niggers monopolized the day, on that occasion.[27] A good many white citizens of the city, who were present, did not seem to relish the 'exercises' the best in the world. As the boys, sometimes say, they looked "chawed."[28]

We are all deeply mortified to learn of the death of President Lincoln. The sorrow of our army, and at the same time, the indignation felt over the outrageous affair, are inexpressible. The universal cry, goes up from our soldiers, demanding that the criminals and instigators in this most heinous crime, be speedily and summarily brought to justice. And woe to that man, that utters, in their hearing, one word of praise or commendation in favor of the act. He would be shot quicker than thought. I trust Booth may be caught and burned alive.

Your affectionate husband,
Henry

May 3, 1865

Near Montgomery, Alabama

Dear Cimbaline,
Paroled prisoners from Lee's army in Virginia, are daily arriving here, in small squads of from two or three to eight or ten. They are all on their way home, generally in Alabama or Mississippi. They universally express themselves as tired of the war, and think the Confederacy has played out. Should the war continue, none of these men, or at least very few, could ever be brought into the field again.

5 o'clock p.m.

---

26. "Down with the traitor, up with the star" comes from the chorus of "The Battle Cry of Freedom," one of the most popular Union anthems of the war. Root, *Battle Cry of Freedom*, Notated Music, https://www.loc.gov/item/ihas.200001814, accessed December 9, 2023.

27. The Montgomery press reported that the fleet included ten ships and "a large number of the *chasseurs d'Afrique*." Its arrival "attracted an immense crowd of spectators on the wharves," presenting "an imposing and enlivening scene." "Arrival of the Fleet," *Montgomery Daily Mail*, May 1, 1865, 1.

28. A newspaper report two weeks later illuminated the depths of violent anger unleashed by the collapse of slavery and the arrival of Black troops. That brief dispatch read: "Several negroes of both sexes have come into the city lately with their ears cut off and large pieces torn from their heads. Such acts, inhuman and unchristian like, are execrated by all good men, and will entail on the perpetrators swift and condign punishment." "Shocking Brutality," *Montgomery Daily Mail*, May 15, 1865, 2.

On the 1st inst., was a solemn day in our entire camp. From sunrise to sun-set cannon were fired every half hour, and between 12 & 1 o'clock, one every minute. This was in honor of the death of President Lincoln. At dress-parade, in the afternoon, every regiment marched to the parade ground with 'reversed arms' and muffled drums beating the funeral march, while the colors were draped in mourning. The parade exercises were brief; and prayer was offered by the various Chaplains. The scene was one of deep solemnity, and caused the sorrowful team to dampen the cheek of many a weather-worn veteran.

Tell Ellie I shall expect her to be almost reading by the time I return home. I want her to learn fast, and I will buy her another nice book when I come.

All are well.

Your affectionate husband,

Henry.

May 6, 1865

Near Montgomery, Alabama

Dear Cimbaline,

We have about finished "policing" up our camp, and digging wells, and every thing presents a neat and comfortable appearance. The men are now receiving plenty of rations, and seem to be well satisfied to stay here awhile. Our "mess" is doing well. We have ample abundance. I fancy we live about as well as you folks at home. . . . Yesterday, I went in charge of a foraging party, into the country some four or five miles from town, for corn and fodder. We went down the river, to the plantation of C. T. Pollard,[29] a very wealthy planter (or rather he has been wealthy) There were no white persons on the places,—but plenty of niggers, some 80 or 90 in all. We found any amount of forage. And while the boys were loading up the wagons, I got all the nice cool buttermilk I wanted to drink from the nigger "boss." I asked "Aunt Car'line" if she couldn't gather me some sweet peas, as I saw they had an abundance in the garden. "O, yes, massa, I can do dat," she replied, and soon mustered up about a dozen little

---

29. The 1860 federal census noted that Charles T. Pollard owned real estate worth $215,000. His personal property, valued at $350,000, was even greater, with most of that wealth tied to the 116 men, women, and children he enslaved. United States Federal Census (hereafter USFC), 1860; U.S. Federal Census, Slave Schedules, 1860.

niggers, who all pitched into the pea-patch, and soon had me a sack full of peas, and greens. To-day we have been enjoying a good dinner as one of the results of yesterday's expedition. . . . The citizens, here, are now becoming a little more familiar than they were at first. They now come out upon the streets considerably; and all seem very anxious to have peace again restored. The inevitable loss of their niggers, some seem to regard as a heavy blow upon themselves, while others express a gladness that they are gone, and that they will never be troubled again with the blighting curse of slavery.

Last night I dreampt I was at home with you and Ellie, where every thing looked so natural and pleasant. I wish my dreams may soon be changed into living realities. Our boys are now getting uneasy and impatient. Every thing looks so much like peace, that they feel the war is over and that they are no longer needed, and they begin to want to go home.

Your affectionate husband,
Henry

May 7, 1865
Near Montgomery, Alabama

Dear Cimbaline,
We have all kinds of rumors about leaving here. They all tend to confirm the same story, that our corps is to leave Montgomery soon, and be sent around by way of New Orleans, and up the Mississippi river to military post, north, preparatory to being mustered out in a short time. If everything is as favorable for the speedy termination of the war as I think, I see no good reason for the government needing our services all the remainder of our term of service; and surely think we shall be mustered out inside of two months. All information we have received or heard, justify this conclusion.

Your affectionate husband,
Henry

May 14, 1865
Near Montgomery, Alabama

Dear Cimbaline,
I saw in the papers yesterday, the welcome intelligence that Genl. Grant is making arrangements to soon muster out four hundred thousand

(400.000) of the troops, and thus materially lessen the enormous expenses of the Government. This, I think, is a prudent and sensible move; and one that the army with us will most heartily endorse.

The rebel soldiers, paroled in Virginia, continue to come in here daily in small squads, on foot. Within an hour past, forty-one have passed along the road just in front of my tent. They come in without any disturbance, and pass along without any molestation more than having to stop and answer the numers [numerous] questions of our boys, propounded to them as they go by. They all tell the same story—tired of the war, glad that peace draws nigh, and think they will never be caught in the army again.

Your affectionate husband,
Henry

May 17, 1865

Near Montgomery, Alabama

Dear Cimbaline,

My health remains as good as usual. Times are somewhat dull in camp as respects news. Yet, last night, we had one of the liveliest times in camp I have experienced in many a day. It resulted from the reception of a telegraphic dispatch, at Genl. Smith's Head Quarters, from Genl. Wilson in Georgia, who telegraphed that he had captured Jeff. Davis and several other prominent secessionists, and sent them to Washington.[30] Our boys ran wild over the news. It reached us just at dark, and the shout was immediately raised in camp; and soon guns were fired. In the course of thirty minutes hundreds and thousands of candles were lighted, and torch light processions were formed. Hundreds and hundreds of the men climbed the tall pine trees and fixed their candles to the limbs, which made the most beautiful spectacle that the eye could behold. Crowds assembled at all the different headquarters and called for speeches from the officers. After a speech would be made, the boys would strike up "John Brown's body lies mouldering in the grave." "Hang Jeff Davis on a sour-apple tree" &c. &c. In the 6th Minnesota Volunteer Regiment, which has a good many half breed Indians in it, was got up the regular Indian war-dance,

---

30. Lieutenant Colonel Benjamin Pritchard and the 4th Michigan Cavalry captured Jefferson Davis shortly after daylight on May 10, in Irwinville, Georgia. "Capture of Jefferson Davis," *Chicago Tribune*, May 15, 1865, 1.

in which many of the men participated.[31] This, and hundreds of other means the boys resorted to, to express their joy, and "carried on" in this style, until a late hour. This news, I presume, you have heard by this time. It is almost too good to credit; yet, we believe it to be true.

Your affectionate husband,
Henry

May 25, 1865

Near Montgomery, Alabama

Dear Cimbaline,
To-day was observed in our regiment, in accordance with the proclamation of President Johnson, to observe it as a day of humiliation and prayer.[32] The regiment assembled the regimental chapel, and united in the exercises of the hour, which consisted of prayer, music, instrumental & vocal, and brief addresses. The exercises lasted about two hours, and were quite interesting.[33]

I want you to get sound and hearty by the time I come home, and be able to tramp around considerably. Tell mother, too, to begin to make calculations and preparations to accompany us. It is my intention for us to take a tour of general and extensive visiting among our relatives and friends. . . . When I return home, my friends generally should board me for about three or four months; for I intended to "board around." . . . The citizens from the surrounding country have commenced coming into the city in considerable numbers. Our camp being located immediately upon one of the public highways leading into the city, I am often reminded of scenes I witnessed, fifteen or twenty years ago, of market wagons passing along the road through Mascoutah, on their way to mar-

---

31. The most detailed history of the 6th Minnesota Infantry offers no indication whether its ranks included men of Native American ancestry. The regiment's initial deployment to suppress the Dakota Uprising, which engulfed Minnesota in the summer of 1862, offers a more likely explanation for this pantomime. One member of the 6th Minnesota described that service as "an interposition of Providence" against "redskins," "savages," and "Indian rascals." Minnesota Board of Commissioners, *Minnesota*, 304–305.

32. President Johnson originally scheduled the "National Day of Humiliation and Mourning" in observance of Lincoln's death for Thursday, May 25, but rescheduled it to June 1 to accommodate the Christians who honored that original date for the ascension of Christ into heaven. "No Paper To-Morrow," *Ohio Statesman*, June 1, 1865, 2.

33. Miller and Risdon Moore were among the members of the 117th Illinois who spoke. Ezekiel Thomas Willoughby Diary, May 25, 1865.

ket at St. Louis. Owing to the ravages of the war, the people, here, have little else than a few chickens, eggs and a little butter or honey to bring for sale. Most of the commodities in this line that our mess consumes, are purchased from these people.

Your affectionate husband,
Henry

June 1, 1865
Near Montgomery, Alabama

Dear Cimbaline,

To-day we received *most glorious* news, to us. We are to be *mustered out immediately*. The order came from the War Department, at Washington, by telegraph, dated May 29, 1865, via New Orleans, May 31. This order directs all regiments that came out under the July call of 1862, and which were mustered into the U.S. service prior to Sept. 30 1862 to be mustered out forthwith.... I do not yet know whether we shall be mustered out here, or sent home to Illinois to be mustered out. We don't care which way, so the authorities attend to the matter without delay. However, this is a thing that requires some time to attend to. All the Government property in the hands of the company commander, and various officers of the regiment has to be disposed of, by turning the same over to the proper officers to receive it. Then, our muster-out-rolls have to be prepared, which is a tedious job, inasmuch as five copies for each company are required. I think, if things move off glibly as they should, that we all will be home in four weeks from this date—five or six weeks at the very outside. You may make your calculations on that.

Our boys feel so well over the state of affairs, that they do not know how to contain themselves. I can not begin to tell or express the many antics they 'cut' over the matter.

Your affectionate husband,
Henry

June 6, 1865
Near Montgomery, Alabama

Dear Cimbaline,

We had expected to be on our way to Mobile by this time, and very likely should have been, had not the arrival here, of a corps of paymasters caused a temporary suspension of the order. We shall be delayed only a few days, however, when we shall be off down the river. Of course, we can afford to stop a few days, when our delay is caused by the prospects of receiving a share of greenbacks. . . . Our regiment is to be payed off in the morning, four months' pay from 1st October 1864. I will get only two months', having received two when I was home.

Your affectionate husband,
Henry

June 14, 1865
Near Montgomery, Alabama

Dear Cimbaline,
I was sorry to hear of the slow rate at which your health seems to improve. From what you state, there surely will be a mighty *thinning out* in Mascoutah, this fall, and emigration to Kansas or Missouri. For my part I have not yet settled upon what I think we had better do; and I think I shall not try to come to a final conclusion till I come home and consult with you and Mother on that matter. I feel that *something has to be done, and I shall do it.* You may guess what that is.

You express a desire that I should resign and come home. If I thought we should be held in the service till Sept. 19 . . . through the hot weather, I should make an immediate effort to get out the service. But, I have reasons for thinking that we all will be home in so short a time, that I do not think it hardly worth while to resign. If things should take any such a turn as I have stated, you will see me trying to "unharness" myself. You need not entertain any fear of our going to Texas.[34]

Your affectionate husband,
Henry

June 16, 1865
Near Montgomery, Alabama

Dear Cimbaline,
To-day I was up in the city, and took dinner at the Exchange Hotel. Montgomery has become quite a lively and stirring city, within the last month.

---

34. The *Montgomery Daily Mail* likewise challenged the rumor that U.S. troops under General Smith would soon go to Texas to deter aggressive action by French troops in Mexico, where Napoleon III had installed a puppet emperor, Maximilian. "Gen. Smith," *Montgomery Daily Mail,* June 12, 1865, 2.

A good number of stores of all kinds have opened, and brisk business is springing up. Hundreds and thousands of the poor people from the country are flocking in with what little produce and marketing they can scare up. There is an endless string of these wagons pouring along by our camp every day. And what shabby teams and wagons they have! Some have old broken down wagons, and some carts. Some of these are drawn by poor poverty-stricken horses or mules, others by one ox or one mule, and sometimes by a yoke of cows. I saw one team of a pair of old jacks. Their wagons have two or three hickory sapplings bent over them, for bows, over which are stretched a homemade coverlet or cotton counterpane to shelter their heads from the intense summer sun, while from underneath this you will discover three or four faces of cadaverous sallow looking females with a "snuff-stick" protruding from the corner of their mouths, and whose "frail tenements" seem, to all appearances, to be enveloped in nothing more than the outer dress which you see. Such is the "poor white trash" of the South. I pity them from the bottom of my heart. They who have been so duped and lead on by the aristocrats of the South. These poor people have scarcely any thing to bring to market.

Your affectionate husband,
Henry

June 18, 1865

Near Montgomery, Alabama

Dear Cimbaline,
We have seen and heard of so many orders and circulars pertaining to the muster-out and detention of troops; rumors of difficulties about to spring up between the United States and Mexico; trouble with England, and a dozen other stories, that I do not pretend to know how the matter rests just now. I guess it will all come out straight and correct in the course of time.

Your affectionate husband,
Henry

June 20, 1865

Near Montgomery, Alabama

Dear Cimbaline,
In both your letters received this evening you again refer to a desire for me to resign and come home. Do you want me to come home "in

fact"? Are you not joking? I do not know that my resignation would be accepted, should I offer it. However, I will state, that under the circumstances, I have concluded to make an effort to get out the service I shall commence getting up my documents to that effect, to-morrow. It will require some time to get such an application through the military channels. . . . Should I be as successful as I might desire, you need not look for me home earlier than the 15" or 20" of July. But, in truth, I do not want you to put too great expectations on my success, for I might not succeed.

Your affectionate husband,
Henry

June 21, 1865

Near Montgomery, Alabama

Dear Cimbaline,
I wrote out my application, tendering my immediate and unconditional resignation, basing it principally upon a medical certificate of physical disability. I took my papers to Brigade Headquarters this afternoon, but had to let them remain there till to-morrow morning, owing to the absence of the Brigade Surgeon, from camp to-day, who has to approve my medical certificate. Genl. Gilbert told me that he would approve my papers. I saw the Division Surgeon this afternoon, and he said he would approve my documents. So it would appear that I am making a very good "start" in the matter. I hope I may be successful, on your account. I shall shove things along again to-morrow, and report my success to-morrow night.

Your affectionate husband,
Henry

June 23, 1865

Near Montgomery, Alabama

Dear Cimbaline,
You spoke of Mr. Denson's family having removed to Centralia to live. I think, when I come home, we shall have to go out there, and around among our Marion County Copperhead kinsfolk.[35] You spoke as though

---

35. Marion County, Illinois, which includes the town of Centralia, sits about forty miles east of Mascoutah.

you thought you would hardly be able to stand the three or four months tour of visiting. That will be the very thing to cure you, and make you hale and hearty.

    Your affectionate husband,
    Henry

July 4, 1865
Near Montgomery, Alabama

Dear Cimbaline,
This day is the glorious old Fourth of July, but a rather dull day it has proven to me. There was a kind of celebration in the city this morning, among a part of the Third Division of our Corps, and a few citizens on the part of the city, but the thing, I learn, proved a fizzle.[36] Our boys don't care much about celebrating the 4" in the army. All they think of is getting home. I expect all you people throughout the North had a fine time of it to-day. O my! the speeches that must have been made, and the lemon-ade and lager beer that have been swallowed since sunrise!

    My health continues to improve slowly. I feel I am gaining some strength.

    Your affectionate husband,
    Henry

July 6, 1865
Near Montgomery, Alabama

Dear Cimbaline,
The health of our regiment remains about the same. The ailment consists mostly in chills and attendant fevers. We had one man die in Division Hospital a day or two ago. . . . The encampment we lately moved to, I think, is a great improvement on the old one.

    I have just returned from town—did not see my men;—and so, I bought a couple of shirts and returned to camp. Two niggers are to be publicly

---

36. The *Montgomery Daily Post* reported, "The Fourth of July passed off very quietly and orderly in this city," with an early dawn salute followed by an "imposing military procession" that passed Commerce Street to the western part of town, where M. J. Saffold delivered a "patriotic and eloquent" address. "The Fourth," *Montgomery Daily Post,* July 6, 1865, 3.

executed here to-morrow, by shooting. Their crime is murder.[37] We have plenty of musquitoes here, to annoy us during our slumbers. Our remedy in the case, is to build up about a dozen 'smokes,' around our camps, and then go to sleep, and we are not much pestered till about day light.

Your affectionate husband,
Henry

July 9, 1865
Near Montgomery, Alabama

Dear Cimbaline,

I am going to try to write you a letter, but I don't know that I shall succeed; for I am either mad, aggravated, out of humor, or something the matter with me, that renders me incompetent to do a letter justice. And all this grows out of the fact that *my papers have not yet come.* I hardly know what to think about the delay. A mail was received last evening from New Orleans, and I thought *sure they would come.* I waited till this afternoon, and heard nothing; so, about two hours ago I rode to Corps Headquarters to investigate the matter, when I found it as stated. . . . If they do not come within a few more days, I shall change my "tactics," and apply for a leave of absence based upon a surgeon's certificate of physical disability. A leave of absence for such reason, can be granted by Genl. A. J. Smith; and if I determine to make that effort I can put it through in a couple of days. . . . I am sorry to think I can not get home as soon as I first calculated. But we know disappointments are the common lot of all. However, *I am going to put this thing through.* I have never yet failed when I set my head to anything of this kind, since I have been in the service, and *I don't intend to fail in this undertaking,* now that I have carried it thus far. *I am bound to get out of this hot* country. And if I once get out, you'll not catch me here again soon. Do you understand my meaning? . . . Now, I am going to stop right here, because I have nothing else to write. I am going to "fight" that resignation business "through," and keep out of humor till I succeed.

Your affectionate husband,
Henry

---

37. The *Daily Post* reported that the men executed, Jerry and Ma[?]er, were found guilty of murdering a local man named Micajah Thomas. Henry's diary entry of July 7 noted that they were convicted by a military commission. "Execution," *Montgomery Daily Post,* July 8, 1865, 3.

Epilogue
"Nothing New. Fine Weather"

Mascoutah, Illinois, to Warrensburg, Missouri
1865 and Beyond

Two months passed before Henry overcame the feverish illness that stalked his regiment during that desultory Alabama summer.[1] Cimbaline, like young Ellie, was doubtless relieved to have him home, but her exact reactions have been lost to history, as the return of peace brought an end to the lengthy correspondence that had nourished her remarkable voice. Henry's diary reveals that the family quickly settled into familiar rhythms of work, church, and socializing. In addition to resuming his leadership of the local Sunday school, Henry also revived the Mascoutah Lyceum and spent much of the fall helping Nathan Land conduct the state census in St. Clair County. After fear-steeped years of separation and loneliness, the Fikes could take comfort in the unhurried days spent in each other's company, which Henry's diary entries only recounted as "Nothing new. Fine weather."[2]

In February 1867 the family made good on a long-debated plan to leave Mascoutah. Nudged by their unsettled finances and the number of kinfolk who had already moved west, they removed to the railroad town of Warrensburg, Missouri, not far from where the 117th Illinois had marched two years earlier. To a reader of Henry's Civil War letters, their destination, the oft-romanticized prairies of the Osage Valley, was hardly surprising. The stream of neighbors who joined them in western Missouri included the families of Ausby Fike and Charles Rayhill, along with Nathan and Moses Land, who partnered with Henry to erect a flour mill, which soon prospered. Mercantile success likely influenced Henry's decision not to return to the classroom, but he maintained an

---

1. See Henry C. Fike Diaries (hereafter HFD), July 10–12, 1865; Ezekiel Thomas Willoughby Diary, July 10–15, 1865.
2. See HFD, September 18, October 21, and November 15 for entries that include those four words and nothing else.

active interest in local schools, serving on both the Warrensburg board of education and the board of regents for the state Normal School No. 2, founded in 1871.

Cimbaline and Henry continued to marvel at Ellie's growth and took great pride when their daughter, the child whose precocious shenanigans once breathed levity into their heavy wartime exchanges, enrolled in the local college. The journal that Ellie began to keep upon turning eighteen conjured echoes of her parents' Civil War papers. Like her father, she proved to be a meticulous diarist, an avid musician, and a passionate member of the local temperance society. She also expounded on her place within family and community affairs with a self-possession that her mother surely appreciated. Ellie, like Cimbaline, also battled neuralgia, chronic pain, and undisclosed ailments, what she called her "same old trouble," that interrupted her schooling and work. "Ma and Pa think I had better take care of my health," she wrote during one pause, "that it is worth more to me than gaining more knowledge." Cimbaline's own health struggles continued, a fact that likely influenced her daughter's decision to stay in Warrensburg. "Ma needed me at home—housecleaning, sewing & work generally, as we had no girl nor could procure one," she noted.[3] Ellie never married nor had children but remained a vital presence in her parents' household. On Christmas Day in 1880, she helped to organize a party honoring their silver wedding anniversary. With nearly a hundred neighbors in attendance, the survival of Cimbaline and Henry's marital union, tested by war and preserved through the written word, was a cause for celebration indeed.[4]

---

3. Ellie Fike Diaries, September 11, 1879; January 1, 1884.

4. After more than two decades in Warrensburg, Henry found work as an auditor for the Missouri Pacific Railroad, the same route that had borne him west as a soldier and later brought his family to their new western home. He later took a position with the Internal Revenue Service in Kansas City, some sixty miles away. Cimbaline and Henry died in 1906 and 1919, respectively, and are buried together in Warrensburg. *History of Johnson County*. LeSueur, *Official Manual*, 130.

Bibliography

Primary Sources

Manuscripts

Lois Watkins Barr Collection, 1817–1910, Abraham Lincoln Presidential Library, Springfield, Illinois.

James A. Black Diary, 1862–1865, Abraham Lincoln Presidential Library, Springfield, Illinois.

James F. Drish Papers, 1861–1865, Abraham Lincoln Presidential Library, Springfield, Illinois.

Ellie Fike Diaries, 1879–1892, State Historical Society of Missouri, Columbia, Missouri.

Henry C. Fike Diaries, 1851–1919, State Historical Society of Missouri, Columbia, Missouri.

Henry C. and Lucy C. Fike Papers, Kenneth Spencer Research Library, University of Kansas, Lawrence, Kansas.

Benjamin R. Hieronymous Diary, 1862–1863, Abraham Lincoln Presidential Library, Springfield, Illinois.

Benjamin S. Hood Papers, 1839–1889, Abraham Lincoln Presidential Library, Springfield, Illinois.

Humphrey H. Hood Papers, 1851–1903, Abraham Lincoln Presidential Library, Springfield, Illinois.

James Krafft Papers, 1864–1865, courtesy of Dean Blackmar Krafft, https://krafftfamily.org/.

David McFarland Papers, 1862–1864, Abraham Lincoln Presidential Library, Springfield, Illinois.

William A. McLean Letters, 1861–1862, Abraham Lincoln Presidential Library, Springfield, Illinois.

Monroe Joshua Miller Papers, 1846–1865, Missouri History Museum, St. Louis, Missouri.

Orange Parret Diary, 1863–1865, Abraham Lincoln Presidential Library, Springfield, Illinois.

Sidney Robinson Papers, 1862–1913, Abraham Lincoln Presidential Library, Springfield, Illinois.

Ezekiel Thomas Willoughby Diary, 1864–1865, Abraham Lincoln Presidential Library, Springfield, Illinois.

Adolphus Wolf Collection, 1861–1962, Lovejoy Library, Southern Illinois University, Edwardsville, Illinois.

Otto E. Wolf Collection, 1863–1865, Lovejoy Library, Southern Illinois University, Edwardsville, Illinois.

Census, Marriage, and Family Records

Ancestry.com, https://www.ancestry.com.
Find a Grave, https://www.findagrave.com.
Fold3, https://www.fold3.com.
Illinois State Census, 1855, Illinois State Archives.
Illinois State Marriage Index, Illinois State Archives.
Kennedy, Joseph C. G. *Agriculture of the United States in 1860; Compiled from the Original Returns of the Eighth Census.* Washington, D.C.: Government Printing Office, 1864.
———. *Population of the United States in 1860: Compiled from the Original Returns of the Eighth Census.* Washington, D.C.: Government Printing Office, 1864.
United States Federal Census, 1850, Population Schedules, National Archives and Records Administration.
United States Federal Census, 1860, Population Schedules National Archives and Records Administration.
United States Federal Census, 1860, Slave Schedules, National Archives and Records Administration.
United States Federal Census, "Census Bulletin: Population of Missouri Counties and Minor Civil Divisions," 1901.
Walker, Francis A. *A Compendium of the Ninth Census.* Washington, D.C.: Government Printing Office, 1872.

Newspapers

Alton (Illinois) *Telegraph*
Champaign County (Illinois) *Gazette*
Chicago Tribune
(Columbus) *Ohio Statesman*
Gallipolis (Ohio) *Journal*
The (Greensboro) *Alabama Beacon*
The (Grove Hill, Alabama) *Journal*
Harper's Weekly
(Kansas City) *Western Journal of Commerce*
Memphis Daily Union Appeal
Mobile Evening News
(Mobile) *Weekly Advertiser and Register*
Montgomery Daily Mail
Montgomery Daily Post

Nashville Daily Union
(Springfield) *Illinois Daily State Journal*
(St. Louis) *Daily Missouri Republican*
Woodstock (Illinois) *Sentinel*

Military Records

Civil War Soldiers and Sailors System Database, National Park Service.
Delap, Fred. Illinois Civil War Muster and Descriptive Rolls Database, Illinois State Archives, Office of the Illinois Secretary of State, https://www.ilsos.gov/isaveterans/civilMusterSearch.do.
Illinois Adjutant General, Regimental and Unit Histories, Containing Reports for the Years 1861–1866, Illinois State Archives.
Index to Compiled Service Records of Volunteer Union Soldiers Who Served in Organizations from the State of Illinois, Record Group 94, M539, National Archives and Records Administration.
Pension Applications of Widows and Other Dependents of Civil War Veterans, Record Group 15, National Archives and Records Administration.
Record Group 393: Records of U.S. Army Continental Commands, 1821–1920, Military Division of the Missouri, 1866–91, Letters Received, 1861–67, National Archives and Records Administration.
United States War Department. *Revised Regulations for the Army of the United States.* Philadelphia: J. G. L. Brown, 1861.
United States War Department. *The War of the Rebellion: A Compilation of the Official Records of the Union and Confederate Armies.* Washington, D.C.: Government Printing Office, 1880.

Published Primary Sources

Berlin, Ira, Barbara J. Fields, Thavolia Glymph, Joseph P. Reidy, and Leslie S. Rowland, eds. *Freedom: A Documentary History of Emancipation, 1861–1867*, ser. I, vol. I: The Destruction of Slavery. Cambridge: Cambridge University Press, 1985.
Berry, Stephen, and Angela Esco Elder, eds. *Practical Strangers: The Courtship Correspondence of Nathaniel Dawson and Elodie Todd, Sister of Mary Todd Lincoln.* Athens: University of Georgia Press, 2017.
Casino, Joseph J. "'Plenty of Work to Do': Correspondence of an Illinois Farm Girl during the American Civil War." *Civil War History* 65, no. 1 (March 2019): 73–91.
Christ, Mark K., ed. *Getting Used to Being Shot At: The Spence Family Civil War Letters.* Fayetteville: University of Arkansas Press, 2002.
Dickens, Charles. *American Notes for General Circulation*, vol. 2. London: Chapman and Hall, 1842.
Donohoe, Patricia A., ed. *The Printer's Kiss: The Life and Letters of a Civil War Newspaperman and His Family.* Kent, Ohio: Kent State University Press, 2014.

Ellis, Michael, and Michael Montgomery. *Private Voices. Corpus of American Civil War Letters Project*, n.d. https://altchive.org.

Flotow, Mark, ed. *In Their Letters, In Their Words: Illinois Civil War Soldiers Write Home*. Carbondale: Southern Illinois University Press, 2019.

Galbraith, Loretta, and William Galbraith, eds. *A Lost Heroine: The Diaries and Letters of Belle Edmondson*. Jackson: University of Mississippi Press, 1990.

Gould, Benjamin Apthorp. *Investigations in the Military and Anthropological Statistics of American Soldiers*, vol. 2. New York: Hurd and Houghton, 1869.

Grant, Ulysses S. *The Personal Memoirs of Ulysses S. Grant: The Complete Annotated Edition*. Edited by John F. Marzalek, with David S. Nolen and Louie P. Gallo. Cambridge, Massachusetts: Harvard University Press, 2017.

Johannson, M. Jane., ed. *Widows by the Thousand: The Civil War Letters of Theophilus and Harriet Perry, 1862–1864*. Fayetteville: University of Arkansas Press, 2000.

Joiner, Gary D., ed. *Little to Eat and Thin Mud to Drink: Letters, Diaries, and Memoirs from the Red River Campaigns*. Knoxville: University of Tennessee Press, 2007.

———. "'No Pardons to Ask nor Apologies to Make': The Journal of William Henry King." *Louisiana History* 53, no. 1 (Winter 2012): 30–50.

Keating, Ryan W., ed. *The Greatest Trials I Ever Had: The Civil War Letters of Margaret and Thomas Cahill*. Athens: University of Georgia Press, 2017.

LeSueur, A. A. *Official Manual of the State of Missouri for the Years 1893–1894*. Jefferson City: Tribune Printing Company, 1893.

"Letters from the Battle of Lexington: 1861." *Missouri Historical Review* 56, no. 1 (October 1961): 53–58.

McCausland, Susan A. "The Battle of Lexington as Seen by a Woman." *Missouri Historical Review* 6, no. 3 (April 1912): 127–135.

McElligott, Mary Ellen, ed. "'A Monotony Full of Sadness': The Diary of Nadine Turchin, May 1863–April 1864." *Journal of the Illinois State Historical Society* 70, no. 1 (February 1977): 27–89.

Minnesota Board of Commissioners. *Minnesota in the Civil and Indian Wars*. St. Paul: Pioneer Press Company, 1890.

Myers, Lana Wirt, ed. *The Diaries of Reuben Smith, Kansas Settler and Civil War Soldier*. Lawrence: University Press of Kansas, 2018.

Phifer, Louisa Jane, and Carol Benson Pye. "Letters from an Illinois Farm, 1864–1865." *Journal of the Illinois State Historical Society* 66, no. 4 (Winter 1973): 387–403.

Roberts, Timothy Mason, ed. *"This Infernal War": The Civil War Letters of William and Jane Standard*. Kent, Ohio: Kent State University Press, 2018.

Root, George F. *The Battle Cry of Freedom*. Chicago: Root & Cady, 1862.

Silber, Nina, and Mary Beth Sievens, eds. *Yankee Correspondence: Civil War Letters between New England Soldiers and the Home Front*. Charlottesville: University Press of Virginia, 1996.

Secondary Sources

Aley, Ginette, and Joseph L. Anderson, eds. *Union Heartland: The Midwestern Home Front during the Civil War.* Carbondale: Southern Illinois University Press, 2013.

Allardice, Bruce S. "'Illinois Is Rotten with Traitors!' The Republican Defeat in the 1862 State Election." *Journal of the Illinois State Historical Society* 104, nos. 1–2 (Spring–Summer 2011): 97–114.

Anderson, William M. "The Fulton County War at Home and in the Field." *Illinois Historical Journal* 85, no. 1 (Spring 1992): 23–36.

Andrews, C. C. *History of the Campaign of Mobile; Including the Cooperative Operations of Gen. Wilson's Cavalry in Alabama.* New York: D. Van Nostrand Co., 1889.

Arliskas, Thomas M. "The First Brigade of Illinois Militia: Three Months Volunteers." *Journal of the Illinois State Historical Society* 105, nos. 2–3 (Summer–Fall 2012): 173–182.

Ash, Steven V. *When the Yankees Came: Conflict and Chaos in the Occupied South, 1861–1865.* Chapel Hill: University of North Carolina Press, 1995.

Astor, Aaron. *Rebels on the Border: Civil War, Emancipation, and the Reconstruction of Kentucky and Missouri.* Baton Rouge: Louisiana State University Press, 2012.

Attie, Jeanie. *Patriotic Toll: Northern Women and the American Civil War.* Ithaca, New York: Cornell University Press, 1998.

Bahde, Thomas. "'Our Cause Is a Common One': Home Guards, Union Leagues, and Republican Citizenship in Illinois, 1861–1863." *Civil War History* 56, no. 1 (March 2010): 66–98.

Ballantyne, David T. "'Whenever the Yankees Were Gone, I Was a Confederate': Loyalties and Dissent in Civil War-Era Rapides Parish, Louisiana." *Civil War History* 63, no. 1 (March 2017): 36–67.

Barry, Peter J. "Colonel Mitchell's Wars: Confederates, Copperheads, and Bushwackers." *Journal of the Illinois State Historical Society* 107, nos. 3–4 (Fall–Winter 2014): 346–369.

Bell, Jack. *Civil War Heavy Explosive Ordnance: A Guide to Large Artillery Projectiles, Torpedoes, and Mines.* Denton: University of North Texas Press, 2003.

Bercaw, Nancy D. *Gendered Freedoms: Race, Rights, and the Politics of the Household in the Delta, 1861–1875.* Gainesville: University of Florida Press, 2003.

Bergeron, Arthur W. "General Richard Taylor as a Military Commander." *Louisiana History* 23, no. 1 (Winter 1982): 35–47.

Berry, Stephen W. *All That Makes a Man: Love and Ambition in the Civil War South.* New York: Oxford University Press, 2003.

Blake, Kellee Green. "Aiding and Abetting: Disloyalty Prosecutions in the Federal Civil Courts of Southern Illinois, 1861–1866." *Illinois Historical Journal* 87, no. 2 (Summer 1994): 95–108.

Blanton, DeAnne, and Lauren M. Cook. *They Fought Like Demons: Women Soldiers in the American Civil War.* Baton Rouge: Louisiana State University Press, 2002.

Bleser, Carol K., and Lesley J. Gordon, eds. *Intimate Strategies of the Civil War: Military Commanders and Their Wives.* New York: Oxford University Press, 2001.

Bleser, Carol K., and Frederick M. Heath. "The Impact of the Civil War on a Southern Marriage: Clement and Virginia Tunstall Clay of Alabama." *Civil War History* 30, no. 3 (September 1984): 197–220.

Blevins, Brooks. *A History of the Ozarks*, vol. 2: *The Conflicted Ozarks*. Champaign: University of Illinois Press, 2019.

Boatner, Mark Mayo. *The Civil War Dictionary*. New York: Vintage, 1991.

Bohn, Roger E. "Richard Yates: An Appraisal of His Value as the Civil War Governor of Illinois." *Journal of the Illinois State Historical Society*, 104, nos. 1–2 (Spring–Summer 2011): 17–37.

Boman, Dennis K. *Lincoln and Citizens' Rights in Civil War Missouri*. Baton Rouge: Louisiana State University Press, 2011.

Browning, Judkin, and Timothy Silver. *An Environmental History of the Civil War*. Chapel Hill: University of North Carolina Press, 2020.

Brownlee, Richard S. "The Battle of Pilot Knob, Iron County, Missouri, September 27, 1864." *Missouri Historical Review* 59, no. 1 (October 1964): 1–25.

Buck, Stephen J. "'A Contest in Which Blood Must Flow like Water': DuPage County and the Civil War." *Illinois Historical Journal* 87, no. 1 (Spring 1994): 2–20.

Burke, Eric Michael. "Egyptian Darkness: Antebellum Reconstruction, 'Republicanization,' and Southern Illinois in the Republican Imagination, 1854–61." *Civil War History* 67, no. 3 (September 2021): 167–199.

Bynum, Victoria E. *The Free State of Jones: Mississippi's Longest Civil War*. Chapel Hill: University of North Carolina Press, 2001.

Cashin, Joan, ed. *The War Was You and Me: Civilians in the American Civil War*. Princeton, New Jersey: Princeton University Press, 2003.

Castel, Albert. *General Sterling Price and the Civil War in the West*. Baton Rouge: Louisiana State University Press, 1993.

Cimprich, John. *Fort Pillow, a Civil War Massacre, and Public Memory*. Baton Rouge: Louisiana State University Press, 2011.

Clarke, Frances M. *War Stories: Suffering and Sacrifice in the Civil War North*. Chicago: University of Chicago Press, 2011.

Clinton, Catherine. *The Other Civil War: American Women in the Nineteenth Century*. New York: Hill and Wang, 1999.

Clinton, Catherine, and Nina Silber, eds. *Battle Scars: Gender and Sexuality in the American Civil War*. New York: Oxford University Press, 2006.

———. *Divided Houses: Gender and the Civil War*. New York: Oxford University Press, 1992.

Cohen, Joanna. "'You Have No Flag Out Yet?': Commercial Connections and Patriotic Emotion in the Civil War North." *Journal of the Civil War Era* 9, no. 3 (September 2019): 378–409.

Cole, Arthur Charles. *The Centennial History of Illinois: The Era of the Civil War, 1848–1870*, vol. 3. Springfield: Illinois Centennial Commission, 1919.

Cooling, Benjamin Franklin. *To the Battles of Franklin and Nashville and Beyond:*

Stabilization and Reconstruction in Tennessee and Kentucky, 1864–1866. Knoxville: University of Tennessee Press, 2011.

Cornish, Dudley Taylor. *The Sable Arm: Black Troops in the Union Army, 1861–1865*. Lawrence: University Press of Kansas, 1987.

Cott, Nancy F. *Public Vows: A History of Marriage and the Nation*. Cambridge, Massachusetts: Harvard University Press, 2000.

Cowan, Walter Greaves, and Jack B. McGuire. *Louisiana Governors: Rulers, Rascals, and Reformers*. Jackson: University Press of Mississippi, 2008.

Coulter, E. Merton. *William G. Brownlow: Fighting Parson of the Southern Highlands*. 1937; reprint, Knoxville: University of Tennessee Press, 1999.

Cozzens, Peter. *The Darkest Days of the War: The Battles of Iuka and Corinth*. Chapel Hill: University of North Carolina Press, 1997.

Cuccia, Phillip. "'Gorillas' and White Glove Gents: Union Soldiers in the Red River Campaign." *Louisiana History* 36, no. 4 (Autumn 1995): 413–430.

Daniel, Larry J. *Conquered: Why the Army of Tennessee Failed*. Chapel Hill: University of North Carolina Press, 2019.

Dayton, Aretas A. "The Raising of Union Forces in Illinois during the Civil War." *Journal of the Illinois State Historical Society* 34, no. 4 (December 1941): 401–438.

Downs, Jim. *Sick from Freedom: African-American Illness and Suffering during the Civil War and Reconstruction*. New York: Oxford University Press, 2012.

Doyle, Don Harrison. *The Social Order of a Frontier Community: Jacksonville, Illinois, 1825–70*. Urbana: University of Illinois Press, 1978.

Duerkes, Wayne N. "I for One Am Ready to Do My Part: The Initial Motivations That Inspired Men from Northern Illinois to Enlist in the U.S. Army, 1861–1862." *Journal of the Illinois State Historical Society* 105, no. 4 (Winter 2012): 313–332.

Earle, Jonathan, and Diane Mutti Burke, eds. *Bleeding Kansas, Bleeding Missouri: The Long Civil War on the Border*. Lawrence: University Press of Kansas, 2013.

Eicher, John H., and David J. Eicher. *Civil War High Commands*. Stanford, California: Stanford University Press, 2001.

Ellis, Michael. *North Carolina English, 1861–1865: A Guide and Glossary*. Knoxville: University of Tennessee Press, 2013.

Epps, Kristen. *Slavery on the Periphery: The Kansas–Missouri Border in the Antebellum and Civil War Eras*. Athens: University of Georgia Press, 2016.

Etcheson, Nicole. *Bleeding Kansas: Contested Liberty in the Civil War Era*. Lawrence: University Press of Kansas, 2004.

———. *The Emerging Midwest: Upland Southerners and the Political Culture of the Old Northwest, 1787–1861*. Bloomington: Indiana University Press, 1996.

———. *A Generation at War: The Civil War Era in a Northern Community*. Lawrence: University Press of Kansas, 2011.

Faragher, John Mack. *Sugar Creek: Life on the Illinois Prairie*. New Haven, Conn.: Yale University Press, 1986.

Faust, Drew Gilpin. *Mothers of Invention: Women of the Slaveholding South in the American Civil War*. Chapel Hill: University of North Carolina Press, 1996.
Finley, Angela Wallace. "Fort Wright." Tennessee Encyclopedia, Tennessee Historical Society, March 1, 2018. https://www.tennesseeencyclopedia.net/entries/fort-wright/.
Foley, William E., Lawrence O. Christensen, and Gary R. Kremer, eds. *Dictionary of Missouri Biography*. Columbia: University of Missouri Press, 1999.
Frank, Lisa Tendrich, and LeeAnn Whites, eds. *Household War: How Americans Lived and Fought the Civil War*. Athens: University of Georgia Press, 2020.
Franklin, John Hope. "James T. Ayers, Civil War Recruiter." *Journal of the Illinois State Historical Society* 40, no. 3 (September 1947): 267–297.
Fredette, Allison Dorothy. *Marriage on the Border: Love, Mutuality, and Divorce in the Upper South during the Civil War*. Lexington: University Press of Kentucky, 2020.
Gallagher, Gary W., ed. *The Shenandoah Valley Campaign of 1864*. Chapel Hill: University of North Carolina Press, 2006.
———. *The Union War*. Cambridge, Massachusetts: Harvard University Press, 2011.
Gallman, J. Matthew. *Defining Duty in the Civil War: Personal Choice, Popular Culture, and the Union Home Front*. Chapel Hill: University of North Carolina Press, 2015.
———. *The North Fights the Civil War: The Home Front*. Chicago: Ivan R. Dee, 1994.
Gerlach, Russell L. *Settlement Patterns in Missouri: A Study of Population Origins*. Columbia: University of Missouri Press, 1986.
Gerling, Edwin G. *117th Illinois Infantry Volunteers, 1862–1865*. Self-published, 1992.
Gerteis, Louis S. *The Civil War in Missouri: A Military History*. Columbia: University of Missouri Press, 2012.
———. *Civil War St. Louis*. Lawrence: University Press of Kansas, 2001.
———. *From Contraband to Freedman: Federal Policy toward Southern Blacks 1861–1865*. Westport, Connecticut: Greenwood Press, 1973.
Giesberg, Judith. *Army at Home: Women and the Civil War on the Northern Home Front*. Chapel Hill: University of North Carolina Press, 2009.
Gillispie, James M. *Andersonvilles of the North: The Myths and Realities of Northern Treatment of Civil War Confederate Prisoners*. Denton: University of North Texas Press, 2008.
Girardi, Robert I. "'I Am for the President's Proclamation Teeth and Toe Nails': Illinois Soldiers Respond to the Emancipation Proclamation." *Journal of the Illinois State Historical Society* 106, nos. 3–4 (Fall–Winter 2013): 395–421.
Glymph, Thavolia. "'I'm a Radical Black Girl': Black Women Unionists and the Politics of Civil War History." *Journal of the Civil War Era* 8, no. 3 (September 2018): 359–387.
———. *The Women's Fight: The Civil War's Battles for Home, Freedom, and Nation*. Chapel Hill: University of North Carolina Press, 2019.

Goodwin, Doris Kearns. *Team of Rivals: The Political Genius of Abraham Lincoln.* New York: Simon and Schuster, 2005.
Gosnell, H. Allen. *Guns on the Western Waters: The Story of River Gunboats in the Civil War.* Baton Rouge: Louisiana State University Press, 1949.
Grasso, Christopher. *Teacher, Preacher, Soldier, Spy: The Civil Wars of John R. Kelso.* New York: Oxford University Press, 2021.
Grossberg, Michael. *Governing the Hearth: Law and the Family in Nineteenth-Century America.* Chapel Hill: University of North Carolina Press, 1985.
Guelzo, Allen C. *Gettysburg: The Last Invasion.* New York: Vintage, 2014.
Guldi, Jo. *Roads to Power: Britain Invents the Infrastructure State.* Cambridge, Massachusetts: Harvard University Press, 2012.
Hacker, J. David. "Economic, Demographic, and Anthropometric Correlates of First Marriage in the Mid-Nineteenth-Century United States." *Social Science History* 32, no. 3 (Fall 2008): 307–345.
Hager, Christopher. *I Remain Yours: Common Lives in Civil War Letters.* Cambridge, Massachusetts: Harvard University Press, 2018.
Hamilton, James A. "The Enrolled Missouri Militia: Its Creation and Controversial History." *Missouri Historical Review* 69, no. 4 (July 1975), 413–432.
Harrelson, Danny W., Nalini Torres, Amber Tillotson, and Mansour Zakikhani. "Geological Influence of the Great Red River Raft on the Red River Campaign of the American Civil War." In *Military Aspects of Geology: Fortification, Excavation, and Terrain Evaluation,* edited by E. P. F. Rose, J. Ehlen, and U. L. Lawrence, 267–273. London: Geological Society, 2018.
Harris, Norman Dwight. *The History of Negro Servitude in Illinois, and of the Slavery Agitation in That State, 1719–1864.* Chicago: A. C. McClurg & Co., 1904.
Hartog, Hendrik. *Man and Wife in America: A History.* Cambridge, Massachusetts: Harvard University Press, 2002.
Hazlett, James C., Edwin Olmstead, and M. Hume Parks. *Field Artillery Weapons of the Civil War.* Urbana: University of Illinois Press, 2004.
Hess, Earl J. *The Civil War in the West: Victory and Defeat from the Appalachians to the Mississippi.* Chapel Hill: University of North Carolina Press, 2012.
———. "The Early Indicators Project: Using Massive Data and Statistical Analysis to Understand the Life Cycle of Civil War Soldiers." *Civil War History* 63, no. 4 (December 2017): 377–399.
———. *Liberty, Virtue, and Progress: Northerners and Their War for the Union.* New York: Fordham University Press, 2020.
———. *Storming Vicksburg: Grant, Pemberton, and the Battles of May 19–22, 1863.* Chapel Hill: University of North Carolina Press, 2020.
Hesseltine, William B. *Lincoln and the War Governors.* New York: Alfred A. Knopf, 1955.
Hicken, Victor. *Illinois in the Civil War.* Urbana: University of Illinois Press, 1966.
History of Cole, Moniteau, Morgan, Benton, Miller, Maries, and Osage Counties, Missouri. Chicago: Goodspeed, 1889.

History of Johnson County, Missouri. Kansas City: Kansas City Historical Association, 1881.
History of St. Clair County, Illinois. Philadelphia: Brink, McDonough, & Co., 1881.
Hollandsworth, James G. *Pretense of Glory: The Life of General Nathaniel P. Banks.* Baton Rouge: Louisiana State University Press, 1998.
Hubbart, Henry Clyde. "'Pro-Southern' Influences in the Free West, 1840–1865." *Mississippi Valley Historical Review* 20, no. 1 (June 1933): 45–62.
Hulbert, Matthew C. *The Ghosts of Guerrilla Memory: How Civil War Bushwhackers Became Gunslingers in the American West.* Athens: University of Georgia Press, 2016.
Jamieson, Perry D. *Spring 1865: The Closing Campaigns of the Civil War.* Lincoln: University of Nebraska Press, 2015.
Jimerson, Randall C. *The Private Civil War: Popular Thought during the Sectional Conflict.* Baton Rouge: Louisiana State University Press, 1994.
Johnson, Ludwell. *Red River Campaign: Politics and Cotton in the Civil War.* Baltimore, Maryland: Johns Hopkins University Press, 1958.
Joiner, Gary D. *Mr. Lincoln's Brown Water Navy: The Mississippi Squadron.* Lanham, Maryland: Rowman and Littlefield, 2007.
Jordan, Daniel W. *Operational Art and the Campaigns for Mobile: A Staff Ride Handbook.* Fort Leavenworth, Kansas: Combat Studies Institute Press, 2019.
Keehn, David C. *Knights of the Golden Circle: Secret Empire, Southern Secession, Civil War.* Baton Rouge: Louisiana State University Press, 2013.
Kemmerly, Phillip R. "'Fighting and Dying in a Frozen Hell': The Impact of Ice, Snow, Fog, and Frozen-Hard Ground on the Battle of Nashville." *Tennessee Historical Quarterly* 74, no. 2 (Summer 2015): 74–103.
———. "Rivers, Rails, and Rebels: Logistics and Struggle to Supply U.S. Army Depot at Nashville, 1862–1865." *Military History* 84, no. 3 (July 2020): 713–746.
Klement, Frank L. "Copperhead Secret Societies in Illinois during the Civil War." *Journal of the Illinois State Historical Society* 48, no. 2 (Summer 1955): 152–180.
———. *The Copperheads in the Middle West.* Chicago: University of Chicago Press, 1960.
———. *Dark Lanterns: Secret Political Societies, Conspiracies, and Treason Trials in the Civil War.* Baton Rouge: Louisiana State University Press, 1984.
Kirsch, George B. *Baseball in Blue and Gray: The National Pastime during the Civil War.* Princeton, New Jersey: Princeton University Press, 2003.
Lamphier, Peg A. *Kate Chase and William Sprague: Politics and Gender in a Civil War Marriage.* Lincoln: University of Nebraska Press, 2000.
Lang, Andrew F. *In the Wake of War: Occupation, Emancipation, and Civil War America.* Baton Rouge: Louisiana State University, 2017.
Lash, Jeffrey N. "'The Federal Tyrant at Memphis': General Stephen A. Hurlbut and the Union Occupation of West Tennessee, 1862–1864." *Tennessee Historical Quarterly* 48, no. 1 (Spring 1989): 15–28.
Lause, Mark A. *Price's Lost Campaign: The 1864 Invasion of Missouri.* Columbia: University of Missouri Press, 2011.

Lawson, Melinda. *Patriot Fires: Forging a New American Nationalism in the Civil War North*. Lawrence: University Press of Kansas, 2002.

———. "'A Profound National Devotion': The Civil War Union Leagues and the Construction of a New National Patriotism." *Civil War History* 48, no. 4 (December 2002): 338–362.

Leonard, Elizabeth. *Yankee Women: Gender Battles in the Civil War*. New York: Norton, 1994.

Lippmann, Ellen, and Martin McMahon. "Professionalism and Politics in the Procurement Process: United States Civil War Early Years." *Accounting Historians Journal* 44, no. 1 (June 2017): 63–76.

Lystra, Karen. *Searching the Heart: Women, Men, and Romantic Love in Nineteenth-Century America*. New York: Oxford University Press, 1992.

Manning, Chandra. *Troubled Refuge: Struggling for Freedom in the Civil War*. New York: Alfred A. Knopf, 2017.

———. *What This Cruel War Was Over: Soldiers, Slavery, and the Civil War*. New York: Vintage, 2007.

Marshall, Anne E. *Creating a Confederate Kentucky: The Lost Cause and Civil War Memory in a Border State*. Chapel Hill: University of North Carolina Press, 2013.

Marten, James A. *The Children's Civil War*. Chapel Hill: University of North Carolina Press, 2000.

Maslowski, Peter. *Treason Must Be Made Odious: Military Occupation and Wartime Reconstruction in Wartime Nashville, Tennessee, 1862–1865*. Millwood, New York: KTO Press, 1978.

Massey, Mary Elizabeth. *Women in the Civil War*. Lincoln: University of Nebraska Press, 1966.

Mathews, Mitford M. *A Dictionary of Americanisms on Historical Principles*, vol. 1. Chicago: University of Chicago Press, 1951.

Mathisen, Erik. *The Loyal Republic: Traitors, Slaves, and the Remaking of Citizenship in Civil War America*. Chapel Hill: University of North Carolina Press, 2018.

Mattei, Eileen. "A Tale of Two Forts on Mobile Bay: Fort Gaines and Fort Morgan." *On Point* 20, no. 2 (Fall 2014), 38–42.

McCurry, Stephanie. *Confederate Reckoning: Power and Politics in the Civil War South*. Cambridge, Massachusetts: Harvard University Press, 2010.

———. *Women's War: Fighting and Surviving the American Civil War*. Cambridge, Massachusetts: Belknap, 2019.

McPherson, James. *Battle Cry of Freedom: The Civil War Era*. New York: Oxford University Press, 1988.

———. *For Cause and Comrades: Why Men Fought in the Civil War*. New York: Oxford University Press, 1997.

———. *War on the Waters: The Union and Confederate Navies, 1861–1865*. Chapel Hill: University of North Carolina Press, 2012.

McPherson, James, and William J. Cooper. *Writing the Civil War: The Quest to Understand*. Columbia: University of South Carolina Press, 1998.

McWhirter, Christian. *Battle Hymns: The Power and Popularity of Music in the Civil War.* Chapel Hill: University of North Carolina Press, 2012.

Meier, Kathryn S. "'No Place for the Sick': Nature's War on Civil War Soldier Mental and Physical Health in the 1862 Peninsula and Shenandoah Valley Campaigns." *Journal of the Civil War Era* 1, no. 2 (June 2011): 176–206.

Meiners, Fredericka. "Hamilton P. Bee in the Red River Campaign of 1864." *Southwestern Historical Quarterly* 78, no. 1 (July 1974): 21–44.

Mercker, David, and Adam Taylor. "Firewood Harvesting as a Forest Management Tool." May 2020, 1–16. https://utia.tennessee.edu/publications/wp-content/uploads/sites/269/2023/10/PB1880.pdf.

Merrill, James M. "Cairo, Illinois: Strategic Civil War River Port." *Journal of the Illinois State Historical Society* 76, no. 4 (Winter 1983): 242–256.

Miller, Jason. "To Stop These Wolves' Forays: Provost Marshals, Desertion, the Draft, and Political Violence on the Central Illinois Home Front." *Journal of the Illinois State Historical Society* 105, nos. 2–3 (Summer–Fall 2012): 202–224.

Milligan, John D. *Gunboats Down the Mississippi.* Annapolis, Maryland: United States Naval Institute, 1965.

Mintz, Steven. *A Prison of Expectations: The Family in Victorian Culture.* New York: New York University Press, 1983.

Mintz, Steven, and Susan Kellogg. *Domestic Revolutions: A Social History of American Family Life.* New York: Simon and Schuster, 1989.

Mitchell, Reid. *Civil War Soldiers.* New York: Viking, 1988.

———. *The Vacant Chair: The Northern Soldier Leaves Home.* New York: Oxford University Press, 1993.

Mountcastle, Clay. *Punitive War: Confederate Guerrillas and Union Reprisals.* Lawrence: University Press of Kansas, 2009.

Mueller, Richard. "Jefferson Barracks: The Early Years." *Missouri Historical Review* 67, no. 1 (October 1972), 7–30.

Murdock, Eugene Converse. *Patriotism Limited, 1862–1865: The Civil War Draft and the Bounty System.* Kent, Ohio: Kent State University Press, 1967.

National Park Service. "From Regiment to President: The Structure and Command of Civil War Armies," https://www.nps.gov/articles/from-regiment-to-president-the-structure-and-command-of-civil-war-armies.htm.

Nelson, Scott Reynolds, and Carol Sheriff. *A People at War: Civilians and Soldiers in America's Civil War.* New York: Oxford University Press, 2007.

Neely, Jeremy. *The Border between Them: Violence and Reconciliation on the Kansas-Missouri Line.* Columbia: University of Missouri Press, 2007.

Neely, Jeremy, and Trevor Martin, eds. "'The Terrors and Trials of War': The Civil War Papers of Henry and Cimbaline Fike." *Missouri Historical Review* 115, no. 2 (January 2021), 107–133.

Neely, Mark E. *The Civil War and the Limits of Destruction.* Cambridge, Massachusetts: Harvard University Press, 2009.

Nelson, Megan Kate. *Ruin Nation: Destruction and the American Civil War.* Athens: University of Georgia Press, 2012.

Niepman, Ann D. "General Orders No. 11 and Border War during the Civil War." *Missouri Historical Review* 66, no. 2 (January 1972), 185–210.

Oertel, Kristen. *Bleeding Borders: Race, Gender, and Violence in Pre-Civil War Kansas.* Baton Rouge: Louisiana State University Press, 2009.

Osterud, Nancy Grey. *Bonds of Community: The Lives of Farm Women in Nineteenth-Century New York.* Ithaca, New York: Cornell University Press, 1991.

Parks, Joseph H. "A Confederate Trade Center under Federal Occupation: Memphis, 1862 to 1865." *Journal of Southern History* 7, no. 3 (August 1941): 289–314.

Pellet, Elias P. *History of the 114th Regiment, New York State Volunteers.* Norwich, New York: Telegraph and Chronicle, 1866.

Peterson, William S. "A History of Camp Butler, 1861–1866." *Illinois Historical Journal* 82, no. 2 (Summer 1989): 74–92.

Phillips, Christopher. *The Rivers Ran Backward: The Civil War and the Remaking of the American Middle Border.* New York: Oxford University Press, 2016.

Rael, Patrick. *Black Identity and Black Protest in the Antebellum North.* Chapel Hill: University of North Carolina Press, 2002.

Ramsay, Robert L. *Our Storehouse of Missouri Place Names.* Columbia: University of Missouri Press, 1973.

Raus, Edmund J. *Banners South: A Northern Community at War.* Kent, Ohio: Kent State University Press, 2005.

Risch, Erna. *Quartermaster Support of the Army: A History of the Corps.* Washington, D.C.: Quartermaster Historian's Office, 1962.

Robinson, Michael D. *A Union Indivisible: Secession and the Politics of Slavery in the Border South.* Chapel Hill: University of North Carolina Press, 2017.

Rose, Anne C. *Victorian America and the Civil War.* Cambridge: Cambridge University Press, 1994.

Rotundo, E. Anthony. *American Manhood: Transformations in Masculinity from the Revolution to the Modern Era.* New York: Basic Books, 1993.

Ruminski, Jarret. *The Limits of Loyalty: Ordinary People in Civil War Mississippi.* Oxford: University Press of Mississippi, 2017.

Sacher, John M. "'Our Interest and Destiny Are the Same': Gov. Thomas Overton Moore and Confederate Loyalty." *Louisiana History* 49, no. 3 (Summer 2008): 261–286.

Sampson, Robert D. " 'Pretty Damned Warm Times': The 1864 Charleston Riot and 'The Inalienable Right of Revolution.'" *Illinois Historical Journal* 89, no. 2 (Summer 1996): 99–116.

Sanders Jr., Charles W. "Jefferson Davis and the Hampton Roads Peace Conference: 'To Secure Peace to the Two Countries.'" *Journal of Southern History* 63, no. 4 (November 1997): 803–826.

Schroeder, Walter A. *Presettlement Prairie of Missouri*. Jefferson City: Missouri Department of Conservation, 1982.

Schwalm, Leslie. *Emancipation's Diaspora: Race and Reconstruction in the Upper Midwest*. Chapel Hill: University of North Carolina Press, 2009.

Sebastian, Jonathan W. "A Divided State: The 1862 Election and the Illinois Response to Expanding Federal Authority." *Journal of the Illinois State Historical Society* 106, nos. 3–4 (Fall–Winter 2013): 381–394.

Seip, Terry L. "Slaves and Free Negroes in Alexandria, 1850–1860." *Louisiana History* 10, no. 2 (Spring, 1969): 147–165.

Sheehan-Dean, Aaron, ed. *A Companion to the U.S. Civil War*. Chichester, U.K.: Wiley, 2014.

Shoemaker, Floyd C. "Dedication of Missouri's Capitol, October 6, 1924." *Missouri Historical Review* 19, no. 2 (January 1925) 300–303.

Silber, Nina. *Daughters of the Union: Northern Women Fight the Civil War*. Cambridge, Massachusetts: Harvard University Press, 2005.

Simpson, Brooks D. *Ulysses S. Grant: Triumph over Adversity*. Boston: Houghton Mifflin, 2000.

Sinisi, Kyle. *The Last Hurrah: Sterling Price's Missouri Expedition of 1864*. Lanham, Maryland: Rowman and Littlefield, 2015.

Sizer, Lyde Cullen. *The Political Work of Northern Women Writers and the Civil War, 1850–1872*. Chapel Hill: University of North Carolina Press, 2003.

Smith, Michael Thomas. "'For Love of Cotton': Nathaniel P. Banks, Union Strategy, and the Red River Campaign." *Louisiana History* 51, no. 1 (Winter 2010): 9–26.

Stanley, Matthew E. *The Loyal West: Civil War and Reunion in Middle America*. Urbana: University of Illinois Press, 2016.

Sterling, Robert E. "Civil War Draft Resistance in Illinois." *Journal of the Illinois State Historical Society* 64, no. 3 (Autumn 1971): 244–266.

———. "Discouragement, Weariness, and War Politics: Desertions from Illinois Regiments during the Civil War." *Journal of the Illinois State Historical Society* 82, no. 4 (Winter 1989): 239–262.

Sternhell, Yael A. *Routes of War: The World of Movement in the Confederate South*. Cambridge, Massachusetts: Harvard University Press, 2012.

Syrett, John. *The Civil War Confiscation Acts: Failing to Reconstruct the South*. New York: Fordham University Press, 2002.

Taylor, Amy Murrell. *The Divided Family in Civil War America*. Chapel Hill: University of North Carolina Press, 2005.

———. *Embattled Freedom: Journeys through the Civil War's Slave Refugee Camps*. Chapel Hill: University of North Carolina Press, 2018.

Taylor, Lenette. *"The Supply for Tomorrow Must Not Fail": The Civil War of Captain Simon Perkins, Jr., Union Quartermaster*. Kent, Ohio: Kent State University Press, 2004.

Taylor, Paul. *"The Most Complete Political Machine Ever Known": The North's Union Leagues in the American Civil War.* Kent, Ohio: Kent State University Press, 2018.

Taunton, Thomas Henry. *Portraits of Celebrated Racehorses of the Past and Present Centuries,* vol. II, *From 1797 to 1824.* London: Sampson Low, Marston, Searle & Rivington, 1887.

Tomblin, Barbara Brooks. *The Civil War on the Mississippi: Union Sailors, Gunboat Captains, and the Campaign to Control the River.* Lexington: University Press of Kentucky, 2016.

Urban, William. "Monmouth College in the Civil War." *Journal of the Illinois State Historical Society* 71, no. 1 (February 1978): 13–21.

Varon, Elizabeth. *Appomattox: Victory, Defeat, and Freedom at the End of the Civil War.* New York: Oxford University Press, 2014.

Vinovskis, Maris A., ed. *Toward a Social History of the American Civil War: Exploratory Essays.* Cambridge: Cambridge University Press, 1990.

Waugh, John C. *Reelecting Lincoln: The Battle for the 1864 Presidency.* New York: Crown, 1997.

Weber, Jennifer. *Copperheads: The Rise and Fall of Lincoln's Opponents in the North.* New York: Oxford University Press, 2006.

Weigley, Russell F. *A Great Civil War: A Military and Political History, 1861–1865.* Bloomington: Indiana University Press, 2000.

Weir, Rebecca. "'An Oblique Place': Letters in the Civil War." In *The Edinburgh Companion to Nineteenth-Century American Letters and Letter-Writing,* edited by Celeste-Marie Bernier, Judie Newman, and Matthew Pethers, 271–286. Edinburgh: Edinburgh University Press, 2016.

Whites, LeeAnn. *The Civil War as a Crisis in Gender: Augusta, Georgia, 1860–1890.* Athens: University of Georgia Press, 1995.

Whites, LeeAnn, and Alecia P. Long, eds. *Occupied Women: Gender, Military Occupation, and the American Civil War.* Baton Rouge: Louisiana State University Press, 2009.

Whittington, G. P. "Rapides Parish, Louisiana, A History, X." *Louisiana Historical Quarterly* 18, no. 1 (January 1935): 5–39.

Wiley, Bell. *The Life of Billy Yank: The Common Soldier of the Union.* Baton Rouge: Louisiana State University Press, 1952.

———. *The Life of Johnny Reb: The Common Soldier of the Confederacy.* Baton Rouge: Louisiana State University Press, 1971.

Wills, Brian Steel. *The River Was Dyed with Blood: Nathan Bedford Forrest and Fort Pillow.* Norman: University of Oklahoma Press, 2014.

Wilson, Keith P. *Campfires of Freedom: The Camp Life of Black Soldiers during the Civil War.* Kent, Ohio: Kent State University Press, 2002.

Winters, John D. *The Civil War in Louisiana.* Baton Rouge: Louisiana State University Press, 1963.

Woods, Michael E. *Emotional and Sectional Conflict in the Antebellum United States.* Cambridge: Cambridge University Press, 2014.

Woodworth, Steven E., and Charles D. Grear, eds. *The Tennessee Campaign of 1864.* Carbondale: Southern Illinois University Press, 2016.

Index

6th Minnesota Infantry, 201–202
13th Army Corps (Union), 117, 121, 185, 190
16th Army Corps (Union), 177; campaigns in Alabama, 181, 185, 190, 197n25, 200, 207; Red River expedition, 13, 103, 108, 117–120
17th Army Corps (Union), 120
19th Army Corps (Union), 117–118
32nd Wisconsin Infantry, 45
48th Ohio Infantry, 50
117th Illinois Infantry, 2, 5–7, 10–11, 74, 209; Camp Butler, 19–22, 25, 30, 35, 39, 42; march through central Mississippi, 13, 102–103, 106; march through Missouri, 14, 128, 130, 133, 136; movements in Alabama, 15, 180–188, 199, 202, 204, 207; Nashville campaign, 14–15, 156–157, 162, 166–172; New Orleans, 177–178; occupation of Memphis, 11, 44, 50–60, 67–71, 83, 98; Red River Expedition, 14, 103, 112–113, 118
120th Illinois Infantry, 50
130th Illinois Infantry, 118
178th New York Infantry, 174

African Americans, 10, 13, 56, 199, 207–208; celebration of Black soldiers, 15, 90, 182, 197–198; contrabands, 73–74, 89; hostility toward, 78n11, 82–83, 90, 182; laborers, serving Henry and officers, 64, 81, 89, 98–100, 109, 188; residents of Memphis, 46–47, 63, 90–92, 107; soldiers, in field, 123n31, 174, 190; soldiers, organization of, 12, 67–69, 73, 90, 110. *See also* racism, anti-black; slavery; United States Colored Troops
Appleby, John, 71
Army of Northern Virginia (Confederate), 192n20, 195. *See also* Lee, Robert E.
Army of Tennessee (Confederate), 156n1, 157, 172n26, 195n24. *See also* Hood, John Bell
Army of the Potomac (Union), 55n19, 181

Banks, Nathaniel P., 103–104, 112–119, 122n30, 123n31
Barth, Ellen, 27n18
battles: of Franklin (Tenn.), 157n1, 159; of Mansfield, 13, 103, 117n24; of Nashville, 14, 15n40, 156–157, 161–164; of Pleasant Hill, 13, 103–104, 118–119; of Sabine Crossroads, 103, 117n24, 118n25; of Spanish Fort, 187–192; of Westport, 130
Beath, Charles, 48, 51
Beauregard, Pierre Gustave Toutant, 195
Blake, Martha, 35, 40
boarding, as source of income, 19, 27–28, 35, 40; by Cimbaline, 13, 53–54, 58, 104, 123
boats, 110, 124, 126; hospital boats, 115; rebel gunboats, 111, 187, 189; rebel transports, 111, 187; Union gunboats, 108n12, 117–123, 159, 185, 187, 195; Union transports, 116–120, 121n29, 187, 195, 197. *See also* steamboats
Border West, 9–10
Britt, Mary, 32
Britt, William, 32
Brown, Rev., 35

Brownlow, William G. "Parson," 35–36
bushwhackers, 145, 151, 153. *See also* guerrillas

Camp Butler, 11, 21–22, 27, 40–43, 47, 52
Canby, Edward R. S., 180
Carr, Mr. (renter), 32
Chalmers, James Robert, 68
children: impact of war on, 33, 84, 104, 141, 194; observers of military movements, 132, 139, 197; presence among refugees, 50, 73, 78; vulnerability to illness, 6, 74, 87, 89. *See also* Fike, Ellie; parenting
Christmas, 5, 12, 61, 98, 165, 210; plans for celebration, 56, 142
civilians, southern, 39, 73, 82, 196, 198, 200; accusations of Union depredations, 49, 51; hardships suffered by, 43, 94, 164–165; pity for, 7, 49–50, 157, 164; poor whites, 124, 193, 205; war weariness among, 94, 200. *See also* occupation, military; refugees
Confederates. *See* secessionists
conscription. *See* draft
Copperheads, 71, 171; hostility toward, by Cimbaline, 8, 72, 79, 85, 100; presence near Mascoutah, 12, 67, 79, 81, 206. *See also* secessionists
cotton, 103n3, 125, 194n23; trade of, 12, 46–47, 73, 94
Crane, Isaac, 166
Crane, Mary, 166
crime: attempted burglaries, 40, 48, 51, 74; increase of, in Mascoutah, 9, 20, 37, 72, 88; murders, 83n20, 207–208; thefts, in Memphis, 13, 82–83
Curtis, James, 29n21, 57
Curtis, Mary, 29, 52
Curtis, Samuel R., 66, 150
Curtis, Thomas, 69–70, 90

Davis, Jefferson, 26, 66, 72, 85, 172–173, 201
Davis, Jerry, 109
Day, Amos, 34, 37, 41, 51, 97, 146
debts, 14, 34, 48, 51, 130, 148–149; frugality as means to escape, 34, 58, 148–149; money owed to Henry and Cimbaline, 31, 38, 52, 58, 140n23, 141. *See also* farms; income; marriage: financial strains on
Densons (Unionist landlords), 124
dental problems, 6, 74, 98–99, 135. *See also* sickness
desertion, 66, 146n36, 186
destruction of property, 13, 49, 102–106, 164–165, 175
disease. *See* sickness
domestic labor. *See* housekeeping
draft, 8, 14, 131; avoidance by hiring substitutes, 8, 129, 134–135, 140, 142, 146
dreams, 47n8, 52, 70, 123, 200
Dupuy, Jesse, 98
duty, 8–9, 11, 37, 41, 74, 141; invocations of, by Henry, 26, 28, 34, 84, 126, 163

Edwards, Riley, 31
emancipation, 9–10, 56, 182, 200; Emancipation Proclamation, 12, 44, 63n26, 74n6; military as agents of, 13, 44
encampments, military, 1, 4, 6, 11; Alabama, 183, 196–197, 207; Arkansas, 93; Louisiana, 178–179, Missouri, 132, 138, 142, 145, 150; Tennessee, 45, 49, 67, 123
enlistment, 5–8, 23, 156–157, 180; criticisms of those who refused, 56, 60, 85; Henry, 10–11, 19, 28, 92, 157, 163

farms, 4, 10, 13, 64, 147; cultivation by formerly enslaved people, 73, 89, 141; management of, 19, 30–34, 37–38, 58–62, 130, 141; renting, as source of income, 38, 68, 140–141, 169
Farragut, David, 180
Fike, Anderson (nephew), 34, 40, 47–48, 56, 135, 167
Fike, Ausby (brother), 30, 58, 144, 149n40, 152, 209; descriptions as selfish, 149; failure to assist Cimbaline, 69, 74–75, 79; sickness, 166–167, 171,

173; source of potential assistance, 31, 34, 52, 62
Fike, Doniphan (nephew), 30, 111
Fike, Ellie (daughter), 5, 21n6, 30, 55, 65; descriptions of Henry's service, 8, 70, 87, 93, 107, 171; education of, 199, 210; gifts for, 120, 124, 127, 152, 193; mischief of, 33, 37–38, 47, 64, 75, 168; missing Henry, 33, 65, 104–108, 127, 135, 148; nighttime rituals with Cimbaline, 48; object of longing, by Henry, 46, 64, 91, 139, 175; play, by, 27, 37–38, 107, 148; prayers for safekeeping, 122; recovery from sickness, 24, 27, 99, 107; sickness, 6, 23–27, 79–81, 124–126, 131–135, 210; stays with extended family, 15, 158, 173; visits to South, 11–13, 44, 46, 52–58, 62, 124. *See also* children; Fike, Nancy; parenting
Fike, James A. (nephew), 32, 35
Fike, John W. (nephew), 49, 152
Fike, Mary Jane (niece), 48
Fike, Nancy (mother), 21n6, 35, 69, 131, 142, 146; dependence on Cimbaline for letters, 26; disagreements with Cimbaline, 193; disappointment with family, 30, 33, 152; interactions with Ellie, 47, 65, 70, 146; source of advice, 42, 56–58, 96, 141, 204; visits by, 135, 166, 175, 202
Fike, Polly Ann (sister-in-law), 91, 93, 148, 152; sickness and recovery, 166–167, 171, 173
firewood: consumption by households, 34, 59, 142; consumption by soldiers, 43, 54, 157, 164, 172; consumption by steamboats, 39, 115
Fitch, Dr., 58, 86
flags, 12, 72, 77, 80, 85, 145
Flannery, Thomas A., 141
flogging, 13, 83, 182
fodder, 34, 106, 153–154, 157, 195, 199
food, 182, army rations, 25, 56, 92–93, 157, 174, 199; items produced in Illinois homes, 71, 77; produce of southern farms, 93, 112–113, 125, 176, 194–196, 199
foraging, 93, 106–113, 153–157, 164, 195, 199; clothing, 125
Forrest, Nathan Bedford, 172, 185–186
forts: DeRussy, 103, 112; Donelson, 23n11, 26, 156n1; Gaines, 184; Morgan, 180–187; Pickering, 10–12, 17, 43, 50, 73, 102; Pike, 183; Spanish Fort / Fort Spanish, 186–192
Fourth of July. *See* Independence Day

gender: challenges to notions of, 72, 85, 94–96; manhood, 4, 8, 51, 84, 95; womanhood, 4, 133; women's independence as result of war, 34, 51, 54, 74, 79, 104
General Order Number 130, 151n43
George (laborer), 188
German Americans, 31, 74, 88, 135, 138, 169
Gibbs, Celia, 29
Gilbert, James, 192, 206
Gillham, John D., 57
Gilmore, Frank H., 83
Grant, Ulysses S.: campaigns in West, 26n15, 63n27, 68, 73; as general-in-chief of Union forces, 102, 172, 192, 195n24, 197, 200
Gregg, Martin B., 25
Griffin, John, 170
guerrillas: presence in trans-Mississippi West, 103n4, 124n32, 130, 145, 151n43; threats to Memphis, 11, 45, 63
gun: acquired for self-defense, 51, 54, 56, 94; use by Cimbaline against potential burglar, 74, 95

Hawes, Alexander G., 66
Hawkins, Mary Josephina, 94
Hilworth, John, 146
Hoit, John, 51
Hood, John Bell, 156–164, 168, 172. *See also* Army of Tennessee
horses, 46n7, 115, 182, 205; acquisition and use by Henry, 10, 30, 46, 51, 197; Cimbaline, request for, 30; Ellie, gift

INDEX

horses (*continued*)
  for, 120, 127, 152, 188; property seized by armies, 114, 140, 142; use by Union army, 106, 164, 179n31. *See also* livestock
hospitals, 80n14, 99, 150, 191, 207
housekeeping, 10; African American laborers, 4, 100; Cimbaline, 38, 59, 80; Ellie, 210
humor, 44–45, 51, 66, 93, 96, 174
Hurlbut, Stephen A., 81–83

income, 29; farm, 5, 31, 58; payment for soldiers, 19, 31, 197, 204
Independence Day, 12, 15, 84, 181, 196, 207; controversy over flag, 72, 85. *See also* patriotism; secessionists; unionism
Irving Block, 80
Jim (laborer), 81, 98
Johnson, Andrew, 144n31, 195n24, 202
Johnson, James, 139
Johnston, Joseph, 192, 195

Land, Garrett C., 76
Land, Moses, 209
Land, Nathan, 13, 29n21, 57n21, 209
landforms, 7, 108, 160; beaches, 184, 186; Ozark hills, 142; prairies, 4, 130, 143–144, 150–151, 209; swamps, 63n27, 114, 194, 196
Lee, Robert E., 15, 160n10, 181, 192–193, 197–198; Army of Northern Virginia, 192n20, 195
Lincoln, Abraham, 21n5, 67n30, 83n19, 116, 173n27; assassination of, 181, 196, 198–199, 202n32; election of 1864, 14, 103n3, 130, 144, 152–156. *See also* emancipation
Lindsey (laborer), 89
lint, picking, 44, 48, 53
livestock, 187, 195; cattle, 39, 43, 142, 164, 191, 205; hogs, 93, 164, 191; mules, owned by southerners, 98, 115, 205; mules, used by Union army, 7, 43, 46, 106, 191; oxen, 205; poultry, 93, 106, 113, 142, 203; sheep, 191. *See also* horses

manhood. *See under* gender
maps, 33, 37, 86, 147, 177, 188
marching, 13–15; Alabama, 194; Louisiana, 117, 120–121; Mississippi, 108; Missouri, 128, 139, 153; Tennessee, 162–167. *See also* soldiering
Marmaduke, John Sappington, 136, 151
marriage, 3–4, 61, 84, 91, 210; affection, 3, 59, 127; financial strains on, 14–16, 19, 44, 99, 130, 149; tensions, 40–41, 54, 57
Mathews, Addy, 40
McClure, Narcissa, 141
McDonald, Charles, 47
McGowan, John, 169
McKendree College, 5–6, 11
McPonles, Milt, 52
McWilliams, Robert, 152
medical treatments: Cimbaline, 58, 85–86, 99, 124, 167, 173; Henry, 55, 81. *See also* physicians; sickness
Merriam, Jonathan, 67, 160, 189
migration: desire by Cimbaline, 97, 131, 158, 171, 178; neighbors leaving Mascoutah, 139, 204; plans to move, 86, 175; relocation after war, 209
militias, 12n34, 129, 132n6, 136, 138, 142
Miller, Monroe Joshua, 52–53n17, 74, 157, 159n9, 179n31, 202n33
mines (torpedoes), 187–190
Moore, Risdon, 21, 49, 98, 108n12, 202n33
Moore, Thomas O., 113
Mosar, John, 27, 81

neighbors, 6, 8–9, 12–14, 19–20, 87; divisions between, 29, 35–37, 52, 58, 91–96, 146–147
newspapers, 5, 13, 133, 136, 140; publications in South, 88, 179–182, 190, 200

occupation, military: banishment of disloyal civilians, 66, 130, 151; Memphis, 12, 43, 61, 73, 102–104; Missouri, 129;

INDEX

Montgomery, 196; use of loyalty oath, 22, 73, 81–82, 93, 197
officers: privileges of, 6n12, 20, 64; quarters, 39, 43, 45, 53, 100; visits by family, 46, 52–56, 60–64, 82, 97

Padfield, Elizabeth, 51
Padfield, James, 51, 135, 170n24
parenting, 11, 27, 48, 65; delight in children, 64, 93, 104; disciplining children, 33, 47, 107; loss of children, 5–6, 55, 74, 78, 87
paroles of soldiers, 45, 140, 182, 197–198, 201
patriotism, 7–8, 11, 33, 144–145, 207n36. *See also* unionism
Payne, Dr., 98
Peace: hopes for, 73, 84–85, 94, 144, 172–173, 180–181; return of, 192, 195–197, 200–201, 209
physicians, 6, 77, 99, 166. *See also* medical treatments; sickness; surgeons
Pike, E. C., 142
Pittes, John, 90
plantations, 41, 113–116, 175–176, 188, 199. *See also* slavery
Pleasanton, Alfred, 140n30, 150, 152
plunder, 139–140, 142–143, 157
Pollard, Charles T., 199
Postel, Philip H., 37–38, 58, 89, 175n28
Price, Sterling, 129–132, 136–152
prisoners, 49, 60, 68, 73, 111; captured in battle, 68, 112–114, 121, 151, 162, 190–191; eastern theater, 193, 197–198; held in Illinois, 22–23, 26

quartermaster, 108, 109n13; acquisition of materiel, 22–28, 43, 46–47, 50–54, 124; appointment of Henry as, 2, 6–7, 20–21; distribution of materiel, 56–57, 113; paperwork, 7n13, 74, 76, 115; potential for corruption, 28, 47n8, 89–90

racism, anti-black, 10, 44, 73, 182
railroads, 131, 145, 166, 178, 209; destruction of, 13, 106, 145, 181, 186; target of military operations, 102, 106; use by Henry, 30; use to send messengers, 24; use to transport materiel, 26, 151; use to transport refugees, 73, 78; use to transport troops, 20–21, 37–38, 90, 133, 136–138, 143–144
Rainforth, Thomas, 35, 96
Randall, Andrew J., 168
Rayhill, Charity (sister), 41n40
Rayhill, Charles (brother-in-law), 41n40, 141, 168, 209
Rayhill, Helen, 29
real estate, 144, 147, 158, 175, 178
recreation, 186; fishing, 76; making music, 23, 25, 33, 39, 56, 182; reading, 167, 182; sleighing, 168–171; swimming, 67, 76, 182, 184; "town-ball," 182–183
Reeves (straggling soldier), 56, 59–60
refugees, 12–13, 73, 77–78, 83n19, 89, 114
religion, 25, 188; camp meeting, 5; church, 35, 40, 47, 55, 65, 135; prayer, 59, 63, 122, 127, 163–164, 202; sermons, 25, 34–35
Rentchler, Elizabeth, 170
resignation, by Henry, 16, 86–87, 183, 204–208
Risley, Frank, 29, 35, 40
rivers: Atchafalaya, 111–112; Big Black, 106; Cumberland, 26n15, 156, 157n1, 168; Fish, 186; Gasconade, 142; Kaskaskia, 5, 38n39; Mississippi, 37, 50, 67, 73, 76, 114; Mississippi, Henry travels along, 7–14, 43, 116–120, 128, 152, 200; Missouri, 143, 147, 153; Mobile, 177, 180; Osage, 143; Red, 13, 103, 108–116, 119–126, 157, 188; Tennessee, 164–168, 171; Tensaw, 180
roads: Alabama, 188, 195, 201–202; Louisiana, 117, 178; Missouri, 138–139, 145, 154; Tennessee, 49, 162, 164; turnpike, 130, 138, 164
Rosecrans, William, 129, 136
Ross, Aledy, 35
Ross, Alexander, 81, 85, 169, 171

rumors, 112, 172, 186, 191–196; invasion by Sterling Price, 14, 129–137, 150–152, 161–163, 186; location of next deployment, 108, 126, 152, 165, 200; Mascoutah, 14, 51, 72, 89–91; movement, Confederates in Louisiana, 117; movement, Confederates near Memphis, 60, 68; movement, Confederates near Nashville, 161; peace, 173, 181, 195; success of military operations elsewhere, 63, 68, 80, 91, 192–193; tensions, over Mexico, 204–205; Union soldiers, taken prisoners, 146

Scheve, Julius, 61
Schiermeier, Minna, 27n18, 35, 40
school, 41, 69, 143, 210; Henry, employment with, 2, 5, 19–20, 76; teachers, 21, 29, 141
secesh. *See* secessionists
secessionists, 43, 49, 60, 82n17, 112–113, 154; disdain for, 7, 36, 157–158, 165, 197; prisoners, 22, 26, 49, 66, 111, 201; sympathizers near Illinois, 21, 66, 72, 77, 79, 85
Seward, William, 196
Shelby, Joseph, 130, 134, 136
Sheridan, Philip, 133
Sherman, William Tecumseh, 68, 102–103, 106n10, 123n31, 142n26, 156n1
sickness, 135, 166, 183, 210; carbuncles, 74, 95; chronic pain, 14, 94, 210; diarrhea, 183; fever, 6, 166–167, 207–209; headaches, 6, 15, 158, 166, 173; neuralgia, 210; smallpox, 6, 15, 55–58, 74, 158, 166–167; soldiers, among, 35, 51, 99, 109, 207, 209; unspecified complaints, 6, 58, 60, 74, 124, 210; vision problems, 86; whooping cough, 6, 74, 89. *See also* children; dental problems; Fike, Ellie
sieges, Mobile; 187–189; Vicksburg, 7, 15, 75n8, 105–106
Silverspar (Captain), 50
Slade, William, 31

slavery, 35n35, 44, 113–116, 181n2, 198n28, 200. *See also* plantations
sleep, lack of, 29, 32, 48, 109, 143, 163; difficult conditions for, 39, 84, 102, 162–163
Smith, Andrew J., 168; campaigns in Alabama, 181, 190n18, 197n25, 201, 204n34, 208; pursuit of Sterling Price, 132, 144, 152; Red River expedition, 103, 111, 120, 126
Smith, Edmund Kirby, 128
soldiering, 4, 7, 20, 126, 157, 163; boredom, 15, 116, 121, 167, 186, 201; combat, 118–119, 161–162, 188–191; complaints about commanders, 119–120, 153; drilling, 25, 43, 50; garrison duty, 13, 69, 73, 152, 181; hardships, anticipated, 28, 33, 84; hardships, experienced, 105, 125, 153–154, 162; lodging, other, 25–26, 43, 169, 172, 182; lodging, tents, 25, 45, 131–132, 169–171, 201; skirmishing, 106, 112, 117–123, 138, 160, 185. *See also* African Americans: soldiers; marching; United States Colored Troops
songs, 25, 33, 116, 182, 197–198, 201
South, 7–13, 16, 102, 128, 181–182
steamboats, 43, 49, 156, 166, 175, 177; *Belle Memphis*, 66; *Empire City*, 177; *Empress*, 39, 41, 65; *Hannibal*, 124–126; *Missouri*, 174–176; *Mollie McPike*, 158; *Stephen Decatur*, 128; *Tarascon*, 186; *Thomas E. Tutt*, 110–111, 113–114; *Woodford*, 115, 116n23. *See also* boats
Steele, Frederick, 103n4, 117n24, 124
Stock, Jacob, 48
substitutes. *See* draft
surgeons, 83n20, 150, 171, 175, 206, 208. *See also* medical treatments; physicians; sickness
surrenders, 15, 130, 181, 184n13, 189, 192–197

taxes, 69, 74–75, 79
Taylor, Richard, 103–104, 115n20, 117n24, 121n29, 181

INDEX

Tegermen, Nancy, 51
telegraph, 24, 30, 192, 201, 203
Thomas, George, 156–157, 164, 171–174
Thomas, Lorenzo, 67n33, 68
Todd, George, 145
torpedoes, 187–190
trees: cottonwood, 42; elm, 175; evergreen, 61, 125, 176; oak, 196; orange, 176; pine, 123, 171, 181, 189, 194–196, 201; sycamore, 42

unionism, 2, 8, 12, 19, 100, 130; southern Unionists, 82, 88, 104, 112, 114, 124; Union Leagues, 8, 12, 72–77, 81–84, 91. *See also* patriotism
United States Colored Troops, 10, 12, 44, 73, 182. *See also* African Americans; patriotism; soldiering; unionism

Vanwinkle, Lucinda, 170
vigilantism, 12–13, 83, 88
vision problems, 86
visiting, family: Cimbaline, in Memphis, 11–12, 44, 53–57, 60–64, 99; Cimbaline, near Mascoutah, 141, 146, 155, 158, 170–173; at Jefferson Barracks, 14, 131–132; plans for postwar, 202, 207; solution for loneliness, 32, 38, 60, 175

Wallis, William, 66, 89
weather, 113, 116, 175–178, 184, 209; extreme cold, 165, 168; flooding, 57–58, 155; heat, 124, 128, 153, 204; heavy rain, 25, 57–58, 63n27, 117, 162–167, 177; snow, 14, 130, 153–154, 165–169
Webb, Loren, 23
Welsch, Wolfgang, 166–167
"Western boys," 81
White, James M., 95
Whittaker, William, 57n21, 90
widows, 50; "war widows," 9, 50, 52
womanhood. *See* gender

Yankees, 81, 122, 181–182, 194, 197
Yates, Richard, 22, 129

New Perspectives on the Civil War Era

Practical Strangers: The Courtship Correspondence of Nathaniel Dawson and Elodie Todd, Sister of Mary Todd Lincoln
edited by Stephen Berry and Angela Esco Elder

The Greatest Trials I Ever Had: The Civil War Letters of Margaret and Thomas Cahill
edited by Ryan W. Keating

Prison Pens: Gender, Memory, and Imprisonment in the Writings of Mollie Scollay and Wash Nelson, 1863–1866
edited by Timothy J. Williams and Evan A. Kutzler

William Gregg's Civil War: The Battle to Shape the History of Guerrilla Warfare
edited and annotated by Joseph M. Beilein Jr.

Seen/Unseen: Hidden Lives in a Community of Enslaved Georgians
edited by Christopher R. Lawton, Laura E. Nelson, Randy L. Reid

Radical Relationships: The Civil War–Era Correspondence of Mathilde Franziska Anneke
translated by Victorija Bilic
edited by Alison Clark Efford and Viktorija Bilic

Private No More: The Civil War Letters of John Lovejoy Murray, 102nd United States Colored Infantry
edited by Sharon A. Roger Hepburn

Heartsick and Astonished: Divorce in Civil War–Era West Virginia
edited by Allison Dorothy Fredette

When Slavery and Rebellion Are Destroyed: A Michigan Woman's Civil War Journal
edited by Jack Dempsey

A Union Tested: The Civil War Papers of Cimbaline and Henry Fike
edited by Jeremy Neely

Milton Keynes UK
Ingram Content Group UK Ltd.
UKHW041856241124
3056UKWH00002B/131